A Troublesome Commerce

ROBERT H. GUDMESTAD

A Troublesome Commerce

The Transformation of the Interstate Slave Trade

LOUISIANA STATE UNIVERSITY PRESS BATON ROUGE

Manufactured in the United States of America
First printing
04 06 08 10 12 11 09 07 05 03
2 4 5 3 1

DESIGNER: Barbara Neely Bourgoyne
TYPEFACE: Janson Text
TYPESETTER: Coghill Composition, Inc.
PRINTER AND BINDER: Thomson-Shore, Inc.

Library of Congress Cataloging-in-Publication Data:

Gudmestad, Robert H., 1964–
A troublesome commerce : the transformation of the interstate slave trade / Robert H. Gudmestad.
p. cm.
Includes bibliographical references and index.
ISBN 0-8071-2884-8 (cloth : alk. paper) — ISBN 0-8071-2922-4 (pbk. : alk. paper)
1. Slave trade—United States. I. Title.
E442.G83 2003
381'.44'0973—dc21

2003009434

The paper in this book meets the guidelines for permanence and durability of the Committee on Production Guidelines for Book Longevity of the Council on Library Resources. ♾

For Beth

CONTENTS

ILLUSTRATIONS

MAP

PHOTOGRAPHS AND DRAWN ART

(following page 86)

ACKNOWLEDGMENTS

The favors that I have begged during this project are legion. Numerous people assisted me on my research trips by providing food, shelter, companionship, and encouragement. I can never repay their kindness, generosity, and hospitality but can only stress my deep appreciation to them for going far beyond what was necessary. Likewise, the staffs of the archives I visited were consistently courteous and helpful. I gratefully recognize their help. Especially vital to the completion of the project were the diligent, professional, and impeccable staffs of the interlibrary loan departments at Louisiana State University and Southwest Baptist University. Sylvia Frank Rodrigue is a tremendous asset for LSU Press. She has been most patient and helpful during this process. Mark Brown, Angie Smith, and John Lancaster at the Belmont Mansion supplied unexpected and useful information in the last stages of writing. John deserves special recognition for taking me on a fascinating tour of Fairvue's grounds. The staff in the rare book room at the University of North Carolina supplied a necessary illustration with grace and good humor. Bill vanHoornbeek took time from his busy schedule to draw the map for this book.

An endeavor of this type draws upon the guidance and assistance of numerous scholars. I thank William J. Cooper Jr., Gaines Foster, Stanley Hilton, and Paul Paskoff for their assistance while this project was a dissertation. Bertram Wyatt-Brown, Robert Remini, and Walter Johnson read portions of the manuscript and provided valuable help. The outside reader at LSU Press was crucial in shaping the direction of this work. My largest debt, and one that I can never repay, is to Charles Royster, who was my dissertation adviser. His encouragement, humor, trenchant analysis, and sound advice have been invaluable and greatly appreciated.

My family and friends have been particularly patient and supportive through the many stages of this project. They have had to suffer through my numerous explanations of what slave traders did and why they are important to understanding the antebellum South. My parents provided the laptop computer upon which this book was written. More importantly, they have been my role models and sources of love and encouragement throughout my life. My son Samuel has been an incredible joy and inspiration. The person to whom I am most grateful is my wife, Beth, who has had to live in the loathsome world of the slave traders longer than she cares to remember. As a meager acknowledgment of her patience, support, sacrifice, and love, I dedicate this book to her.

ABBREVIATIONS

DU	Perkins Library, Duke University, Durham, N.C.
JER	*Journal of the Early Republic*
JSH	*Journal of Southern History*
LSU	Hill Memorial Library, Louisiana State University, Baton Rouge
MDAH	Mississippi Department of Archives and History, Jackson
NCDAH	North Carolina Division of Archives and History, Raleigh
TSLA	Tennessee State Library and Archives, Nashville
UNC	Southern Historical Collection, University of North Carolina, Chapel Hill
UV	Alderman Library, University of Virginia, Charlottesville
VHS	Virginia Historical Society, Richmond

A Troublesome Commerce

Routes of the Interstate Slave Trade

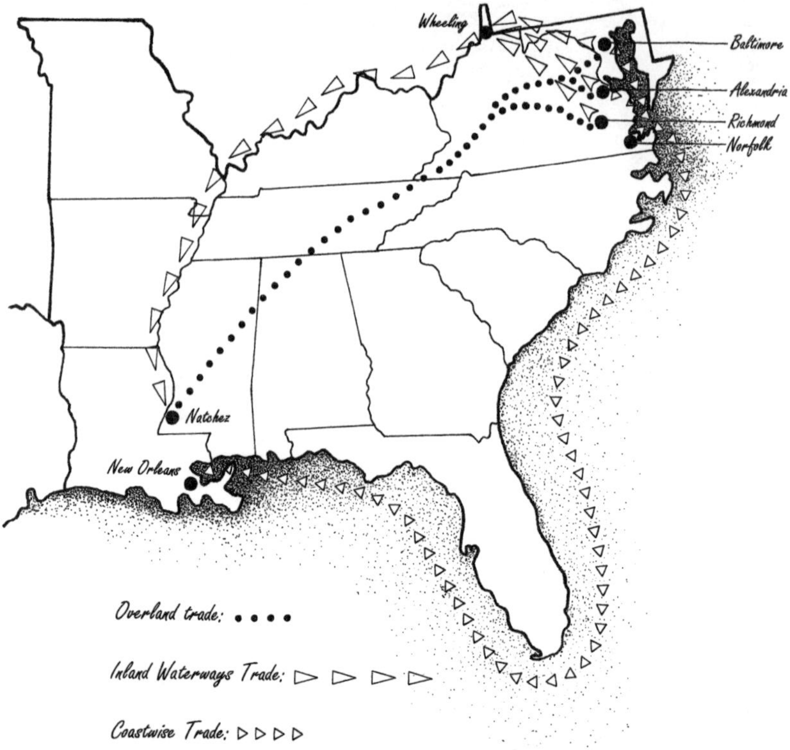

INTRODUCTION

The Problem of Speculation

On April 27, 1846, Isaac Franklin died of "congestion of the stomach" on his plantation in West Feliciana Parish, Louisiana. His widow made arrangements to have the body preserved in alcohol and then accompanied it to his favorite plantation, Fairvue, in Sumner County, Tennessee. Franklin, fifty-seven years old at his death, owned six properties in Louisiana and the one in Tennessee. His entire estate, which included over 10,600 acres and seven hundred slaves, was valued at over half a million dollars. The passing of arguably the richest man in the South attracted attention. One newspaper commented on Franklin's "perseverance and steadiness of purpose, and that address and tact, in the management of business, for which he became afterwards so remarkable." Another memoriam reached the same conclusion and noted his success in his "peculiar calling."[1]

Franklin's "peculiar calling" was a particularly disagreeable portion of the peculiar institution: the interstate slave trade. Variously known as speculators, nigger traders, or soul drivers, Franklin and others like him bought slaves in one state, transported them to another state, and sold them. He teamed with John Armfield to build the largest slave-trading firm on the continent, one that sent ships from Alexandria, Virginia, to New Orleans

1. *Succession of Isaac Franklin* (n.p., n.d.), 27–51, 293 (first quotation), 482, 700–708; *New Orleans Daily Picayune*, October 7, 1846 (second quotation); *New Orleans Daily Delta*, December 19, 1849 (third quotation); Wendell Holmes Stephenson, *Isaac Franklin: Slave Trader and Planter of the Old South* (Baton Rouge, 1938); Steamboat receipt of the Steamer *Tennessee*, May 24, 1846, Natchez Trace Steamboat Collection, Center for American History, University of Texas, Austin, Texas.

and Natchez twice a month during the prime shipping season of October through March. Franklin and Armfield, as the company was known, speculated on a massive scale, having $250,000 in bills receivable after the 1831–32 trading season and selling over $100,000 worth of slaves the next year. Franklin was not bragging when he observed that his business sold more slaves than all the other traders put together. Armfield put the number at one thousand in 1833 and expected an even higher figure the next year. The two men were clearly and inextricably associated with the interstate slave trade.[2]

Given the size and prominence of Franklin's slave-trading empire, it seems unusual that none of the newspaper stories mentioned his specific means of making a living. They did not describe him as a slave trader or even mention slavery, as if Franklin made his fortune through the sheer force of his personality. The papers wanted to avoid all association with the interstate slave trade, suggesting that southerners were reluctant to accept the fact that slave trading was based on speculation. Selling slaves for profit was particularly galling because it could lead to personal debasement. Slaveowners came to assume that slave trading was rare despite evidence to the contrary. When trading occurred, southerners attributed it to circumstances beyond their control. They blamed the slaves for being unmanageable, debt for being remorseless, traders for being greedy, and abolitionists for corrupting slaves by meddling where they did not belong. Crude stereotypes of speculators and the slave trade masked the fact that slaveholders themselves were primarily at fault for the degradation of bondservants. Even though slave trading was ubiquitous by the time of Franklin's death, speculators had become the subjects of a ridiculous stereotype, as had the trade and the slaves. Such caricatures were the means by which slaveholders separated themselves from the most objectionable portions of slavery. These stereotypes served as a way for southerners to avoid facing the brutal realization that slaves were everywhere in their society degraded, scorned, and oppressed.

This study charts the changing perceptions towards speculators, the slave

2. Isaac Franklin to Rice C. Ballard, December 25, 1833, Rice C. Ballard Papers, UNC (quotation); *Washington Daily National Intelligencer*, November 6, 1835; *Genius of Universal Emancipation*, March 1834, 39; "Interview with Gen. W. T. Martin," Frederic Bancroft Papers, Box 92, Southern Trip Notes (1902), 3:249, Butler Library, Columbia University, New York, N.Y.

trade, and slavery. In the late eighteenth and early nineteenth centuries, there was no consensus on the place of the slave trader in southern society because there was no agreement about the trade itself. There was much discussion of its efficacy, especially as it grew in scale and became more open in the years following the War of 1812. It was difficult to distinguish the trade from other forms of slave movement in the South. Ultimately, though, the interstate slave trade became distinct when a class of slave traders pioneered the use of business practices that facilitated its growth. The increased visibility of traders who captured and sold free blacks or those slaves with a term of years to serve troubled many in the new republic. Others resented the notion that traders made money through speculation on slaves' misery. The scenes of bondservants upon the auction block clashed with the ideas of those southerners who imagined slavery to be a benevolent institution. Just as bad were the sights and sounds of traders' coffles headed south and west, especially when whites knew that the trade tore apart slave families. Activities of bondspeople to resist speculation were strong reminders of the negative consequences of the trade. Evangelical Christians acted upon their beliefs and worked to keep slave trading at a minimum. Residents of slave-exporting states were divided as to the trade's virtue, alarmed at its growth, and uncertain of its proper place in society.

This variety of opinions betrayed a divided mind over speculation. Most people registered their disapproval through individual efforts that had no direction or cohesion. Some refused to deal with speculators, others looked askance at their neighbors who did not refuse, and many denounced the most offensive aspects of the trade. These unfocused and usually unorganized actions shied away from government interference and extreme solutions but hoped instead that the slave trade, and possibly slavery itself, would somehow go away. Southerners who harbored doubts about servitude, no matter how small, were most likely to be troubled by the interstate slave trade. Those who did not believe in slavery absolutely could not believe in the absolute power of the slaveholder. Their conditional acceptance of slavery did not include unqualified approval of the slave trade. It is a measure of their frustration that they could provide no viable alternative to a commerce that was becoming vital to the South's expansion.

Perceptions of the slave trade, and reactions to it, varied over time and place. While coffles and family separations bothered many in the Upper South, those states that imported a significant number of slaves had other concerns. An increase in the number of slaves, citizens in these states believed, raised the specter of a powerful and restive slave population that might one day repeat the experience of Haiti. Residents of the importing states, usually the Lower, or Deep, South, complained that they received the castoffs and the worst slaves from the other states. They responded in various ways, such as trying to limit the importation of slaves, controlling the types of bondservants who crossed their borders, or creating strict rules for the conduct of all slaves. A significant number of masters in Alabama, Mississippi, and Louisiana went to Virginia or Maryland on their own slave-buying expeditions. Although their activities were virtually the same as commerce in slaves, they drew a sharp distinction between themselves and speculators.

Even as southern reactions to the slave trade varied, speculators changed their business practices in response to criticism. They distanced themselves from the seamier portions of their business, making both it and themselves more accepted in southern society. Traders carefully cultivated the idea that it was possible to separate speculation from the men who engaged in it. They successfully created the idea that there were different types of traders who had distinct places in southern society. As a result, southerners could blame a lowly class of itinerant traders for slavery's abuses while fully accepting the activities of prosperous speculators. Southern attitudes about the interstate slave trade were a partial result of the complex interaction between trader and slave.

Even as speculators changed their tactics to make their business more palatable, the trade became the basis of repeated attacks by abolitionists, who assaulted slavery at its weakest point. Speculators were a convenient target, since they often committed heinous offenses. Beset from the outside, most southerners were unwilling to question the interstate slave trade and readily converted speculators into scapegoats as a means to avoid responsibility for the worst of slavery's abuses. These stereotypes became a way to define the shape of slavery. Ultimately, the need for the trade conquered most slaveholders' qualms about the negative consequences of the peculiar institution. Southerners, when confronted with evidence of the slave trade's brutality, managed to convert this challenge to slavery into a bastion of support for it. In so doing, they refused to acknowledge any spot or blemish in slavery.

For the purposes of this study, a slave trader or speculator is a man who bought slaves in one state and sold them in another on a regular basis as the sole or principal source of his income. The terms *slave trader*, *trader*, and *speculator* will be used interchangeably, as will the terms *interstate slave trade*, *speculation*, and *slave trafficking*. Obviously, other persons, such as brokers, auctioneers, and commission merchants, sold slaves, but were not primarily concerned with the interstate market and the transportation of bondspeople. At times, slaveholders brought slaves into other states and sold them, but not as their principal or steady income. Such distinctions might seem artificial to the modern reader, and, in a sense, they are. Southerners of the nineteenth century, however, would have found nothing contrived about perceiving the various types of slave transactions in different terms. For them, it was necessary.

CHAPTER I

The Strands of Forced Migration

When the charter members of the American Colonization Society met in 1816, they wanted to select a prominent slaveholder to lead the organization. Their choice of Bushrod Washington, most thought, was an inspired one. He was the nephew of the country's first president and a Virginia slaveholder who could bring instant credibility to the society. The ACS thought that Washington's reputation would convince masters to join them in their goal of transferring emancipated slaves to Africa. Official statements of the ACS expressed the hope that slaves would voluntarily go overseas, but privately many members were willing to deport not only bondservants, but free African Americans as well. This precarious coalition of slaveowning southerners and antislavery northerners hoped to smother the peculiar institution by gradually reducing the number of slaves while simultaneously eliminating the nation's black population.[1]

Washington, who lived at Mount Vernon, ostensibly shared many of these same attitudes. He ran into financial difficulties, however, and his subsequent actions belied his involvement in the ACS. Like many other plantations in Virginia, Mount Vernon failed to be profitable enough to keep up with its owner's spending. In 1821 Washington took a drastic step to buoy

1. P. J. Staudenraus, *The African Colonization Movement, 1816–1865* (New York, 1961); Early Lee Fox, *The American Colonization Society, 1817–1840* (Baltimore, 1919); Ira Berlin, *Slaves without Masters: The Free Negro in the Antebellum South* (New York, 1975), 200–12; John G. West Jr., *The Politics of Revelation and Reason: Religion and Civic Life in the New Nation* (Lawrence, Kans., 1996), 110–12.

his declining fortune by selling fifty-four slaves to two men from Louisiana. He netted $10,000 on the transaction. Washington knew he had to keep the sale a secret lest he damage his reputation as president of the ACS. It would be unseemly for the leader of an organization dedicated to freeing and then deporting slaves to unload them for cash. His hopes were in vain. The transportation of slaves was difficult to conceal, and someone spotted Washington's bondservants trudging through Leesburg, Virginia, in chains. A local paper printed an account of Washington's "unhappy wretches" passing through the town in the midst of a coffle of one hundred slaves. Other papers picked up the story, and soon Washington was under attack by newspapers along the Chesapeake seaboard, with the implication being that he sold his slaves to speculators. The *Baltimore Morning Chronicle* accused Washington of separating families and pronounced him guilty of speculation and "hoarding up wealth." The *Chronicle* demanded an explanation.[2]

Washington shot back with an angry letter defending his actions. He charged that no one had the right to question his authority to dispose of property which was lawfully his. Not only were his actions perfectly legal, but he resented the accusation that he had separated families. Washington took great pains to avoid such unhappy occasions, he said, and made sacrifices to keep families together, including selling the slaves for $2,500 less than their market price. The slaves, he explained, were not sorry to go. In fact, they cheerfully consented to go with their new purchasers after being assured they would have a good owner. He sold them to two "gentlemen" from Louisiana who lived on the Red River. The new owners promised to preserve slave families by not reselling the bondservants. Washington pointedly denied any involvement in the interstate slave trade in his letter. He made the case that his slaves were not subject to speculation by resale, but were merely being transferred to another part of the country. Washington claimed, moreover, that the actions of the slaves justified their sale. The final straw was their insubordination and disregard of authority that rendered them useless. When the slaves learned that Washington would never

2. *Niles' Weekly Register*, September 1, 1821, 1–2 (first quotation); *Baltimore Morning Chronicle*, August 25, 1822, as quoted in the *Genius of Universal Emancipation*, August, 1822, 25–26 (second quotation); *Liberator*, March 22, 1834, 45; Gerald T. Dunne, "Bushrod Washington and the Mount Vernon Slaves," *Supreme Court Historical Society Yearbook* (1980): 25–29; Donald M. Sweig, "Northern Virginia Slavery: A Statistical and Demographic Investigation" (Ph.D. diss., William and Mary College, 1982), 234; Staudenraus, *African Colonization Movement*, 173.

emancipate them, three bondspeople tried to escape. Washington feared that the rest of his workforce would do the same.[3]

Washington's actions were legal, and if his account is correct, he did his best to prevent his slaves from falling into the clutches of speculators. The sale, however, was too similar to the interstate slave trade to prevent unfavorable comparisons to that controversial business. One hundred bondservants marching in chains looked like the trade even if the slaves consented to the move. Washington's troubles illustrate a real problem in southern society during the early republic—differentiating between the different types of forced migration. The interstate slave trade, movement with migrating owners, and Deep South planters buying slaves in the Upper South combined to coerce approximately one million bondservants to cross state lines between 1790 and 1860. Between 1810 and 1840, almost 350,000 slaves left Delaware, Maryland, Virginia, North Carolina, and South Carolina. Forcible separations destroyed about one-third of all first slave marriages in the Upper South, and cut the ties between spouse and spouse, between parent and child, between sibling and sibling, and between others in the kindred network. Clearly, forced migration took a heavy toll on the lives of slaves.[4]

Disentangling the various strands of forced migration is like trying to untie the Gordian knot. Migration with owners, planter purchase, and the interstate trade blended together to form a seamless whole. It is problematic to precisely isolate how much each component contributed to the overall movement of bondservants because they were indistinguishable on a practical level. But even if each portion cannot be clearly delineated, it is clear that the proportions changed over time. Migration with owners predominated until the 1820s. Before that time, the African trade supplied much of the labor need for the expanding areas of settlement. As the international trade ebbed and the agriculture of the Upper South struggled, an increasing number of Deep South planters journeyed north to buy slaves. More impor-

3. *Niles' Weekly Register*, September 29, 1821, 70–72 (quotation); *Liberator*, March 22, 1834, 45.

4. Herbert Gutman and Richard Sutch, "The Slave Family: Protected Agent of Capitalist Masters or Victim of the Slave Trade?" in *Reckoning with Slavery: A Critical Study in the Quantitative History of American Negro Slavery*, by Paul A. David et al. (New York, 1976), 99; Peter D. McClelland and Richard J. Zeckhauser, *Demographic Dimensions of the New Republic: American Interregional Migration, Vital Statistics, and Manumissions, 1800–1860* (New York, 1982), 159–64; Michael Tadman, *Speculators and Slaves: Masters, Traders, and Slaves in the Old South* (Madison, 1989), 133–78.

tantly, the proportion of slaves who marched for a speculator also increased. It was this growth of speculation that created problems for many southerners. Speculation challenged the comfortable conclusion that slavery had little or no negative impact on slaves themselves. This very public example of slavery's brutality compelled southerners to create artificial distinctions between the types of forced migration in order to cope with the growth of speculation. They had to find some way to distance themselves from a public and repellent aspect of slavery that did not easily coexist with assumptions about slavery's benign nature. The growth of the interstate slave trade, then, called into question some of the basic opinions of slavery itself.

Slave migration with masters was responsible for the bulk of forced migration in the decade after Andrew Jackson's victory at New Orleans. White migrants who brought slaves with them to establish a new settlement relied upon a variety of methods to accomplish their purposes. Some forced all of their slaves to accompany them during their westward migration and did not augment their workforce prior to leaving. When Thomas H. Dent moved from South Carolina to Alabama, for example, he took all the slaves from his rice plantation. A move like Dent's was an arduous ordeal for most bondservants. One traveler estimated he saw a thousand slaves "worn down with fatigue" as they walked with their masters to Alabama and Mississippi. The owners accommodated the needs of those bondservants who could not keep pace with the rest by allowing them to ride in wagons. Because forced migration was so physically demanding, many white migrants of the early-nineteenth-century South judiciously altered the composition of their workforce before moving south or west. Most masters were selective in the slaves they brought, selling others to family members or neighbors. They did so, most obviously, in order to facilitate the process of settlement in one way or another. Some owners realized the harmful effects the migration would have on the bondservants and tried to ease the transition by keeping their slaves' families intact as much as possible. A migrant on his way to Georgia told a curious observer that it was common for planters to sell bondservants who had a personal attachment to their home and did not want to leave. Rather than selling bondservants, other owners bought new slaves in order to head off trouble. James Williams, an escaped slave, recalled how his former master "took great pains" to buy the spouses of those bondservants who married off the plantation. The owner wanted to make sure that the 214 slaves who made the trip would be relatively content and not have to be chained together. Others who made purchases prior to moving were not as concerned with their slaves' welfare. Before moving to Florida, a Fredericksburg, Virginia, resident said he wanted to buy a few slaves for his own use. He simply wanted to assemble a strong and productive workforce.[5]

Masters who changed the composition of their workforce sometimes behaved in a fashion similar to speculators, as the example of Leonard Covington demonstrates. When he learned that he had received an appointment as commander of a company of light dragoons in the Mississippi Territory in 1809, he carefully planned his move. Covington, who had made a name as an Indian fighter and a member of Congress, decided to divide his slave force in two. The first group remained on his Maryland farm so they could grow another year's worth of crops. The other slaves joined Covington's brother Alexander at the new land and prepared it for cultivation. Covington sent thirty-one slaves to Mississippi and kept twenty-five for himself. The slaves who went to Mississippi were, on the whole, noticeably younger than those they left behind. Of the thirty-six bondservants under the age of twenty, two-thirds went west. By contrast, seven of the nine slaves over thirty years old remained in Maryland. Similarly, John Blakely went through Elbert County, Georgia, on his way to Alabama. The conscientious Blakely registered his bondservants with the Richmond County clerk as stipulated by the laws of Georgia. He brought twenty-three slaves, the eldest of whom was thirty-five. Fifteen of his slaves were less than sixteen years of age, hardly reflective of the age composition of the southern slave population. He likely purchased some of the younger slaves prior to setting out.[6]

5. George W. Featherstonhaugh, *Excursion through the Slave States, from Washington on the Potomac to the Frontier of Mexico* (New York, 1844; reprint, 1968), 152 (first quotation); James Williams, *Narrative of James Williams, an American Slave* (New York, 1838), 37 (second quotation); Basil Hall, *Travels in North America in the Years 1827 and 1828*, 2 vols. (Philadelphia, 1829), 2:128–29; Adam Hodgson, *Letters from North America, written during a Tour in the United States and Canada*, (London, 1824), 1:113–14, 138; Tyrone Power, *Impressions of America during the Years 1833, 1834, and 1835*, 2 vols. (Philadelphia, 1836), 2:80–83; John Melish, *Travels through the United States of America, in the Years 1806 and 1807, and 1809, 1810, and 1811* (London, 1818), 341; *Fredericksburg, Virginia Herald*, August 30, 1826; Ann Patton Malone, *Sweet Chariot: Slave Family and Household Structure in Nineteenth-Century Louisiana* (Chapel Hill, 1992), 211; James Benson Sellers, *Slavery in Alabama* (University, Ala., 1950), 36; Edward E. Baptist, *Creating an Old South: Middle Florida's Plantation Frontier before the Civil War* (Chapel Hill, 2002), 62–67.

6. Nellie Wailes Brandon and W. M. Drake, eds., *Memoir of Leonard Covington by B. L. C. Wailes* (1861; reprint, n.p., 1928), 53–59; Joel D. Trese, ed., *Biographical Directory of the American Congress, 1774–1996* (Alexandria, 1997), 869; Affidavit of John Blakely, September 21,

Migrants like Covington and Blakely weighed their options carefully. They wanted young slaves who would be able to withstand hard work, labor for many years, and quickly procreate. Since these slaveholders had highly selective purchasing patterns, they could be accused of dabbling in speculative activities. It was well established that traders trafficked in young slaves, thus breaking up families in the process. Migrants, though, would have denied any such connection to slave trading. This idea is especially true once speculation gained strength and notoriety in the 1820s and beyond. Private citizens did not want to be tainted by the interstate slave trade.[7]

As the Lower South became more settled, a significant number of planters took on the burden of finding their own slaves in the Upper South. These men united the desire to exert greater control over their slave force with a passion to save money. They wanted to avoid buying slaves who might be "convicts, the inhabitants of jails, drunkards, rogues, and vagabonds" by going directly to Maryland and Virginia. Not only was it more prudent to buy slaves in the Upper South, but it was more profitable. When Tennessee resident Marius R. Robinson took a four-month tour of the South, he learned that a large number of planters used this strategy to save money. Southerners routinely blamed speculators for keeping slave prices artificially high. It is doubtful that traders charged exorbitant prices, but they were in the business to make money. After paying for food, clothing, transportation, lodging, and other expenses, traders had to tack on a fee that made speculation worth the risk. The trade's profit rates varied enormously, depending on the time, location, and type of slave being sold. A figure of somewhere between 20 and 30 percent was common in the years between 1820 and 1836, meaning that speculators who brought slaves from Maryland to Louisiana in 1830 could add up to two hundred dollars to the price of the slave. Planters who took on the responsibility of finding their own bondservants could thus save a substantial amount of money, sometimes up to half of the total purchase price. If they waited until after the height of the

---

1833, Slave Importation Register, Elbert County, Georgia, Drawer 2, Box 76, Georgia Department of History and Archives, Atlanta.

7. Gail S. Terry, "Sustaining the Bonds of Kinship in a Trans-Appalachian Migration, 1790–1811: The Cabell-Breckinridge Slaves Move West," *Virginia Magazine of History and Biography* 4 (1994): 455–76; Tadman, *Speculators and Slaves*, 228–36; Baptist, *Creating an Old South*, 67–73.

slave-buying season, usually September 1, they could save even more money. Prices tended to fall once the slave traders left the market.[8]

Not all planters from the Deep South, however, were satisfied with their savings. Andrew Durnford traveled from his plantation outside of New Orleans to Richmond in order to buy slaves at the lowest possible price. After depositing $8,312 in a local Richmond bank, the free man of color set out to find some bargains. Much to his chagrin, he found the prices of slaves to be quite high because of all the Deep South planters in the city. "Even the negro traders," Durnford grumbled, were "surprised at the prices demanded." He pessimistically concluded that he would buy fewer slaves than he intended because other buyers were driving up the prices. The frugal Durnford eventually bought twenty-five bondservants for $6,876.[9]

Some planters like Durnford went in search of slaves while others waited for sellers to come to them. They customarily placed advertisements in local papers after checking into a local hotel. Such men consistently reiterated their desire for "likely young negroes," which meant healthy slaves under twenty-five years of age. They took care to differentiate themselves from traders by emphasizing that any slaves they purchased were for their "own use and *not for sale*." Many went further and declared they were gentlemen who desired more slaves. Planters revealed their identity to gain an advantage when buying slaves. It quickly became known that Chesapeake farmers

8. Undated *Natchez Ariel*, as quoted in *Genius of Universal Emancipation*, July 4, 1827, 7 (quotation); *Liberator*, May 17, 1834, 77; Samuel Coburn to Abram Barnes, July 10, 1828, Barnes-Willis Family Papers, Natchez Trace Slavery Collection, Center for American History, University of Texas, Austin; Ethan A. Andrews, *Slavery and the Domestic Slave-Trade in the United States* (Boston, 1836), 174; Tadman, *Speculators and Slaves*, 204–7, 292–95; Herman F. Freudenberger and Jonathan B. Pritchett, "The Domestic United States Slave Trade: New Evidence," *Journal of Interdisciplinary History* 21 (1991): 447–77; Robert Evans Jr., "Some Economic Aspects of the Domestic Slave Trade, 1830–1860," *Southern Economic Journal* 27 (1961): 332; William C. Calderhead, "The Role of the Professional Slave Trader in a Slave Economy: Austin Woolfolk, a Case Study," *Civil War History* 23 (1977): 201; Robert W. Fogel and Stanley L. Engerman, *Time on the Cross: The Economics of American Negro Slavery* (Boston, 1974), 1:70; Joseph H. Ingraham, *The South-West by a Yankee*, 2 vol. (1835, reprint Ann Arbor, 1966) 2:244.

9. Andrew Durnford to John McDonogh, June 9, June 25 (quotation), July 6, 1835, John McDonogh Papers, Howard-Tilton Memorial Library, Tulane University, New Orleans; David O. Whitten, *Andrew Durnford: A Black Sugar Planter in the Antebellum South* (New Brunswick, N.J., 1995); David O. Whitten, "Slave Buying in 1835 Virginia as revealed by the Letters of a Louisiana Sugar Planter," *Louisiana History* 11 (1970): 231–44.

treated planters differently from slave traders, especially regarding the price of slaves. Maryland slaveowners gained a reputation for having two prices for their bondservants, one for private citizens and a higher one for traders. They gladly hiked up prices by a third or a half in order to separate speculators from their money.[10]

Planters who advertised for slaves usually indicated their desire to buy families. Doing so gave them a significant advantage over traders, who commonly bought slaves singly rather than in families or in mixed age groups. Planters emphasized that they were protecting bondservants by ensuring that they could preserve slave families. The advertisers repeated that they were gentlemen who bought slaves for noble reasons other than to make a profit. One man, who described himself as a gentleman from Louisiana, wanted to purchase fifteen or twenty slaves at a fair cash price. He added that he wanted the bondservants in families and would not resell them. There is a degree of tension in his words—mentioning cash but declaiming any speculative interests. Planters who purchased slaves tacitly acknowledged the contradiction in slavery between the slave as person and the slave as property. Buyers underscored their desire to purchase families of slaves so that they might shield themselves from slavery's ill effects. They separated themselves from speculators by playing on the paternal pretensions of slave sellers. Individual owners, then, went to great pains to prove they were not speculators. Doing so was a form of self-reassurance that they were not acting from selfish motives and blatantly exploiting their slaves.[11]

The claim of preserving family relations was a bit of sophistry, since most bondspeople, even if they were sold south with their immediate families, left behind aunts, uncles, cousins, or grandparents, not to mention close friends and their homes. The implicit claim of sheltering slave families from speculation was a rather invidious device used by planters to spare prospective sellers from uneasiness. If masters could be persuaded that the sale of their slaves was not so disruptive as might first appear, then those

10. *Easton Republican Star*, July 2, 1822 (first quotation); *Baltimore American*, August 25, 1831 (second quotation, emphasis in original); *Nashville Whig*, March 19, 1817; *Norfolk American Beacon*, June 18, 1818; *Baltimore American*, August 23, 1820; *Easton Republican Star*, May 18, 1824; *Richmond Enquirer*, July 12, 1825; *Washington Daily National Intelligencer*, May 31, 1826; "Estimates of the Value of Slaves, 1815," *American Historical Review* 19 (1914), 818; *Cambridge Chronicle*, December 24, 1836, as quoted in Bancroft Papers.

11. *Richmond Enquirer*, January 25, 1823; *Washington Daily National Intelligencer*, April 6, 1832; Tadman, *Speculators and Slaves*, 52–55.

who had misgivings about the process would be more likely to part with their bondservants. Bushrod Washington seemed to believe as such. Just as importantly, buyers who purchased an entire family could get such slaves at a reduced price, since slaves sold singly tended to have a higher purchase price than those sold in family units. The "gentlemen" who bought slaves for their own use considered themselves to be engaged in nobler conduct than speculation. Even though their activities mirrored the slave trade, they could convince themselves of their pure motives, especially in comparison to speculators. A gentleman would not destroy families or force slaves to move to the Deep South against their will. The fiction of a benevolent purchaser defined the limits of acceptable behavior in the South and enabled slaveholders to disregard reality in favor of a patronizing illusion of benevolence. It was also a means to erect a wall between speculators and slaveowners.

Although such planters fancied themselves as being enlightened because they spared their slaves the ravages of speculation, the difficulties associated with bringing the bondservants home might have lessened the glow of their supposed self-sacrifice. Unless a planter bought all of his slaves at one time, he had to make arrangements to detain his initial purchases. Some hotels and city jails were available for this purpose, especially in larger cities. John W. Smith of the Southern Hotel in Alexandria advertised that his establishment had everything necessary that "gentlemen from the SOUTHERN COUNTRY" would need, including security facilities. Traders normally provided the same service, for a fee, of course. Lewis Collier let it be known to Deep South planters that he had comfortable rooms for them and a jail for their slaves. Despite Collier's promises, private citizens tended to shy away from slave pens because of their reputation for disease. Andrew Durnford, for instance, refused to purchase a family of eight because he did not want to put them in a slave jail and risk illness.[12]

Arranging for the temporary detention of slaves was easier than making arrangements for their transportation. This process was more difficult than it appeared at first glance. The cheapest option was an overland march. A planter, though, had to buy food, horses, wagons, and other supplies—a daunting task for a novice. Walking south also had the disadvantage of being time-consuming and physically demanding. Despite these obstacles,

12. *Alexandria Phenix Gazette*, April 5, 1825 (quotation); *Richmond Enquirer*, March 19, 1833; Andrew Durnford to John McDonogh, June 25, 1835, McDonogh Papers.

the land trip was the most popular choice of planters because, according to a man familiar with such things, it required only two good mules, one or two horses, and a wagon. This veteran even provided his friend with a detailed set of directions from Petersburg, Virginia, to Clinton, Mississippi.[13]

Transporting slaves downriver was another option. Durnford used this alternative when his original plans to use the oceangoing transportation fell through. After much hesitation, he took the advice of a fellow traveler and rented a wagon, bought some horses, and transported his slaves across Virginia to a port on the Ohio River. From there, they floated down to New Orleans. Even though it cost him money he had not planned to spend and took twenty-five days, it was cheaper and faster than making the whole trip by land. Yet river transportation did have its risks. An Alabama planter warned his father to be especially careful on the Ohio. He said the best precaution was anchoring the boats midriver at night lest abolitionists board the vessels and free the bondspeople.[14]

Shipping slaves in seagoing vessels, also called coastwise travel, could also be effective, despite Durnford's experience. Although he avoided the Louisiana heat, Durnford bought his slaves during a lull in the shipping season. James Byers of Rapides Parish, Louisiana, by contrast, had no difficulty arranging for coastwise transportation of his slaves. In 1822 he sent 37 bondservants from Richmond to New Orleans, arriving with them in Louisiana during the first week of February. It is obvious he wanted young slaves, since 16 of his purchases were less than ten years old and only 1 was over twenty years of age. Likewise, Wilfred Dent left his Louisiana home and traveled to Maryland to buy slaves in 1827. After purchasing 29 bondservants, 20 of them aged nineteen or less, he loaded them on a ship in Annapolis and sailed for home. Like the other methods of transportation, coastwise shipping closely mirrored the interstate slave trade. Benjamin Ballard and Samuel T. Barnes, for instance, sent a total of 224 slaves from Norfolk to New Orleans in 1819. They wanted to be certain that they would not be confused with speculators. In the margins of the ship's manifest, each of them testified they were "not a dealer in human flesh." Owners did what they could to avoid any tangible association with speculation.[15]

13. John H. Faulkner to William C. Fitzhugh Powell, September 14, 1835, William C. Fitzhugh Powell Papers, DU; Baptist, *Creating an Old South*, 72–73.

14. Andrew Durnford to John McDonogh, June 10, 15, July 6, 1835, John McDonogh Papers; James Tutt to Richard Tutt, September 19, 1839, James Tutt Papers, DU.

15. U.S. Customs Service Records, Port of New Orleans, Louisiana, Inward Slave Manifests, Shipments of February 2, 1822, and January 7, 1827, microfilm in LSU; Ulrich Bonnell

Planters like Ballard and Barnes who wanted to compete in the slave-buying market had to come up with a ready stock of cash or pay higher prices in credit transactions. Slave traders constantly emphasized their ability to pay in cash or on short credit, which proved to be an enormous advantage, since the seller did not have to worry about collecting a debt. In an age when banks were notoriously unreliable, slave sellers who accepted long terms of credit invited financial ruin. The unpredictability of agriculture, moreover, was another reason to favor the immediacy of cash over the uncertainty of credit. A northern traveler heard that some planters brought up to $20,000 or even $50,000 with them for purchases. One way to raise such a staggering amount was to market a crop immediately before heading north. Durnford, for instance, sold his sugar before going to Virginia. Those with sizable holdings could also secure loans to finance their slave-buying trips. Ethan Andrews toured the South while doing research for his book on the internal slave trade. While traveling from Washington to Richmond, he fell in with a planter from Louisiana who had just purchased 155 slaves, the entire workforce of a Virginia plantation. The man, who spent $75,000 to stock a new farm in his home state, was concerned that if cotton fell below ten cents a pound he could not make his loan payments. As we have seen, such men who did bring rolls of cash with them were usually quick to note that they were not speculators. The presence of much cash was often a sign of trading activity, so planters who competed on this level were risking being labeled a speculator.[16]

The number of slaves purchased by Deep South planters will never be known, owing to the absence of solid records. Although it is an overstatement to claim that Gulf South planters controlled the market, their presence had a substantial impact. When Pryor McNeill moved to Mississippi in 1825, the first thing he noticed was that "the money has nearly all disappeared" from the area because so many planters went to the Upper South to buy bondservants. It is safe to say that such expeditions were a normal part of life. Planters so commonly made trips to the Chesapeake that one Virginia auction house advertised in a Natchez paper. It notified Mississippi

---

Phillips, *American Negro Slavery: A Survey of the Supply, Employment, and Control of Negro Labor as Determined by the Plantation Régime* (New York, 1918), 182 (quotation).

16. Tadman, *Speculators and Slaves*, 52–55; Ingraham, *South-West by a Yankee*, 2:244; Andrew Durnford to John McDonogh, June 9, 1825, McDonogh Papers; Andrews, *Domestic Slave-Trade*, 171–72.

planters that a judicial decree would force it to sell at least 150 slaves at Royallton Mills, about forty miles from Richmond. Joseph Ingraham, who visited the Natchez slave market in 1834, learned that the phrase "'he is gone to Virginia to buy negroes,' or 'niggers,' as is the elegant and equally common phraseology, is as often applied to a temporarily absent planter, as 'he is gone to Boston to buy goods,' to a New-England country merchant."[17]

One measure of the number of planters who bought slaves in the Upper South is the reaction of speculators. Traders took this challenge to their livelihood seriously. Franklin, for one, warned fellow speculator Rice C. Ballard to expect more southern planters than usual if Alabama passed a law banning the interstate trade. He knew that the planters would go after slaves in Baltimore, Alexandria, Richmond, and Norfolk. Franklin further cautioned Ballard that planters "will come in Droves" should a good crop be harvested. Shrewd traders like Franklin viewed such planters as a potential market rather than as a threat to their business. He instructed his agent in Richmond to pursue sales to Louisiana planters. Richmond trader James McFall employed a more elaborate strategy. He advertised in seven newspapers of Louisiana and Mississippi that he could buy slaves in advance and have them ready when planters arrived. James Hutcherson, a speculator who made Alexandria his base of operations, merely offered his expertise. He offered to "visit persons who may be strangers in the market" and counsel them in their search for slaves.[18]

The third type of forced migration for slaves was, of course, the interstate slave trade. Speculation, as it was called, began in the eighteenth century on a sporadic basis. It gained in strength over time, but originally moved few slaves when compared to the other types of forced migration. The trade was sporadic and uncertain at a time before there was the crush for labor in the Old Southwest. It also had much fluidity, with many speculators operating on a part-time basis or selling a variety of goods. Some such individuals were either auctioneers who handled the division of estates or

17. Pryor McNeill to Malcom McNeill, June 10, 1825, Elizabeth Winston Collection, NCDAH (first quotation); Ingraham, *South-West by a Yankee*, 2:234 (second quotation); *Natchez Mississippi State Gazette*, September 5, 1818; Calderhead, "Professional Slave Trader," 202.

18. Isaac Franklin to Rice C. Ballard, February 28, 1831, June 8, 1832, Rice C. Ballard Papers, UNC; *New Orleans Bee*, December 21, 1833; *Washington Daily National Intelligencer*, July 3, 1827 (quotation).

merchants who supplemented their income by arranging slave sales. In 1787, Moses F. Austin, for instance, was a commission merchant in Richmond who advertised for one hundred "Hearty and well made" slaves. Austin, whose son Stephen captured much fame, probably handled slave sales as part of his general business but was not a full-time slave trader. Most men who did become such speculators had no fixed depots for the buying or selling of slaves but roved about the countryside, buying a few slaves from different owners or purchasing them at auctions. When they acquired enough bondservants, these men marched their chattel south or west and sold them to whoever happened to be at hand. A few established themselves in a town and bought slaves from that area. John Stannard, for instance, remained in Fredericksburg, Virginia, long enough to publicize his desire to buy likely slaves. He was the exception, however, as most traders preferred not to advertise their presence prior to 1820. Most notices for slaves were for the sale rather than the purchase of bondservants, and the vast majority involved private individuals rather than professional slave traders.[19]

The relative unimportance of the interstate slave trade changed after serious enforcement of the international slave trade. Even though it is apparent that speculation became more prevalent, the numbers are silent when one tries to separate the interstate trade, movement with masters, and planter purchases. A further complication is the fact that no single source gives a clear view of slave movement. Ship manifests offer a glimpse into the movement of slaves along the nation's coasts, but they do not clearly distinguish between traders and planters. More importantly, they are incomplete. For instance, John Armfield told one observer that his firm

19. Austin's advertisement is quoted in Robert McColley, *Slavery and Jeffersonian Virginia* (Champaign, 1964), 164–65 (quotation); David B. Gracy, *Moses Austin: His Life* (San Antonio, 1987), 22–52; *Fredericksburg Virginia Herald*, September 12, 1810; Steven Deyle, "'By Farr the Most Profitable Trade': Slave Trading in British Colonial North America," *Slavery and Abolition* 10 (1989): 107–25; Chase C. Mooney, *Slavery in Tennessee* (Bloomington, Ind., 1957), 39; Ulrich B. Phillips and John R. Commons et al., eds., *A Documentary History of American Industrial Society*, vol. 2, *Plantation and Frontier Documents*, Ulrich B. Phillips, ed. (Cleveland, 1910), 55–56; Anita S. Goodstein, "Black History on the Nashville Frontier, 1780–1810," *Tennessee Historical Quarterly* 38 (1979): 403–6; Michael Tadman, "The Hidden History of Slave Trading in Antebellum South Carolina: John Springs III and Other 'Gentlemen Dealing in Slaves,'" *South Carolina Historical Magazine* 97 (1996): 6–29; Charles Ball, *Slavery in the United States: A Narrative of the Life and Adventures of Charles Ball, a Black Man* (1837; reprint, New York, 1969), 16–21, 28, 36–50, 66–80, 86–95.

shipped 1,000 slaves out of Alexandria in 1833 and expected to ship 1,200 the next year. Surviving manifests indicate Franklin and Armfield shipped 163 in 1833 and 258 a year later. Not only are many of the manifests themselves missing, but the coastwise trade constituted only a portion of the overall slave trade. Various counties and parishes have records of slave sales that have been analyzed by historians, but, again, they suffer from many of the same deficiencies. The documentary record of the interstate slave trade is simply woefully incomplete. Even when documents exist, there is no certain way to distinguish between traders and planters. Both tended to have younger slaves but there is no sure way to differentiate between the various types of forced migations.[20]

Historians have tried to resolve the matter despite these obstacles, but no consensus has emerged. Estimates place the share of the interstate slave trade at anywhere from 14 to 70 percent. It is likely that the lower figure is more accurate for the years prior to 1820. What is certain is that the number and proportion of slaves who moved westward with white migrants decreased during the nineteenth century. White emigration to Tennessee, Georgia, Florida, Alabama, Mississippi, Arkansas, and Louisiana was most prevalent in the first two decades of the century. According to one estimate, over 95,000 white residents moved into these seven states in the ten years preceding 1820. The number dropped during the next decade, and then plummeted to just under 40,000 between 1830 and 1840. Table 1 in the Appendix presents the complete statistics.[21]

Even as white migration slowed, the movement of slaves into these same states increased. From 1810 to 1820 almost 50,000 black migrants entered this area. During the next decade the number jumped to more than 81,000, and then doubled in the 1830s, a time of extensive growth in the slave trade. The demographic composition of the slaves involved in this great movement also changed. Six out of ten slave migrants in the decade before 1820 were under the age of ten, a figure almost double that of the entire South's population. This percentage dropped steadily over time, especially in the

20. Sweig, "Northern Virginia Slavery," 226; and Charles H. Wesley, "Manifests of Slave Shipments along the Waterways, 1808–1864," *Journal of Negro History* 27 (1942): 155–74. See, for example, affidavit of David C. Michie, January 24, 1832, and affidavit of William B. Howell, June 25, 1832, Natchez Trace Slaves and Slavery Collection, University of Texas.

21. The figures for this and the following paragraphs are taken from McClelland and Zeckhauser, *Demographic Dimensions*, 6, 138–43, 159–64.

1830s, but did not reach the southern norm. Slaves aged between ten and twenty in 1820 increased noticeably, while those aged from thirty to forty declined to half of their figure. The full statistics are found in Table 2 in the Appendix.[22]

The nature of forced slave migration was inextricably linked to the dynamics of white movement. A decline in white emigration created the opportunity for a noticeable growth in the interstate slave trade. It is probable that before 1820, the majority of slave owners brought their bondservants with them to the edge of settlement rather than moving and then buying from a speculator. White migrants appear to have favored young slaves who would provide a high return on their investment, withstand more work, labor for more years, and eventually produce children. As the newer states became settled and white migration abated, fewer bondservants accompanied their masters to new land. As a result, some masters traveled to Maryland and Virginia to buy additional slaves, while others stayed in the Lower South and purchased slaves from speculators. Slave traders tended not to trade in children under ten years of age, but especially bought and sold slaves between fifteen and thirty years old. It is this age grouping that gained strength over time, rising from a quarter of the population in the decade after 1810 to 45 percent in the 1830s. To put it another way, whites who migrated in 1835 as compared to twenty years earlier probably brought an equivalent ratio of slaves with them to their new land, but the number of bondservants declined because there were fewer white migrants. Additionally, those masters who were already in the Southwest needed more slaves for cultivation as they expanded their land holdings, so they relied more on speculators. Rather than being relatively stable in the nineteenth century, the interstate slave trade increased in volume and proportion during the 1820s and 1830s as white migration declined and the demand for labor increased in the Lower South. Although it is unclear exactly how many bondservants traveled in coffles or with migrating masters, what cannot be disputed is the sheer volume of slave movement in the early nineteenth century. One experienced slave trader wondered in amazement at the "spirit

22. Fogel and Engerman, *Time on the Cross*, 44–58; Allan Kulikoff, *The Agrarian Origins of American Capitalism* (Charlottesville, 1992), 228–29, 239–42; Tadman, *Speculators and Slaves*, 11–46, 225–27, 237–82; Gutman and Sutch, "Slave Family," 94–113; Steven H. Deyle, "The Domestic Slave Trade in America" (Ph.D. diss., Columbia University, 1995), 252–66.

for speculation and emigration." He estimated that one-fourth of the Upper South's slave population was in motion, "preparing to go to the south and make cotton."[23]

The advertisements of Chesapeake newspapers clearly reflected the growth of the interstate slave trade. Before 1815, there is a conspicuous absence of something that is a sure sign of trading activity—notices that promised to pay cash for large numbers of slaves. Virtually all of the advertisements dealing with bondservants referred to one or two slaves and asked interested parties to obtain specific information from the printer. Newspapermen routinely handled the slave sales in order to provide a measure of discretion for the transaction. An Annapolis resident, for instance, declared his intention to sell three slaves who were not "corrupted by town habits." In the vague and customary phrase of the day, the seller described the reason for the sale as "no fault." Most people understood the term to mean that the slave had done nothing to provoke the sale. Another possible message was that the owner could not be held responsible for instigating the sale. In other words, the master excused himself from blame for the sale and shielded himself from association with the exploitative side of speculation. The idea of "no fault" implied that the slave sale happened only because of circumstances beyond the owner's control. The assumption was that no one was to blame for "no fault" sales, since the owner sold slaves as a matter of self-preservation.[24]

The situation changed, however, by the end of the 1820s. Although there were still advertisements by individual sellers, speculators signaled their desire to purchase a growing number of slaves. They began using the heading "CASH FOR NEGROES" at the beginning of their advertisements as a means to set themselves apart. Cash gave speculators a distinct advantage because of its immediacy when compared to credit, especially in the wake of the Panic of 1819. Sellers definitely preferred the specie that traders could offer because it was a known quantity that did not fluctuate in value. A multitude of traders competed to buy slaves in ever increasing numbers. In long-running advertisements, Joseph W. Neal pledged "CASH! CASH! CASH!" for his customers. Traders who wanted hundreds of slaves were ubiq-

23. Jordan M. Saunders to David Burford, April 6, 1835, Burford Papers (quotations); Tadman, *Speculators and Slaves*, 234.

24. *Annapolis Maryland Gazette*, September 12, 1810 (first quotation), July 25, 1822; *Baltimore American and Commercial Daily Advertiser*, May 4, 1815 (second quotation).

uitous. In 1836 Robert Fenwick pledged to give the "highest market price" in cash for slaves. The same issue of the paper contained James H. Birch's ad that promised *he* could give the highest cash price for bondservants. The headlines grew bolder, the word *cash* (always in capital letters) became more frequent, the desire for hundreds of slaves was more prominent, and the ads themselves were longer. In the early-to-mid-1820s traders often concealed their identities by asking prospective sellers to inquire of the printer or go to the bar of the local tavern. No longer. Speculators wanted name recognition in the highly competitive market of slave trading. They also made explicit appeals to the pecuniary interests of slaveholders. Excessive use of the word *cash* meant that speculators had reduced the master-slave relationship to one of a purely economic nature rather than something more noble. Such ads seemed to represent the worst side of slavery. Speculation was a blatantly commercial activity that cut across the grain of the traditional conception of the master-slave relationship.[25]

A number of important slave trading routes emerged over time. The first main artery of the interstate slave trade passed through Alexandria, Fredericksburg, Richmond, and Columbia before stopping in Hamburg, South Carolina. Traders on this "upper route" after 1815 probably followed the normal routine of assembling slaves in a coffle, that is, handcuffing the male slaves together in pairs and passing a long chain or rope through all of the manacles to keep them together, much like fish on a stringer. At night, the men slept in their manacles to prevent the more adventurous from trying to escape. Reasoning that females and children were less likely to run away, traders allowed them to plod unchained behind the men. Those too young, old, or feeble to walk rode in a supply wagon. A speculator, or perhaps one of his armed assistants, followed the procession on horseback to dissuade any escape attempts. Once the coffle went far enough south where escape was unlikely, he unshackled the slaves in order to speed up the march.[26]

25. *Washington National Intelligencer*, November 17, 1831 (first quotation), September 30, 1836 (remaining quotations); Baptist, *Creating an Old South*, 72–74.

26. *Baltimore American*, December 25, 1815 (quotation), July 12, 1816; Calderhead, "Professional Slave Trader," 195–211; Dickson J. Preston, *Young Frederick Douglass: The Maryland Years* (Baltimore, 1980), 76–80; Frederic Bancroft, *Slave Trading in the Old South* (1931; reprint, Columbia, 1996), 39–44; Ball, *Slavery in the United States*, 38; Walter Johnson, *Soul by Soul: Life Inside the Antebellum Slave Market* (Cambridge, 2000), 63–77; John W. Blassingame, ed., *Slave Testimony: Two Centuries of Letters, Speeches, Interviews, and Autobiographies* (Baton Rouge, 1977), 704–6; Featherstonhaugh, *Excursion through the Slave States*, 36–37; Henry C. Knight, *Letters from the South and West* (Boston, 1824), 78–79; F. Nash Boney, ed.,

The upper route began to be less traveled as other markets proved more valuable to slave traders. In the mid-1820s Natchez and New Orleans emerged as the two major termini of the interstate slave trade. Whites moved in increasing numbers to a stretch of land across Alabama, Mississippi, and Louisiana, an area that would become known as the Black Belt because of the dark color of the soil and, eventually, the concentration of slaves. Land in the Black Belt was durable, fertile, ideally suited to cotton, often close to excellent water navigation, and cheap. The intense pressure on Native Americans to give up their lands coincided with the desire for more land and more slaves. Most migrants to the Black Belt chose to plant cotton, a crop that produced quick economic dividends. The labor-intensive nature of cotton cultivation meant that slaves were in high demand in developing areas. Traders knew very well that the cotton market was the engine that drove their speculation. The price of slaves, one trader admitted, was regulated "in a great measure" by the price of cotton. Those settlers who chose to plant cotton naturally looked to slavery in the Chesapeake to supply their labor needs. Traders forced more and more slaves to march from the Chesapeake to the Old Southwest as the 1820s progressed. Doing so increased the visibility of the slave trade. It was difficult not to notice processions of up to one hundred slaves clogging the main roads. Virginians traveling west were known to hurl "curses and execrations" at speculators. Once coffles and speculators became a common sight on the roads, citizens cast about for ways to control them, so as to minimize "the most painful feelings" created in bystanders.[27]

With the arising of termini in Natchez and New Orleans, new routes opened up. Some enterprising traders marched their bondservants to the western end of Virginia and then loaded them onto flatboats or steamboats

---

Slave Life in Georgia: A Narrative of the Life, Sufferings, and Escape of John Brown, a Fugitive Slave (Savannah, 1972), 16; Richard Puryear to Isaac Jarratt, March 3, 1834, Jarratt Puryear Papers, DU.

27. Jordan M. Saunders to David Burford, May 24, 1847, Burford Papers (first quotation); Phillips, ed., *Plantation and Frontier Documents*, 2:55 (second quotation); Washington Grand Jury, as quoted in Theodore D. Weld and James Thome, *Slavery and the Internal Slave Trade in the United States of North America* (London, 1841), 206 (third quotation); Joyce E. Chaplin, "Creating a Cotton South in Georgia and South Carolina, 1760–1815," *JSH* 57 (1991): 299–315; Jane Turner Censer, "Southwestern Migration among North Carolina Planter Families: 'The Disposition to Emigrate,'" *JSH* 57 (1991): 407–26; James Oakes, *The Ruling Race: A History of American Slaveholders* (New York, 1982), 69–95.

for a voyage down the Ohio and Mississippi Rivers. Use of boats reduced travel time while simultaneously resting the slaves. Wheeling, Virginia, emerged as the "great thoroughfare" in this route. Other speculators bought slaves in Kentucky and Tennessee on their way downriver. In either case, traders allowed the bondservants, up to seventy-five on a boat, to roam the deck during the trip. If the vessel needed to dock at shore for wood or other provisions, the speculator chained the slaves together in pairs to prevent their escape. Isaac Franklin learned about slave trading from the river trade. As a teenager he transported his brother's produce to New Orleans, and while in Louisiana he witnessed several slave transactions. Franklin began selling bondservants by 1810, but his service as a private in the War of 1812 halted any efforts to establish himself in the slave trade. After the war, the twenty-six-year-old became a full-time speculator, most likely buying slaves in his home state and transporting them downriver to Natchez, where he sold them.[28]

Franklin brought slaves to Natchez just as that city's slave market emerged as one of the most important in the United States. A visitor described the scene in 1817. When he stood at the brow of the two-hundred-foot cliff that overlooked the waterfront, he was amazed to see fourteen flatboats loaded with slaves. The speculators forced the bondservants to wear attractive clothing so that they might convince casual observers to become serious bidders. It was an old trick, the visitor thought, borrowing "the same principle that jockeys do horses upon sale." A few traders sold their slaves right from the boats, but most led their slaves up the steep climb to the town's center. Despite the steep incline, the bondservants moved in single or double files in well-ordered procession. Each carried a bundle, possibly old clothes, often balancing it on his or her head. The speculators brought their slaves to a jail, or pen, which served as a holding facility until they sold the bondservants. Natchez, like most other cities, tightly controlled where traders could build their pens. Slaves clustered in the town's center until 1833, when the city passed an ordinance forcing jails to be out-

28. Samuel Joseph May, *Some Recollections of our Anti-Slavery Conflict* (Boston, 1869), 12; Knight, *Letters from the South and West*, 101–102; Paul Jefferson, ed., *The Travels of William Wells Brown* (New York, 1991), 40–43; *Lexington Kentucky Gazette*, September 29, 1826; *New Orleans Daily Picayune*, October 7, 1846; slave sale receipts dated May 6, 1809, December 30, 1809, and May 29, 1810, in David Weeks and Family Papers, LSU; Byron Sistler and Samuel Sistler, *Tennesseans in the War of 1812* (Nashville, 1992), 200.

side of the city limits. Most speculators moved to an area that became known as the Forks in the Road or Niggerville, a small group of buildings a few miles from Natchez.[29]

While Natchez relied on the overland routes and river trade to supply most of its slaves, New Orleans looked to the ocean. The development of the coastwise trade stimulated the growth of the Crescent City into the largest slave-trading center in the United States. Transporting bondservants in seagoing vessels was the most efficient way to deliver them to the Deep South. While the costs were higher than for an overland journey, so too were the profits, with advantages including a reduced risk of escape, less strain on the slaves, a quicker trip, and a faster time from purchase to resale. Austin Woolfolk was one of the first slave traders to make extensive use of the coastwise trade, but others such as Franklin and Armfield, Abner Robinson, William Fulcher, Joseph Isnard, Edwin Lee, David Anderson, and Bartholomew Accinelly quickly realized the potential of moving slaves in this fashion.[30]

The coastwise trade greatly expanded the interstate movement of slaves by allowing speculators to safely ship more than a hundred bondservants at once without leaving the Chesapeake themselves. A federal law of 1816 stipulated that all slaves shipped in the coastal waters be described by name, sex, and height also benefited the traders by safeguarding their purchases. The captain was responsible for the bondservants until arrival at the port of destination. Speculators arranged for someone to meet the ship at the dock in New Orleans, take charge of the slaves, and sell them on the local market. Woolfolk became a major slave trader by participating heavily in the coastwise trade. Instead of asking for fifteen to twenty slaves to go to the Georgia market, he notified the public in 1821 that he would pay the highest prices

29. Henry B. Fearon, *Sketches of America: A Narrative of a Journey of Five Thousand Miles through the Eastern and Western States of America* (London, 1818), 270 (quotation); Estwick Evans, *A Pedestrious Tour of Four Thousand Miles, through the Western States and Territories during the Winter and Spring of 1818* (Concord, 1819), 213; *Natchez Mississippi Republican*, October 24, 1822; Ingraham, *South-West by a Yankee*, 2:235–47; Jim Barnett and H. Clark Burkett, "The Forks of the Road Slave Market at Natchez," *Journal of Mississippi History* 63 (2001): 168–87.

30. Freudenberg and Pritchett, "Domestic Slave Trade," 472–75; New Orleans Inward Slave Manifests. See also advertisements in the *New Orleans Louisiana Advertiser*, January 3, May 5, 1826, December 9, 1828; *New Orleans Courier*, March 19, November 16, 1825, January 13, 1827.

in gold or silver for one hundred bondservants who would be shipped to New Orleans. Eleven years later he wanted three hundred slaves. It is unlikely that he actually wanted to buy three hundred slaves at one time, but the exaggerated number was a device to attract attention and reflects the trade's increased volume. By all accounts, Woolfolk and his relatives succeeded in their efforts to expand their slave-trading operations, at least during the 1820s. They were acute businessmen who made themselves into the preeminent slave-trading firm in Maryland. Customs manifests reveal that they consistently sent shipments of forty or more slaves to New Orleans several times a year. By the middle of the 1820s, the family dominated the trade out of Maryland, sending, according to one estimate, 2,288 slaves to Louisiana between 1819 and 1832. The Woolfolks handled so much of the Maryland trade that the name Woolfolk became symbolic of the slave trade. Frederick Douglass recalled that slaves on Maryland's Eastern Shore equated being "sold to Woldfolk [*sic*]" with banishment to the Deep South.[31]

Franklin, too, took advantage of the coastwise trade to New Orleans and switched his base of operations to the Chesapeake. Even while establishing himself in Alexandria, Franklin formed a partnership with John Armfield, a former stagecoach driver. The two men signed articles of agreement in February 1828 and three months later leased a house on Duke Street in Alexandria that became the headquarters for their firm. They signaled their intention to be a large trading concern by advertising for 150 male and female slaves aged eight to twenty-five. The firm consistently sought to purchase large numbers of slaves, saying it could pay higher prices than anyone else. Whether or not Franklin and Armfield paid the best prices for slaves is open to debate, but clearly their marketing strategy was efficient and profitable. When the Virginia trade proved too small to contain their ambitions, they expanded into the Baltimore area. Armfield was giddy that they paid less there for slaves than they did in Alexandria. He told a colleague that "Woolfolk's done us a good kindness when he caused us to go into that market." The firm soon cut into Woolfolk's business and helped persuade him to quit the trade.[32]

31. Calderhead, "Professional Slave Trader," 200 (estimate); Preston, *Young Frederick Douglass*, 76 (quotation); New Orleans Inward Slave Manifests, November 25, 1822, December 13, 1824, April 21, 1825, May 5, 1828; Wesley, "Manifests of Slave Shipments," 155–74; *Easton Republican Star*, January 2, 1821; Bancroft, *Slave Trading*, 40.

32. *Alexandria Phenix Gazette*, May 17, 1828; John Armfield to Rice C. Ballard, March 26, 1832, Ballard Papers (quotation); Stephenson, *Isaac Franklin*, 23; Isabel Howell, "John Armfield, Slave-Trader," *Tennessee Historical Quarterly* 2 (1943): 3–29.

Franklin and Armfield offered top dollar for slaves because they eliminated the middlemen by owning and operating their own fleet of four ships. The first ship, the *United States*, was a "fast sailing packet brig" that could hold up to 150 slaves, although it normally carried about a hundred. The firm's second ship, the *Tribune*, was of similar size and had two sections in its hold for housing slaves. The rear section held up to eighty bondservants and normally carried women, while one hundred men could cram into the forward compartment. Two raised platforms, each about five or six feet deep, jutted into the ship's interior. Slaves lay on the ledges "as close as they can stow away." In the 1835 shipping season, one of Franklin and Armfield's ships left Alexandria every other week. On return trips, the ships carried sugar, molasses, whiskey, and cotton. Sailing at consistent intervals, Franklin and Armfield's vessels brought more regularity to the trade, reduced outside costs, and provided revenue on the return voyage. Just as importantly, they freed up Franklin and Armfield to concentrate on marketing slaves rather than spending time transporting them.[33]

The establishment of a permanent headquarters was another vital component to the growth of the interstate trade. In the early years of the trade, speculators had no fixed base of operations but tended to establish temporary lodgings in the seedy taverns of Virginia and Maryland. In the Washington area, the taverns got so full during the trading season that owners devoted specific rooms to holding slaves. The Bell Tavern in Richmond became notorious for having speculators fill up its beds and for holding auctions at its front door. The men who later bought the tavern did so despite the "merited and invidious character universally imputed to it." In 1823 Woolfolk changed things by opening a slave jail at his residence near the Three Ton Tavern on Pratt Street in Baltimore. Using a fixed base of operations rather than staying in taverns enabled him to create a sense of continuity in the increasingly competitive trade. Besides making it easy for purchasers to locate him, the move reduced long-term costs because Woolfolk did not have to pay jailer's fees. Other speculators soon copied the idea and pens became a common sight in the larger towns of the Upper South.

33. *Alexandria Phenix Gazette*, December 22, 1829 (first quotation); William Jay, *Miscellaneous Writings on Slavery* (Boston, 1853), 157–58 (second quotation); *New Orleans Bee*, October 20, 1831; New Orleans Inward Slave Manifests, October 22, 1828; Stephenson, *Isaac Franklin*, 40–44; Janice G. Artemel, Elizabeth A. Crowell, and Jeff Parker, *The Alexandria Slave Pen: The Archaeology of Urban Captivity* (Washington, 1987), 11–56.

Samuel Dawson, for instance, established his pen about eight miles from Fredericksburg. In Richmond, the best location that Lewis Collier could find was near the poor house, while Charles Mills put his facility next to a livery stable. An antislavery organization noted with some satisfaction that most jails were little more than "dilapidated huts" perched on the outskirts of town. While the danger of escapes was always a possibility, the fact that a slave jail drove down property values was motivation enough for residents to restrict their location. Even though the interstate slave trade was increasing in size and establishing a constant presence in the South, it physically remained separate from the best parts of town.[34]

The widespread tendency for speculators to form partnerships coincided with the proliferation of slave pens. Before 1820 it appears that most traders operated alone. Since the trade was so small at that time, splitting the profits between two or three people was not practical. As speculation grew in scale, a joint venture held out the possibility of trading on such a scale where dividing the money would not be onerous. The two ideas, of course, were interrelated. Forming partnerships and dividing the labor meant that speculators could sell more slaves and presumably earn enough money to keep everyone satisfied. Traders became responsible for handling one aspect of the trade—the purchases in the Upper South, movement of the slaves, or the sales in the Lower South. In this fashion traders did not have to suspend purchasing while they accompanied a coffle or waited until selling all of their bondservants. George Kephart knew the advantages of joining forces with other speculators. He mulled over whether to join forces with James Purvis or Thomas McCargo. Kephart wanted to stay in Virginia, admitting that it would be "unpleasant" to be in the selling market. He wanted to ally with someone who could remain in New Orleans and could cultivate the personal relationships necessary to be successful.[35]

34. *Richmond Enquirer*, July 10, 1835 (first quotation); Andrews, *Domestic Slave-Trade*, 80; *Baltimore American*, August 11, December 12, 1823, April 9, 1824; Jesse Torrey, *A Portraiture of Domestic Slavery in the United States* (1817; reprint, St. Clair Shores, Mich., 1970), 41–42; *Liberator*, June 7, 1834, 91 (second quotation); *Fredericksburg Virginia Herald*, April 19, 1826; *Richmond Enquirer*, April 19, November 24, 1833.

35. George Kephart to John Armfield, March 16, 1838, Ballard Papers (quotation); unknown to George Kephart, August 4, 1839, Papers of George Kephart, Raritan Bay Union and Eagleswood Military Academy Collection, New Jersey Historical Society, Newark; Johnson, *Soul by Soul*, 47–49; Tadman, *Speculators and Slaves*, 12–21; Bancroft, *Slave Trading*, 19–25.

In a similar fashion, Woolfolk employed several men in his speculative enterprise once he switched his focus to the coastwise trade. He started with a number of his relatives, men who were probably his brothers. Richard Woolfolk originally sent slaves from Norfolk to New Orleans, but then moved to Maryland for the purpose of buying slaves. Joseph Woolfolk also became an important buyer in Maryland, setting up his operations at Lowe's Tavern in Easton. This location was ideal, since it was close to the site of the county slave auction, the local newspaper offices, the courthouse (where bills of sales were filed), and the local jail (where the sheriff boarded slaves for twenty-five cents a day). Joseph enticed planters to visit him by noting that he had just received "a fresh supply of that much wished for article, CASH." Austin, Richard, and Joseph sent their slaves to New Orleans, where John and Samuel Woolfolk handled all the sales. Even Austin Woolfolk Sr. visited New Orleans and occasionally helped out. The use of relatives was quite common in the slave trade. John Springs III and his brother Eli bought slaves in Maryland and brought them to South Carolina. Samuel and Joseph Meek were involved together, as were Isaac Franklin, his brother James, and his nephew by marriage, John Armfield. Speculators also formed alliances with nonrelatives. Tyre Glen signed an agreement with Isaac Jarratt in 1831 and then with William G. Norton five years later. Whether or not speculators kept their alliances within the family is not as important as what the partnerships reveal. The tendency to ally with others shows the increasing volume of the interstate slave trade. Three men could collectively arrange for the transportation of more slaves from the Upper South to the Lower South than they could separately. More important, the trend towards a corporate structure, albeit a primitive one, indicates an increased emphasis on the commercial nature of the trade. A single speculator often mimicked the actions of white migrants. Slave-trading firms, on the other hand, used methods and tactics alien to the individual slaveholder. It is no coincidence that just as the interstate slave trade was becoming more noticeable it was also becoming blatantly commercial.[36]

36. *Easton Republican Star*, August 2, 1825 (quotation), October 9, 1827, June 17, 1828; New Orleans Inward Slave Manifests, December 17, 1821, May 5, 1822, November 18, 1823; Tadman, "Hidden History of Slave Trading," 21; Joseph Meek Papers, VHS; Stephenson, *Isaac Franklin*, 23; Howell, "John Armfield," 3–6; Agreement of Tyre Glen and Isaac Jarratt, November 13, 1831, and "articles of agreement" between Glen and William G. Norton, June 6, 1836, Tyre Glen Papers, DU.

Not only did speculators form partnerships, but they also employed local agents who were responsible for a specific territory. Woolfolk appears to have been the first trader to use such men, who bought slaves in one or two counties and then sent them to Baltimore for transshipment south. Henry N. Templeman worked the Eastern Shore for Woolfolk in the late 1820s. Like most of the other agents, Templeman lasted only a few years with Woolfolk before he moved on to found his own trading operation. Agents tried to establish themselves as speculators in their own right once they gained a few years' experience. The rapid turnover made it difficult to keep good people. A trader, most likely Woolfolk himself, advertised that he wanted three or four "respectable men" to travel through Maryland "to aid in the disposal of a very popular work." He promised a "liberal compensation" but warned that only those who could provide security for a significant amount of money should apply. Paying in cash was one of the trader's greatest advantages but could be a liability when unscrupulous traders got their hands on large amounts of money.[37]

Another innovation in the trade was the tendency amongst speculators to form loose alliances with one another. Typically a small trader made an affiliation with a large speculator and transported the slaves along the coast so that no one was tied down accompanying a coffle. Ira Bowman, for instance, had a meager slave-trading business out of a hotel in Alexandria. In 1825 he started sending bondservants on consignment to one of the Woolfolks in New Orleans. Both parties gained from the arrangement, as Bowman could stay in Alexandria and Woolfolk did not risk handing over large sums of cash to someone of dubious reputation. Franklin and Armfield made similar arrangements with traders. Armfield, who lured away some of Woolfolk's affiliates, established alliances with speculators in and around Richmond and Warrenton in Virginia, and Easton, Frederick, and Baltimore in Maryland. With these men making most of the purchases, Armfield arranged for the slaves' transportation while Franklin sold them in Natchez and New Orleans. Franklin and Armfield sold the slaves of their affiliates for half the profit, a beneficial arrangement for both parties, since it cut down on overhead. As the largest firm of the day, Franklin and Armfield tried to control both the buying and selling on the slave-trading markets, in

37. Calderhead, "Professional Slave Trader," 197; *Easton Republican Star*, October 9, 1827; *Princess Anne Village Herald*, December 6, 1830, as quoted in Bancroft, *Slave Trading*, 32; Johnson, *Soul by Soul*, 53–55; *Baltimore American*, December 18, 1822 (quotations).

effect establishing a monopoly. Jordan Saunders, Franklin and Armfield's agent in Warrenton, explained to his silent partner how the company operated. He said they hoped to reduce the amount paid for slaves by holding down competition. Once the bondservants reached New Orleans, Saunders bragged that Franklin and Armfield could manipulate the number they offered for sale at one time. Saunders thought the firm could "hold their fellows at $700" despite market pressures to the contrary.[38]

Franklin's arrangement with Rice C. Ballard seems to have been typical of the alliances between traders. The customs invoice that accompanied each coastwise shipment contained enough information to identify the slaves and normally indicated their purchase price. Speculators sent specific instructions on another invoice, as well. In 1836 Tait, Boudar, and Company of Richmond sent twenty-three slaves to Ballard, Franklin, and Company in Natchez. The invoice listed the name, age, height, color, and cost of each of the slaves, and left a space for remarks. Ballard scribbled notes about the specific qualities of many of the slaves on the reverse side. One man was an "excellent marksman—a pretty good cook and also a very smart dining room servant," while there was also "an excellent cook washer & Ironer & a very steady woman" in the group. Specific skills such as these enhanced a slave's value, so traders wanted to ensure that purchasers knew the abilities of any slaves they purchased. Sellers could not always obey the shippers' wishes, however. When Franklin received a shipment of sixty-three slaves from Ballard, he assured the man that he would heed the written instructions but also cautioned that the invoice price was so high that profits would be meager.[39]

It is clear that Franklin and Armfield considered themselves separate from their affiliates. In Richmond, for instance, they kept in constant contact with Ballard. Franklin or his brother gave Ballard frequent information

38. Jordan M. Saunders to David Burford, November 17, 1829 (quotation), and December 13, 1831, Burford Papers; New Orleans Inward Slave Manifests, November 3, 1825, February 6, 1826, March 2, 1827; *Alexandria Phenix Gazette*, May 25, 1825; Michael Ridgeway, "A Peculiar Business: Slave Trading in Alexandria, Virginia, 1825–1861" (master's thesis, Georgetown University, 1976), 19–21; John Armfield to Rice C. Ballard, March 26, 1832, Isaac Franklin to Rice C. Ballard, October 5, November 1, 1833, and James R. Franklin to Rice C. Ballard, November 23, 1832, Ballard Papers.

39. Slave invoice from Tait, Boudar, and Company to Ballard, Franklin, and Company, dated September 23, 1836 (quotations), and Isaac Franklin to Rice C. Ballard, November 5, 1833, Ballard Papers.

as to the state of the slave market in general and the status of Ballard's slaves in particular. Ballard, in turn, concentrated on buying slaves in and around Richmond but did not have to take the time to accompany them to New Orleans or Natchez. Franklin and Armfield made some extra cash for handling a few more slaves. Since they were already established in the Lower South, the cost of taking on new slaves was minimal. There was a limit, however, to how many men could be affiliated with Franklin and Armfield. At one point, Franklin turned down the opportunity to expand his business dealings, explaining that he had as many "concerns & partners as our two men can possibly do justice."[40]

Speculators had to trust one another if such an arrangement was to work properly. Unscrupulous traders in New Orleans could rob their colleagues by claiming a lower selling price for slaves and pocketing the difference. At one point, Ballard grew uneasy about his alliance with Franklin and complained about the terms. Franklin responded with a long letter extolling the virtues of the firm in an effort to convince Ballard to continue the arrangement. His words may have been persuasive, but he also wrote from a position of strength. Franklin knew that Ballard had few choices, since there was a surfeit of corrupt traders. At one point he reminded his colleague that Lewis Collier in Richmond could find no affiliates because he was a thief. Even the best-known speculators resorted to underhanded methods. As Woolfolk began losing business, he started cheating people. Other traders avoided any dealings with him because of his growing reputation for dishonesty.[41]

In the 1820s and beyond, the interstate slave trade grew from paltry beginnings to a vital component of the southern economy. One antislavery writer concluded that before then the trade "was hardly known." During this pivotal decade, speculation moved from something that was sporadic, unorganized, and uncommon to a trade that was regular, organized, and ubiquitous. Slave trading emerged as a major southern commodity market, with active sellers demanding buyers. An increasing number of men became speculators during the decade, and most of the prominent antebellum traders starting selling slaves during this time. Speculators dramatically changed the nature of their business by using innovations such as slave jails, agents,

40. Isaac and James Franklin to Rice C. Ballard, October 9, 1833, Ballard Papers.

41. Isaac Franklin to Rice C. Ballard, August 15, 1832, October 9, 1834, John Armfield to Rice C. Ballard, March 26, 1832, Ballard Papers.

and coastwise transportation to bring a measure of certainty and regularity to the trade. Speculators established headquarters which doubled as pens, so they would no longer have to keep their slaves in local jails, or worse yet, taverns. Buyers in Louisiana, Alabama, and Mississippi who desired labor now had a good indication of when new slaves would arrive and could be assured that they had enough slaves from which to choose.[42]

The emergence of the interstate slave trade paralleled the general economic development of the United States following the War of 1812. Americans dug canals, established corporations, built factories, and generally promoted commercial development. The rapid expansion and increasing sophistication of the interstate slave trade fits into this tendency to promote a capitalist ethos. Slave traders littered their correspondence with references to profit, loss, cash, cost, and expense. Speculators publicly and unabashedly stressed cash transactions and reiterated their ability to pay top dollar for slaves. Slaves were not valued as individuals but perceived as commodities, notable for their age, skill, muscularity, or reproductive capacity. Formulas became supreme, as traders placed slaves into categories such as "#1," "bright," "scrub," and "fancy," or simply sold bondservants by the pound. This message of assertive free enterprise could be a jarring experience for southerners accustomed to framing the master-slave relationship in terms of rights, duties, and responsibilities. Speculation cast aside such notions in favor of impersonal factors.[43]

The transformation of the interstate slave trade from a loose-limbed, speculative enterprise into an advanced and organized business led to significant changes in southern society. Most obviously, an untold number of slaves had to rearrange their lives to accommodate the whims of their masters. The trade produced brutal hardship and suffering for the bondservants swept up in its wake. Speculation's growth also affected southern whites. Before the War of 1812, when speculation was haphazard and small, trading barely entered into the public consciousness. It easily blended with the other types of forced migration. But as speculators succeeded and expanded

42. *Liberator*, March 20, 1838, 62.

43. Charles Grier Sellers, *The Market Revolution: Jacksonian America, 1815–1846* (New York, 1991); Harry L. Watson, "Slavery and Development in a Dual Economy: The South and the Market Revolution," in *The Market Revolution in America: Social, Political, Religious Expressions, 1800–1880*, ed. Melvyn Stokes and Stephen Conway (Charlottesville, 1996), 50–51.

their methods and scope, they brought the trade into contact with countless southerners. Doing so meant that many whites tried to disassociate themselves from the more objectionable features of speculation, such as coffles and the emphasis on cash and profit. Bushrod Washington's experience shows just how defensive southerners could get when accused of behaving in a fashion that mimicked slave trading. Southerners now had to confront the most difficult aspects of the peculiar institution. They had to find some way to explain the presence of the interstate slave trade—clearly exploitative behavior—in the midst of an institution that was supposed to be beneficial for the slaves.

CHAPTER 2

Slave Resistance, Coffles, and the Debates over Slavery in the Nation's Capital

She did not know that she would ignite a national debate when she tried to leap to her death from the third floor of George Miller's Tavern. Miller's seedy establishment had gained a reputation as the most notorious slave depot in Washington. The woman, known only as Anna, jumped because a slave trader purchased her and two of her children but declined to take their siblings and father. The price for her impulsive action was a broken back and two shattered arms. Her crumpled body bore strong testimony to the destructive impact of the interstate slave trade. Anna explained her deed by simply saying, "I did not want to go." When John Randolph learned of the incident, he rose to his feet in the House of Representatives and blasted the inhuman sale of slaves carried on in the District. In so doing, he cast doubt upon the efficacy of the interstate slave trade by closely linking it to abhorrent activities and results. It was the first direct denunciation of the interstate slave trade in Congress. Randolph turned his finger of scorn towards an issue that most others, southerners as well as northerners, would rather avoid or ignore.[1]

The Virginia representative began by pointing to events that were hap-

1. Jesse Torrey to John Randolph, April 29, 1816 (quotation), Deposition of Francis Scott Key, April 22, 1816, and Sworn Statement of Samuel Booker, March 7, 1816, all in Papers of the Select Committee to Inquire into the Existence of an Inhuman and Illegal Traffic in Slaves in the District of Columbia, HR 14A-C.17.4, National Archives, Washington, D.C.; Torrey, *Portraiture of Domestic Slavery*, 42–44; *Debates and Proceedings in the Congress of the United States* (Washington, 1854), 14th Congress, 1st sess., March 1, 1816, 1115; *Washington National Intelligencer*, September 28, 1815, May 7, 1816.

pening under the very noses of his colleagues. Not even on the rivers of Africa, he contended, was such a sin committed before God and man. At least the African trade plucked "savages" from their native wilds, rather than "tearing the civilized, informed negro, habituated to cultivated life" from his family. Lest slaveowners become concerned that Randolph was going to propose drastic measures, he clearly distinguished between the movement of slaves as a natural consequence of ownership and a systematic slave market. The former was not offensive to Randolph, and he thought the government had no business meddling with it; the latter, though, was indeed offensive, and Randolph thought something should be done to rectify the situation. That Washington had become a depot for the nefarious traffic was regrettable. He was mortified when a high-ranking foreigner told him that even though America called itself the land of the free, the workings of the slave trade caused Europeans to be "horrorstruck and disgusted."[2]

Randolph sounded almost like an abolitionist when he described "hard-hearted masters" who sold slaves for pecuniary gain. Employing a technique that would eventually become standard fare with antislavery advocates, he used an emotional plea depicting the struggles of a few heroic slaves as a way to appeal to the finer senses of his listeners. Randolph told the story of a slave who had saved enough money to purchase the freedom of his wife and child. When the man died, his master sold the family anyway, contrary to the standards of decent society. This and other stories put a human face on a trade that treated its subjects as commodities. By ignoring abstract arguments and dwelling on concrete examples, Randolph hoped to prod the House into taking some type of action to prevent the worst abuses of slavery within Washington. At the end of his long diatribe, he moved that the Committee for the District of Columbia devise a speedy means to stop the lawful trading of slaves in the District. If the House declined to act, Randolph, with his characteristic bluster, threatened to undertake the business himself "and ferret out of their holes and corners the villains who carried it on."

Randolph's speech, the subsequent congressional investigation, and further debates on Capitol Hill demonstrate how the slave trade was working

2. *Debates and Proceedings*, 14th Cong., 1st sess., March 1, 1816, 1115–17 (these and the following quotations are from this speech); *Washington National Intelligencer*, March 2, 1816; *Niles' Weekly Register*, March 9, 1816, 30; Russell Kirk, *John Randolph of Roanoke: A Study in American Politics* (Chicago, 1964), 131–39.

its way into the national consciousness. As speculation progressed from its inchoate nature into something more complex, it posed numerous problems for many southerners. They began to struggle with how to reconcile the negative consequences of slave trading with the necessity of its existence. Speculation posed difficult questions concerning property rights in slaves, over whether there was any legitimate distinction between an owner migrating with slaves or a speculator transporting them, and even raised issues about the nature of slavery itself. Two of the most thoughtful categories of southern citizens—politicians and writers—grappled with these issues. The end result was frustration, confusion, and no solid answers.

Northerners, too, were becoming aware of the interstate slave trade's importance to the young nation. Public officials from free states who came to Washington often encountered slavery for the first time. Such contact might be relatively benign: servants, waiters, or footmen. It might also be harsh: ragged clothing, bare feet, or coffles. The grim sight of bondspeople and the heroic acts of resistance by individual slaves helped some northern congressmen break free from the tight grip of racism. They could envision slaves not as property to be exploited but as people to be free.[3]

The debate that began on the street below Miller's tavern indicates the intellectual and ideological distances that many Americans had traveled between the closure of the international slave trade and rise of the internal one. Almost a decade earlier, Randolph had fought desperately to increase the tonnage requirement for the ships that carried slaves in the coastwise trade. His argument was based on a keen desire to prevent the federal government from limiting the authority of masters over their slaves. He wanted no controls placed on slavery or the slaveholder. Randolph's ravings helped win him the reputation as one of the South's foremost defenders of slavery. Now, in 1816, he was asking Congress to end the slave trade in the District of Columbia, a far more drastic step than limiting the tonnage of ships engaged in the coastwise trade. Randolph was doing the very thing he earlier had opposed: asking for controls on the activities and behavior of masters. He was acutely aware that he might be opening a Pandora's box of federal legislation and hastened to explain his about-face. This new policy did not interfere in "the contract between the owner and his slave," he intoned, and pointed out his previous efforts to preserve that relationship. The irascible

3. James L. Huston, "The Experiential Basis of the Northern Antislavery Impulse," *Journal of Southern History* 56 (1990): 609–40.

Virginian went on to explain that the unique status of the District justified an exception to his usual pleas for federal noninterference.

Randolph's new line of reasoning makes sense only in light of previous federal policy regarding the ownership and sale of slaves in Washington. The District, obviously, was under direct control of the federal government and in 1794 Congress asserted its authority over the sale of slaves in Washington. The resulting statute prevented the exchange of bondservants from Virginia and Maryland within the city limits. Eighteen years later Congress amended this law and allowed Alexandria residents to take slaves into the District. Residents of Washington still could not enter Alexandria to buy slaves in order to bring them back to the District to sell or reside. The intended effect of the amendment was to prevent the sale of slaves in the capital. As a consequence, most of the transactions for the purchase or sale of slaves took place in Alexandria, usually in private jails. However, some traders temporarily housed slaves in Washington's taverns or small hotels on the outskirts of town. The nation's capital became a depot for the exhibition of slaves rather than a market, with the large speculators of the 1820s operating out of Alexandria or Baltimore. The perception was that the District of Columbia had a thriving slave trade because of the coffles that marched through the city and because of taverns like George Miller's.[4]

The oversight of commerce within federal territory was, in Randolph's mind, a different matter from regulation of trade between the states. The federal nature of the District set it apart, and Randolph did not ask for regulation of the trade outside of Washington. He shrank from full interference with the trade but wanted to find a moderate solution for a public eyesore. His rhetoric, however, does much to reveal his frame of mind. Randolph referred to a "crying sin before God and man" that separated slave families and drove them through the streets like "beasts." The increased visibility of the interstate slave trade, its obvious brutality, and the vehement reactions of bondservants gave Randolph reason to pause. He had no desire to abolish

4. Francis Hall, *Travels in Canada, and the United States, in 1816 and 1817* (London, 1818), 425; *Mobile Commercial Register*, September 12, 1822; Bancroft, *Slave Trading*, 49–53; Mary Tremain, *Slavery in the District of Columbia* (1892; reprint, New York, 1969), 31–33; Walter C. Clephane, "The Local Aspect of Slavery in the District of Columbia," *Records of the Columbia Historical Association* 3 (1900): 224–28, 235; William T. Laprade, "The Domestic Slave Trade in the District of Columbia," *Journal of Negro History* 11 (1926): 19–21, 27–30; Richard S. Newman, *The Transformation of American Abolitionism: Fighting Slavery in the Early Republic* (Chapel Hill, 2002), 49–59; Ridgeway, "Peculiar Business," 1–95.

slavery or impair the rights of masters, but he did see the worst side of slavery and wanted to remove the most odious aspects of the peculiar institution. Randolph was no abolitionist and was not intending to create a groundswell for the peculiar institution's destruction. Instead, he wanted to strengthen slavery. The best way to preserve the peculiar institution, he felt, was to reform it so that its opponents would have no room for criticism. Randolph was sensitive to the South's reputation, as is obvious from his reference to the foreigner's stinging remark. He also had a regard for the treatment of the slaves themselves, seeing them not as brutes, but as humans who needed the protection of the federal government. Randolph's proposal, according to his line of thought, was good for both the master and the slave. He sought to domesticate domestic slavery.[5]

Randolph's colleagues met his proposal with blank stares and a general sense of apathy. The interstate slave trade was simply an issue that most Americans did not want to confront. Northerners remained mute on the issue, while southerners had little more to say. If northerners wanted to pounce on slavery, now was their chance. If southerners felt compelled to defend the peculiar institution, they had an excuse. Robert Wright of Maryland broke the silence and weakly protested that the laws concerning the trade were sufficient. Referring to the War of 1812, he said that Europeans practiced a worse form of slavery when they impressed sailors, so there was no reason to draw attention to the interstate slave trade. He tried to bury the issue by diverting attention to a noncontroversial topic. Fellow Maryland representative Charles Goldsborough agreed with Randolph's assessment and noted that he, too, had seen coffles in Washington's streets. Goldsborough did not want to limit the trade, though, and observed that laws would be of no value in arresting the trade because they would not be enforced. He advocated doing nothing. When Henry St. George Tucker of Virginia suggested that a select committee would be the best method for addressing the situation, the House readily complied.[6]

After spending two months gathering information, the committee turned over its evidence to the House. Southerners filled four out of the five positions on the committee, and they were able to dictate the results to their liking. The report detailed numerous abuses associated with the interstate

5. Kirk, *John Randolph*, 131–33; Willie Lee Rose, "The Domestication of Domestic Slavery" in *Slavery and Freedom*, ed. William W. Freehling (New York, 1982), 18–36.

6. *Debates and Proceedings*, 14th Cong., 1st sess., March 1, 1816, 1117.

slave trade. It described the typical slave pen in the area as a "dungeon" in which slaves were "confined in their filth." The report also singled out the "atrocious" kidnapping of free persons. Such strong descriptions, however, had virtually no effect. Committee members rejected federal action to deal with the situation. The final report recommended that state authorities deal with the problem, thus precluding any changes in the District. That was a convenient way to dodge the situation, since neither Virginia nor Maryland had direct jurisdiction over Washington. It was also a suggestion that fit well with the traditional southern preference for state authority instead of federal control. The final copy even struck out the word "commerce" in describing the trade and substituted "traffic" in its place. Although this may have been an attempt to portray the trade negatively, it is more likely that it was meant to circumvent the wording of the Constitution that allowed Congress to regulate interstate commerce. The report, however, was not shared with the entire House; it was ordered to lie on the table just before Congress adjourned. The House did not want to take on the seemingly unimportant issue of the interstate slave trade, and most members were content to let the matter die. While there was a vague sentiment against the trade and a slight impulse to reform it, there was not enough of a commitment to actually do anything. Despite its recent growth, the interstate trade was more of a minor irritant to the congressmen than anything else.

Even though Randolph's tirade led to no specific action, this incident reveals how southerners were grappling with the implications of a growing interstate slave trade in the early republic. It is significant that the first direct attack on speculation in the Capitol had come not from a northerner but from a southerner, and one who had a solid reputation as a defender of slavery. Another southerner supported his opinion. This examination of the slave trade also stemmed from the Upper South, while the Lower South remained silent on the issue. Southern members did not defend the trade, justify it, or shift the blame onto the back of the slave trader, as they would do later. Just as importantly, northern members refused to attack the trade as emblematic of the harsh state of slavery in the South or call for an immediate end to slave trading and the abolition of slavery in the District of Columbia. In a few short years, northerners would use the slave trade as the "door to the slave Bastille" because of its effectiveness in illustrating slavery's evil consequences. In 1816 discussions about the slave trade generated no light and no heat. It was not yet a part of the national debate on slavery and hardly entered into most people's consciousness. The trade was still growing in strength and had not reached the point where it caused trouble for southerners.[7]

Despite this slowness to recognize the immense importance of the interstate slave trade, southerners were beginning to realize that it posed a problem when considering the property rights of slaveholders. Randolph wanted the federal government to regulate the movement and sale of slaves in Washington in order to render slavery more benign. He desired an end to abuses associated with bondage. In doing so, however, he had to acknowledge that the interstate slave trade treated slaves as commodities through speculation. This assumption presented two main problems for southerners. It turned the traditional southern presumption about slaveholding on its head by denying that an organic relationship existed between master and slave. An effective way to explain away the exploitative nature of slavery was to assume blithely that masters cared for slaves and looked out for their best interest. Masters could rest easy with slavery if they could convince themselves that their slaves received food, clothing, and shelter in return for their labor. A public and thriving interstate slave trade contradicted this assumption. If slave traders were increasing in number, then many slaveholders must be resorting to speculation and were thus not acting in a way that preserved the master-slave relationship. Such owners had then denied the fundamental premise that allowed them to support and maintain the peculiar institution. Instead of being kind and generous they were cruel and exploitative. Another problem involved the debate about whether the slave trade was a form of commerce. Randolph did not specifically assert that it was, but the implications of his thinking were clear and held out the specter of federal intervention. Article I, Section 8 of the Constitution gives Congress the power to regulate interstate commerce. Should the interstate slave trade become widely known as such, it would create an easy argument for federal oversight. Slaveholders, always concerned to maintain as absolute a power as possible over their slaves, would hardly consent to such a scenario. Their most common rebuttal of this idea was to minimize the volume of the inter-

7. Papers of the Select Committee . . . on the Illegal Traffic in Slaves (quotations); *Debates and Proceedings*, 14th Cong., 1st sess., April 30, 1816, 1465; *Washington Daily National Intelligencer*, May 1, 1816; *Niles' Weekly Register*, May 4, 1816, 165. For later uses of the slave trade in political rhetoric, see David L. Lightner, "The Door to the Slave Bastille: The Abolitionist Assault upon the Interstate Slave Trade, 1833–1839," *Civil War History* 34 (1988): 235–52, and David L. Lightner, "The Interstate Slave Trade in Antislavery Politics," *Civil War History* 36 (1990): 119–36.

state slave trade. Since it was minimal, they asserted, there was no need to monitor speculation. Southerners emphasized the migration of slaves, rather than the forced speculation. That mind-set fit comfortably with the concomitant emphasis on the benevolent aspects of slavery. If the interstate slave trade was minimal, then there was no apparent reason to examine the philosophical underpinnings of the peculiar institution.[8]

It was the jarring actions of some determined slaves and the growth of the interstate slave trade that continually brought the subject to the surface. In the fifteen years or so after the War of 1812 bondspeople shaped the nature of the public debate over slavery. Their bravery in the face of crushing dehumanization injected a new element into the scene—the idea that they were not merely property and deserved a better life. Slaves, of course, had always resisted their situation in one form or another. Speculation, however, created conditions where slaves were more likely to resist servitude because it generated intense emotional reactions in the bondservants. Slave traders, with an eye for profit, used highly selective purchasing practices and tended to buy younger slaves. Such practices may have been necessary for profitability, but were destructive of marriages and families. In the nineteenth century, it is estimated that over half of all the slaves in the Upper South were separated from a parent or child because of forced migration. The slave John Brown, for instance, remembered how his mother begged the speculator to let her kiss her son one last time. Charles Ball's last memory of his mother was her sobbing and beating the shoulders of the speculator who had just purchased him. The sundering of child from parent was just the start. Forcible separation also destroyed approximately one-third of all slave marriages in the Upper South. For Moses Grandy, the slave trade ruined his life. He tried to speak to his wife while a speculator carried her away, but the trader used a pistol to keep Grandy at a distance. Grandy later confided that he could have said very little anyway because his heart was broken. "I have never seen or heard from her from that day to this," he lamented. "I loved her as I love my life."[9]

The interstate slave trade had a shattering impact on bondspeople. It also influenced whites because it was a very public form of slave degradation.

8. David Lightner, "The Founders and the Interstate Slave Trade," *JER* 22 (2002): 46–48.

9. Boney, ed., *Slave Life in Georgia*, 15; Ball, *Slavery in the United States*, 11 (quotations); Moses Grandy, *Narrative of the Life of Moses Grandy, Late a Slave in the United States of America* (Boston, 1844), 11; Tadman, *Speculators and Slaves*, 146–54, 169–77.

Beatings and escapes, for instance, were usually confined to a plantation or a locality. Few outsiders would view them. Revolt scares were fairly common, but rarely could they be construed as being exploitative of slaves. Auctions were another matter, and had been closely associated with slavery since its beginning in North America. Speculation, though, could seem more menacing. Should a slave become the property of a trader, he was definitely going to be torn from everything he knew. That process would normally involve marching in a coffle, something more commonplace by about 1820. Slaves not sold to traders might stay in the local area or move away with their new owners. In the latter case, they did not have the automatic assumption of coffles and brutality. This combination, the unique visibility of the interstate slave trade and the emotional reactions of the slaves, helped force a reappraisal of slavery.

Slaves in the Upper South dreaded the prospect of having to abandon everything they knew. Maryland slaves of the 1820s viewed their removal to Georgia or New Orleans as a virtual death sentence. James Williams, a slave who lived in Powhatan County, Virginia, before escaping, knew that slaves feared the power of their masters to sell them. He wrote that it was an awful threat for Virginia slaves to be sold to the Deep South. Slaves' aversion to the interstate trade was so great that some masters used the threat of sale to Georgia as a means of changing a slave's behavior. Rumors of harsh conditions in distant states swirled through the quarters. Frederick Douglass remembered how his friends were scared of being sold to a trader who would carry them to Georgia. Some slaves whispered stories of having family who marched barefoot for hundreds of miles with a minimum of food and clothing. The words of one song testify to speculation's threat:

> Mammy, is Ol' Massa gwin'er sell us tomorrow?
> Yes, my chile.
> Whar he gwin'er sell us?
> Way down South in Georgia.

It was too much for many slaves to bear; they wept bitterly but found no solace. Henry Box Brown remembered the "frantic screams" and "scalding tears" associated with auctions and coffles. For Brown it was as simple as the declaration that slaves have feelings and knew too well the permanence of family separations.[10]

10. Williams, *Narrative of James Williams*, 32; T. Stephen Whitman, *The Price of Freedom: Slavery and Manumission in Baltimore and Early National Maryland* (Lexington, Ky., 1997), 75; Torrey, *Portraiture of Domestic Slavery*, 61; Preston, *Young Frederick Douglass*, 76; Lawrence

Twenty-first century observers tend to think of the whip as emblematic of slavery's harshness, but the lash "was not the ultimate sanction of the master's authority." Sale or even the threat of sale "may have been the keystone of coercive slave control" because it relied on terror rather than torture. A master's ability to separate slaves irrevocably from their families and loved ones was a punishment that inflicted mental and spiritual anguish far in excess of the physical pain produced by the whip. The sale of disobedient slaves was the most powerful long-term technique of discipline because bondservants feared it more than anything else. This threat of sale seems to contradict owners' impulses to reform slavery by promoting strong families. The concepts, however, could be used to accomplish the same end: control over slaves. An owner who encouraged family development could suddenly revoke that "privilege" and use it as leverage to extract the maximum amount of labor from his slaves. In this way, manipulation of the slave family became one of the owner's most effective tools in maintaining control of his people. It became the "frequent custom" in the Chesapeake area for owners to intimidate their slaves with the threat of sale to distant lands. According to one abolitionist, slave traders became a "boogey man" who could be trotted out to keep slaves in line. When a sale took place, it was a decisive way to jettison difficult slaves. Selling one slave would often be powerful enough to influence the behavior of other slaves in the community. Owners understood very well the dramatic impact that sales had upon their workforce. John Haywood wrote that one of his slave women was becoming discontented and unwilling to work. He could not tolerate her poor example because it encouraged other slaves to avoid their chores. Haywood, who had purchased the woman at a court sale, quickly sold her in order to be rid of the headache and to ward off further idleness. If nothing else, using speculators as part of a scare tactic to intimidate slaves also reduced them to a caricature in the white mind. After all, if masters were to be successful in scaring their slaves, they had to exaggerate the traders' evil qualities. Such efforts to cow their slaves contained the seed that eventually ripened into the stereotype of the evil slave trader.[11]

Levine, *Black Culture and Black Consciousness: Afro-American Folk Thought from Slavery to Freedom* (New York, 1977), 15 (quotation); [Henry Box Brown], *Narrative of Henry Box Brown* (Boston, 1849), 31.

11. George M. Fredrickson, "Masters and Mudsills: The Role of Race in the Planter Ideology of South Carolina," *South Atlantic Urban Studies* 2 (1978): 40 (first and second quotations); Emily West, "Surviving Separation: Cross-Plantation Marriages and the Slave Trade in Antebellum South Carolina," *Journal of Family History* 24 (1999): 212–31; Norrece T.

Once speculators became the personification of evil for slaves, it became clear that bondservants would react unpredictably to such a great threat. Speculators, probably more than most, realized they dealt with a potentially volatile slave population and took steps to prevent opposition. That traders tried to keep a lid on slave resistance obviously stemmed from motives of personal preservation. Another reason, however, dealt with the way southerners perceived the interstate slave trade. If they assumed that traders mainly dealt with unruly slaves, an increasingly common assumption in the Lower South, then the business of slave trading would be threatened. Potential buyers would be loath to purchase slaves if they suspected them to be violent or uncontrollable. The hostile actions of bondservants then, could be a powerful, if unintended, way to shape white attitudes. Speculators countered such unpredictable behavior by asserting control over their commodities. They marched their coffles through cities at night, kept their slaves confined in private jails, and used other methods to exert their authority. The South, in many ways, used slavery as a means of economic and racial control, with slave traders being one mechanism of power. Should traders be capable of controlling their slaves with a minimum of disruption, then they would mesh smoothly in the system. Speculators proved themselves necessary for the maintenance of slavery—removing any slaves who proved nettlesome and inspiring dread in those left behind.

Speculators used a variety of tactics to prevent or minimize slave resistance. A common method was surprise. Traders and masters often worked together to make sure slaves had no time to consider how to thwart a sale. An Alabama planter wrote his agent to use secrecy lest the slave he had just sold try to run away. Reuben Madison was sold so suddenly that he had no chance to say good-bye to his wife. Once traders took possession of slaves, they used numerous measures to reduce the chance of outright revolt and to force compliance. The most obvious was physical punishment. Traders who were dissatisfied with their slaves could flog them, trying to beat them into "looking bright." In the coastwise trade, speculators segregated slaves by sex, prohibited males from seeing the females at night, and confined all

---

Jones Jr., *Born a Child of Freedom yet a Slave: Mechanisms of Control and Strategies of Resistance in Antebellum South Carolina* (Hanover, N.H.: 1990), 3, 37–38; William Dusinberre, *Them Dark Days: Slavery in the American Rice Swamps* (New York, 1996), 126; John Haywood to Mrs. Brickell, April 25, 1815, Ernest Haywood Papers, UNC; Torrey, *Portraiture of Domestic Slavery*, 61 (remaining quotations).

slaves in the ship's hold at night. During the day bondservants normally roamed the deck, lest they become too resentful of being confined in close quarters. Should they prove to be unmanageable, they could be bolted to the deck.[12]

For those slaves forced to march in coffles, some traders tried to lift the spirits of their bondservants, and thus reduce the risk of resistance, by forcing them to sing, dance, or listen to an instrument. Music was not usually sufficient, so traders frequently used chains to keep slaves from fleeing the coffle, fighting one another, or killing the slave trader. These slaves, especially those who had just been forcibly separated from their families, were more likely to feel that they had nothing to lose in an escape attempt. The threat of a beating or even death had no hold over them. Traders knew from experience the necessity of leg irons and handcuffs as means of control. Similarly, traders normally did not permit slaves to speak to one another unless heard by one of the white escorts. They did not want slaves encouraging one another to resort to desperate measures. Others used bribes to obtain cooperation from their slaves. Speculator Obadiah Fields used small presents as incentives for good behavior in the slaves he purchased.[13]

Slaves resisted traders often enough that the threat of rebellion was omnipresent in coffles. Some bondservants just wanted to escape and did not contemplate further violence. Slaves encamped near Raleigh, for instance, fled when one member of the coffle bashed the speculator in the head with a stone. Similarly, traders named Whitfield and Tompkins traveled through North Carolina with a coffle of seventeen bondservants. Near the Chowan River, six armed runaway slaves attacked the group and drove off the speculators. Two of the slaves in the coffle joined the band while the others fled.[14]

More serious were slaves' efforts to kill speculators. In 1826 Austin Woolfolk put twenty-nine Maryland slaves on board the *Decatur*, a ship

12. Deyle, "Domestic Slave Trade," 219; Boney, ed., *Slave Life in Georgia*, 98, 115–16 (quotation); *Niles' National Register*, January 22, 1842, 323–26; Blassingame, ed., *Slave Testimony*, 175, 180, 185.

13. *Southern Agriculturist* 9 (1836): 70–75; List of Slave Sales, February 11, 1828, Obadiah Fields Papers, DU; Deyle, "Domestic Slave Trade," 102.

14. Unidentified Raleigh newspaper, as quoted in *Western Luminary*, November 9, 1825, 279; *Lexington Virginia Intelligencer*, May 29, 1824. Other examples of slave resistance may be found in *Washington National Gazette*, August 6, 1825, as quoted in *Western Luminary*, August 24, 1825, 110; [William H. Blane], *An Excursion through the United States and Canada during the years 1822–23* (New York, 1969), 226–27.

scheduled to sail from Baltimore to New Orleans. Somewhere off the coast of Georgia the slaves mutinied, threw the captain and the mate overboard, and steered the ship towards Haiti. The *Constitution* overtook the *Decatur* and took seventeen slaves off of it, as many as could be safely transferred. Three days later the *Rooke* found the *Decatur* and escorted it to New York. One slave, William Bowser, stood trial in that city for mutiny and murder. After his conviction, Bowser made a farewell speech from the gallows on Ellis Island where he reputedly addressed Woolfolk. Bowser forgave the speculator and said he hoped to see him in heaven. Woolfolk supposedly answered with an angry profanity and muttered that Bowser "was now going to get what he deserved, and he was glad of it." Whether or not Bowser knew it, he was influencing thought about slavery and the slave trade. His actions, if true, showed him to be a better man than Woolfolk. He acted nobly while Woolfolk seemed petty. Even if the details of the story are apocryphal, they show that it was possible to imagine that slaves possessed dignity. The murderer instead of the speculator received sympathetic treatment, at least in the North.[15]

While the homicide of speculators was one extreme form of resistance, slaves used other methods to undermine the trade. Some refused to submit to a sale and killed or maimed themselves or their family members. In Baltimore, for instance, a slave cut his throat in public view on a wharf as he was boarding a ship for New Orleans, while a woman in nearby Snow Hill killed her child and then herself when learning of her sale. Suicide to prevent speculation was frequent enough that it drew the attention of a visitor to Virginia. Such activities worried slaveowners. Slaves who killed themselves illustrated dramatically one of the fundamental problems of speculation, namely, that it was exploitation. Such suicides spoke volumes as to how the trade ruined slaves' lives and were powerful reminders that bondservants were possessors of free wills. The fact that slaves exerted power in such extreme ways also challenged white perceptions of slaves and the slave trade. When southerners read or heard stories of bondservants who attacked spec-

15. Undated *New York Christian Inquirer* as quoted in *Genius of Universal Emancipation*, January 2, 1827, 109–10 (quotation); *Niles' Weekly Register*, May 20, 1826, 262, September 5, 1829, 18–19, December 26, 1829, 277, September 9, 1830, 328; Merton L. Dillon, *Benjamin Lundy and the Struggle for Negro Freedom* (Urbana, 1966); *Genius of Universal Emancipation*, January 1, 1830, 131; *Lexington Kentucky Reporter*, September 9, 1829, as quoted in J. Winston Coleman Papers, King Library, University of Kentucky, Lexington; Edward D. Jervey and C. Harold Huber, "The *Creole* Affair," *Journal of Negro History* 65 (1980): 196–211.

ulators, or of slaves who committed suicide, they had to face the fact that slaves were human and not beasts. The irony is that a business that labored mightily to reduce slaves to just another commodity accidentally promoted the fact of bondservants' humanity. Speculation, moreover, did so in a public way that observers could not ignore. A young woman bound for New Orleans gave powerful testimony to this fact. She carried a young child who had not been sold with her. "When they reached the wharf, she sat down, unconscious of everything but the presence of her infant, upon whose face she continued to gaze, in apparent agony, while affording it nourishment for the last time from her breast." When it came time to depart, her former master took the infant while the mother poured forth with "the most agonizing cries." The bystanders were deeply moved but could do nothing. John Randolph had a similar experience. He said the greatest orator he ever heard was a woman. "She was a slave. She was a mother, and her rostrum was the auction block." Sale, then, is best understood less as a master's prerogative and more as a complex system of negotiation within an exploitative system. It also called into question some of the foundational principles of slavery.[16]

It has been suggested that southerners often created reality and insisted that it be honored, even though it was false. Masters also tried to fashion reality for their slaves. These two ideas merged in the interstate slave trade. Owners wanted to make an artificial world where slaves hardly felt the effects of speculation. Reality could not be more different, and slaves "gave the lie" to masters when they angrily chopped off their hands or sobbed uncontrollably. When bondservants would not accept slaveowners' reality, they called into question what was known and believed about slavery. Slaves' reactions to the interstate slave trade revealed the disparity between what owners wanted the master-slave relationship to be and what actually existed.[17]

16. William Wells Brown, *Narrative of William Wells Brown: A Fugitive Slave* (Boston, 1847), 40; E. S. Abdy, *Journal of a Residence and Tour in the United States of North America*, 3 vol. (London, 1835), 3:350 (first and second quotations); Kirk, *John Randolph*, 147 (final quotation); Benjamin Brand to Martin Dawson, March 17, 1819, Benjamin Brand Papers, VHS; Jordan M. Saunders to David Burford, October 29, 1829, Burford Papers; Whitman, *Price of Freedom*, 77; Christopher Phillips, *Freedom's Port: The African American Community of Baltimore* (Urbana, 1997), 45–54; Johnson, *Soul by Soul*, 176–87.

17. Kenneth S. Greenberg, *Honor and Slavery: Lies, Duels, Noses, Masks, Dressing as a Woman, Gifts, Strangers, Humanitarianism, Death, Slave Rebellions, the Proslavery Argument, Baseball, Hunting, and Gambling in the Old South* (Princeton, 1996), 32–42.

These and other issues would surface during the debates surrounding the admission of the state of Missouri to the United States. An examination of the rhetoric involved in the dispute reveals that northerners and southerners were giving more thought to the consequences of a growing interstate slave trade. For their part, northerners raised the issue as a way to seize the moral high ground and argue that slavery should be prohibited in Missouri. James Tallmadge triggered the discussion when he moved that slaves be prohibited from entering Missouri and slave children born after statehood be free at age twenty-five. His intention was to provide a plan of gradual emancipation for the state. The northern representatives who allied with Tallmadge used their observation of the slave coffles and slavery in the Washington area to bludgeon the South. They depicted the trade as emblematic of slavery and drew the conclusion that such an evil institution must not be allowed to expand. Their experience with the District of Columbia's slave trade became the basis for their remarks about how bondspeople would be treated in Missouri. In the face of this outside attack on slavery and the trade, southerners relied on apologetics to deflect the accusations. They refused to discuss the moral implications of speculation but concentrated instead on the constitutional right of southern migrants to carry bondservants into new territory. Southerners carefully differentiated between speculation and migration in the hopes of keeping the slave trade out of the debates. They had no coherent explanation for the commerce in slaves and were not willing to defend it. The best strategy, they thought, was to deny it.

It was Arthur Livermore of New Hampshire who fired the first salvo when he used the slave trade to denounce the South. In dramatic fashion, he described how the separation of mothers and children led to agonies of grief amongst the slaves. Opening Missouri to slavery would only magnify the pain. Tallmadge then kept up the pressure by refusing to listen to any excuses for the trade. He noted that a slave trader carrying a whip had just driven a coffle past the Capitol. Tallmadge hinted that a providential hand placed the coffle there to provide a dramatic illustration for his argument. He portrayed the slaves positively to his colleagues, observing that the men were prevented from protecting their families from destruction. Tallmadge could not believe such scenes took place in "Republican America." These vivid descriptions were a powerful indictment of slavery's dark side. Livermore and Tallmadge used scenes with which most of their fellow representatives were familiar in order to connect slavery's expansion to speculation. In doing so, they tried to mobilize opposition to the spread of slavery by arguing that the admission of Missouri as a slave state would increase slaves' suffering. The two men hoped to tap into the emotions of their colleagues by describing slavery in the most dismal way possible.[18]

If northern representatives intended to use these condemnations of the trade to aggravate their southern colleagues, they failed. The indictment of slavery via the interstate slave trade drew no heated response from the southern delegates. Only Louis McLane of Delaware directly addressed the issue, and he coolly argued that slavery's expansion had beneficial effects. Dispersing slaves into lands west of the Mississippi River, McLane maintained, would make them less restless. He also tried to convince his colleagues that such bondservants would live better lives because they would be on superior land. McLane apologetically noted that, on a personal level, he would not permit slaves to be sold by traders, or become the objects of profit. As for the microscopic interstate slave trade that did exist, it fell under the purview of the states. His home state, he explained, prohibited the introduction or exportation of slaves for sale. McLane's bland appeal failed to rouse his colleagues to action. No other southern representative referred to the interstate slave trade during the Missouri debates. Even South Carolina senator William Smith, who defended the institution without reservation, did not mention the trade. Southerners' virtual silence suggests that they were quickly learning the lessons their slaves were teaching them. It was becoming all too apparent that speculation exposed slavery for what it was—an ugly stain on humanity. Although they may have had private doubts, there was no room for their expression in the halls of Congress. Southerners would not allow speculation to become an object lesson that illustrated slavery's immorality.[19]

Northern representatives changed tactics once it became apparent their criticism would not draw out southerners. They alleged that the spread of slavery into Missouri would increase the smuggling of Africans into the United States. On this account, they tried to tar the legal interstate trade with the brush of the illegal African trade. John W. Taylor argued that an

18. *Debates and Proceedings,* 15th Cong., 2nd sess., February 16, 1819, 1:1191–92, 1210 (quotation); Glover Moore, *The Missouri Controversy, 1819–1821* (Lexington, Ky., 1953), 33–51; Leonard L. Richards, *The Slave Power: The Free North and Southern Domination, 1780–1860* (Baton Rouge, 2000), 52–82.

19. *Debates and Proceedings,* 15th Cong., 2nd sess., February 17, 1819, 2:1233–34; Don Fehrenbacher, *The South and the Three Sectional Crises* (Baton Rouge, 1980), 9–23.

expansion of slave territory would make the whole country west of the Mississippi River a "market overt for human flesh." The natural consequence of allowing slaves into Missouri, his argument ran, would be to encourage smuggling. On the shores of Africa there would be an increase of unscrupulous men who bought slaves with "a few gewgaws or a bottle of whiskey" and then sold them in New Orleans. Like the earlier attack on slave coffles, this denunciation of the international trade drew a muted response from southerners, who merely asserted that the foreign trade was illegal and they did not wish to revive it.[20]

Although using the interstate slave trade as a moral indictment of slavery and dredging up the African slave trade did not cause southerners to rise to the bait, another tactic did draw a heated response. When northern senators linked the interstate trade with the migration of bondservants across state lines, southerners responded quickly. This method relied on a creative interpretation of the ninth section of the Constitution's first article to argue that Congress could prevent the importation and migration of slaves into new territories or states. This passage was obviously intended for the African slave trade, but, as we have seen, northerners were willing to do almost anything to link the two types of commerce. Timothy Fuller of Massachusetts was the first to try this approach. Again, he injected a moral indictment into his argument by saying he feared that the opening of an extensive slave market in Missouri would "tempt the cupidity" of southerners who might otherwise emancipate their slaves. Philip P. Barbour of Virginia brushed past the allegations of a vast slave market and defended the right of southerners to carry their slaves into Missouri. Prohibiting such movement would effectively prevent slaveholders from settling in the new state. He pointed out that slave labor was necessary to establish farms, and since few slaves would be available for purchase (because, of course, southerners would not stoop to dealing with speculators) there would be no incentive for migration. Barbour tried to avoid the topic of the slave trade, merely noting that only financial necessity or slave criminality induced masters to sell their slaves. Barbour was one of the first southerners to make the connection between the interstate slave trade and southern expansion. The desire for more territory was often foremost in southern thinking, but speculation added a new dimension. Only dimly did slaveholders grasp the true significance of defending speculation as well as migration. The Fif-

20. *Debates and Proceedings*, 15th Cong., 2nd sess., February 15, 1819, 1:1175.

teenth Congress adjourned having accomplished nothing, except to show that southerners were reluctant to face the moral criticisms of slavery and eager to steer the debate to a strict interpretation of the Constitution that defended property rights.[21]

The Missouri debates continued into the next session, but when discussing the movement of slaves, the congressmen continued to talk past one another. Northern representatives continually mentioned the movement of slaves by traders, while their southern counterparts constantly spoke of migration. In the Senate, Jonathan Roberts of Pennsylvania referred to a Louisiana law that outlawed the carrying of slaves into that state unless done by a United States citizen who intended to settle there. Southern senators produced an argument similar to their counterparts in the House. John Elliot of Georgia responded by noting that slaves were not subject to federal restrictions on migration because they had no volition or self-determination. They might be carried, but they did not migrate. The Constitution, he explained, did not allow Congress to inhibit transfer or removal of slaves from one state to another. Such a right lay exclusively in the states, and they would never surrender it. He went on to admit that slavery was an "evil," but sound policy dictated migration because the slave population was safer when it was dispersed instead of being cooped up in a few slave states. Senators from Mississippi, South Carolina, Virginia, and Kentucky all concurred that Congress could lawfully outlaw the importation of slaves from areas outside the United States but could not "regulate the internal distribution" of slaves. They seemed to be caught unawares. They advanced a welter of ideas: slaves were treated well, they were property, they were rarely sold, they were not commerce, they were dangerous. It seems they had not given much thought to speculation.[22]

Northern congressmen were ahead of the southern counterparts in understanding the importance of the interstate slave trade. They had observed how slaves had fought speculation, either in a blind fury or through quiet dignity. It was becoming clear to them that the interstate slave trade was the Achilles' heel of the South. Benjamin Lundy, William Lloyd Garrison, and other abolitionist leaders would also instinctively seize upon the trade to

21. Ibid., February 15, 1819, 1:1183–84, 1188 (quotations); Lightner, "Founders and the Interstate Slave Trade," 47–48.

22. *Debates and Proceedings*, 16th Cong., 1st sess., January 17, 1820, 2:125–26, 129–35 (quotations on 134), January 18, 1820, 1:1010–12, and January 26, 1820, 2:259–64.

heap shame upon the South. Southern congressmen, on the other hand, would not acknowledge the presence of an interstate trade that destroyed slave families and caused untold hardship. Their way of dealing with the situation was to carefully separate speculation from migration. The references to the inhumanity or barbarity of the slave trade were moot, they argued, because most bondservants moved with owners rather than speculators. They also asserted that Congress had no power to regulate the migration of bondservants. The use of the word "migration" was intentional, as it did not paint as harsh a picture of the slaves' conditions and bypassed constitutional questions. Southerners were also beginning to realize that the slave trade was vital to slavery's continued existence. They were not, however, willing to admit publicly that slave owners participated in the trade or even in activities similar to speculation. Southerners were struggling with how to reconcile their defense of slavery with their misgivings surrounding speculation, especially in the face of outside pressure to control slavery.

In the end, of course, Missouri retained slavery, and the interstate slave trade remained unregulated on the national level. What the debates revealed is that the trade was a convenient tool to attack the South. Vivid rhetoric describing the markets of human flesh and the cries of bondservants separated from their families would eventually become standard fare in abolitionist denunciations of slavery. Those who opposed the peculiar institution tried to cut through some of the abstractions and make the discussion personal. They hoped to sidestep the theoretical issues of law and policy by stirring up the emotions of their listeners. Although the Missouri debates may have identified "the doctrine of states' rights with the defense of slavery," the nature of the discussion reveals that the interstate slave trade was excluded from the defense perimeter. More often than not, southerners ignored the issue in the hopes that it would go away. The embryonic nature of the trade in 1820, specifically the fact that it was just developing into a major source of labor for the Deep South, meant that southerners were not yet in a position to defend it or had not fully considered its implications for the defense of slavery. Although they began to recognize the importance of the slave trade—if not through the resistance of slaves or the presence of coffles in the South, then through the persistent attacks of northern representatives—it remained to be seen how southerners could reconcile the trade's brutality with their optimistic assumptions of slavery. The legalistic tactic of ignoring the slave trade by hiding slave movement under the guise of state sovereignty had a hollow ring to it, especially in the face of the heated and emotional indictments. They needed to draw a sharper distinction between migration and the slave trade, because the former was widely regarded as legitimate while the latter was suspect because selfish motives could be imputed to it. The slave trade, furthermore, seemed to contradict one of the main reasons for accepting slavery—that the institution improved bondservants' lives. Eventually most southerners, especially those in the Upper South, would construct more elaborate ways to explain away the existence of the interstate slave trade. For now, as speculation slowly gained force in the South, the issue seemed inconsequential.[23]

Southern congressmen were not the only ones who faced slave resistance and wrestled with the thorny implications of speculation. The contemporary southern literature was troubled when it came to understanding and accepting the interstate slave trade. Southern writers who even attempted to explain the presence of speculation in the early republic were a rare breed. Only two, George Tucker and James P. Kennedy, directly confronted the issues of slave trading and family separation. This paucity stands in stark contrast to the glut of the later antebellum years, when southerners churned out a slew of bad novels that exonerated slave trading.[24]

Tucker, for his part, found it difficult to accept speculation as a legitimate part of slavery. Born in Bermuda, Tucker grew up in Virginia near his distant cousin, Henry St. George Tucker. He failed as a lawyer, but his skill in selecting rich young women to marry ensured that he would have enough money to support his vices of gambling and lavish parties. Tucker served in the state legislature before his election to the United States Congress, where he betrayed his Jeffersonian Republican principles by supporting the Bank of the United States and Henry Clay. His legal and legislative careers, though, seemed to have been a dalliance more than anything, since Tucker aspired to be a writer. In *Letters from Virginia* (1816), he used the well-worn literary device of a fictitious outside observer to satirize society, in this case Virginia's. In his fifth letter, he provided a sentimental description of a coffle of slaves and their cruel trader. Tucker invited the reader's attention by musing whether he was in Norfolk or on "some barbarous coast," implicitly linking the interstate trade to its African forebear. Tucker's French traveler

23. Norman K. Risjord, *The Old Republicans: Southern Conservatism in the Age of Jefferson* (New York, 1965), 220.

24. Tadman, *Speculators and Slaves*, 180–84.

heard and then saw thirty slaves chained together in a coffle. The sight appalled him, and he felt pity for the slaves who clung to one another for emotional and physical support. Especially touching was a woman and her three children, one of whom suckled while the other two held either side of their mother's apron to prevent being separated from her. Tucker described several shades of distress, from a "soft gentle sorrow" to a "grim and threatening despair, that asked for nothing but a grave." A speculator had just bought the slaves at an auction.[25]

Tucker's detailed description makes it clear that he had seen a coffle. His moving portrayal of the scene was intended to provoke emotions of sympathy for the slaves. He noted that they sang a hymn, thus showing their nobility in the face of calamity. Tucker not only described the slaves in the coffle, he imbued them with vivid emotions. Posing as the Frenchman, he wondered how someone could not have a pang of conscience when an innocent child was torn from her mother. He described slaves as human beings so that whites would regard them as such, rather than insensitively dismissing them as brutes. Any person who could not understand the concept was sadly blinded from seeing that bondservants "love their wives, their children, their homes, as well as their masters." Tucker's account could ring true only if slaves had been pushed to the limits of their enslavement.[26]

If the slaves possessed great dignity in Tucker's account, the same cannot be said for the slave trader. The unsavory character sat with apparent ease and indifference as he drank one last brandy. Upon returning to his carriage, he cracked his whip, and forced the "miserable exiles" forward in a "funeral procession." The visitor wanted to call down fire from above "to blast the wretch," even though such thoughts were unchristian. Somewhat confused, the visitor asked a local resident what the slaves did to deserve such a punishment. The man replied that the slaves had done nothing at all, but their master wanted money. Tucker showed how the commercial nature of the slave trade warred against the paternalistic pretenses of slave owners. He wondered how Virginians could tolerate such blatant cruelty that punished the innocent. Even though Tucker knew that Virginians were not "barbarians," their actions gave him reason to reconsider. He feared that habit might make his countrymen callous to such horrors.[27]

25. [George Tucker], *Letters from Virginia, translated from the French* (Baltimore, 1816), 29–30 (quotations); Robert Colin McLean, *George Tucker: Moral Philosopher and Man of Letters* (Chapel Hill, 1961), 3–36.

26. [Tucker], *Letters from Virginia*, 32–33.

27. Ibid., 29–35.

Tucker clearly condemned the slave trader. Like the later southern novels that perpetuated the myth of the slave speculator, his portrait of this man was one-dimensional.[28] There was no room for admiration of the trader's character; he was motivated by money, was lazy, and drank too much. In short, he had no redeeming qualities. What set Tucker's work apart from later novels was his portrayal of witnesses to the coffle and the slaves themselves. Tucker was most critical of the auction's observers, something that was in stark contrast to all of the later antebellum fiction. He singled out the witnesses for rebuke because they allowed reprehensible activities to flourish in their midst. No civilized nation should tolerate such treatment of any part of its population. Those who sold slaves were not merely caught in a web of forces beyond their control, but were willing participants in the destruction of slave families. Like the trader, they were motivated by profit because they received good prices for their slaves. Tucker equated the slaveholder who sold his slaves with the speculator who bought them. Both shared the blame for the slave trade and both had allowed slavery to become repugnant.

The slaves were the real heroes of the description. Tucker's bondservants were different from whites, but any inferiority was from their condition rather than their color. The later accounts of slave sales painted bondservants in stereotypical terms, portraying them as wholly devoted to their owners and blindly accepting the reasons for the auction. Tucker refused to typecast the slaves in his story. They did not show excessive devotion to their masters, and just as importantly, they were not miraculously rescued in the end; they marched southward singing their hymn. The overall lesson that Tucker wanted to teach was that slavery, specifically through the awful means of speculation, exploited the slaves and caused the white mind to "sink."[29]

Tucker's second work, published eight years later, was less critical of Virginia society and more ambiguous about the slave trade. He was more forgiving of those who sold their slaves and depicted a state struggling through difficult economic times. The poor condition of Virginia agriculture forced owners to part with their slaves even as they worked to keep their labor force intact. In *The Valley of the Shenandoah* (1824), Trueheart, an attorney, handled the disposition of Mrs. Grayson's property. Her husband's death

28. Tadman, *Speculators and Slaves*, 180–84.

29. [Tucker], *Letters from Virginia*, 73–101, quotation on 101.

forced Mrs. Grayson to sell her slaves in order to prevent foreclosure. Trueheart conformed to his client's wishes and located a buyer in Georgia who was expanding his cotton holdings. Finding such a man relieved Mrs. Grayson, since the pain of separation from her servants would be softened, since all of them, or at least nearly all, would go to a good master and the structure of their families would be preserved.[30]

The slaves learned of the sale when the domestic servants overheard the conversation between Trueheart and Grayson. One of the oldest slaves approached her owner and asked for a favor. She requested that her daughter and grandchildren not be included in the pending sale because they would be worked too hard in Georgia. Grayson reasoned with the slave and convinced her that slave life in Georgia would not be as bad as imagined. The old slave relented to the sale, but asked that her youngest grandchild be sold to a Virginia farmer. Grayson agreed and called all of the slaves together to officially inform them of the impending sale. She assured her bondservants that none of them would be sold "against their wishes." Three or four slaves indicated their desire to stay in Virginia, so Grayson spared them from the auction. In a final act of "genuine benvolence," she gave her old clothes to her slaves and fed them sugar and molasses.[31]

The slave auction commenced that afternoon, and many people were "extremely shocked" to see fellow human beings "set up for sale to the highest bidder, like horses or cattle." Even those who were accustomed to such things found it disagreeable. Tucker defended the scene, though, asserting that slaves hardly felt their fetters because they had almost everything they wanted. Only "moderate" coercion was necessary to persuade them to take part in the auction, and they did not "feel it to be wrong," since they were members of "a sort of patriarchal family." When one of the slaves cried on the auction block because she would be separated from her husband, the man's new owner bid on her. He risked financial ruin by trying to keep the "hussey" and her husband together. Trueheart came up with a better idea: sell both of the slaves to the Georgia bidder. It was done, and all parties were satisfied. The true crisis of the day came when two slave traders bid for a likely mulatto girl who suited the tastes of the "libertines" of Louisiana. Under orders from Trueheart, the auctioneer slowed down the bidding

30. [George Tucker], *The Valley of the Shenandoah; or, Memories of the Graysons,* 2 vol. (New York, 1824), 2:194–96.

31. Ibid., 2:196–201, 212.

while the attorney authorized a bystander to buy the woman on his behalf. When one of the speculators made a disparaging remark about Trueheart's motives, the local farmers rebuked the man and forced him to leave the auction. The end result was that spouses stayed together, no slaves went to Georgia against their wishes, and the slave traders went away empty-handed.[32]

Tucker's second work was a curious blend of conflicting attitudes. It represents a transitional phase in southern literature. He was not as critical of slavery as in his first novel, but did condemn the institution, or at least its effects. His depiction of the slave trader, the crowd, and the slaves was simplistic. The bondservants, for instance, professed undying devotion to their mistress and instead of crying, wailing, and grimly submitting to the speculator as before, they were almost happy to go to Georgia. Tucker, though, could not just explain away the auction and its blunt intrusion into slaves' lives. He criticized absentee ownership and the separation of families. The auction was shocking to the neighborhood and pointed to a flaw in the peculiar institution. Tucker was one of the few southern novelists to address these issues without apology. He struggled to explain something so horrible as an auction, but ended up deadening its impact. While Tucker commented on the dread of the auction for the slave, he tried to reconcile that situation with the paternalistic view of slaveholders. Slavery was still a "necessary evil," but his second novel softened the harsh edges of the peculiar institution and acquitted those masters who took care of their slaves. The greatest evil of slavery, he concluded by 1824, was the dissolution of slave families from an auction. This result could be, and often was, prevented by the quick thinking and resourcefulness of the upstanding citizens of the South. He came to accept the slave trade's presence by denying its pervasiveness.[33]

Tucker's changing attitudes came, in part, because of success in increasing his slaveholdings. As he prospered, he saw the difficulties of his neighbors and became afraid that Virginia would be swamped with idle slaves. For that reason, he defended slavery's expansion during the Missouri Compromise. Since the spread of slavery to the Southwest would lessen the chance of unrest in Virginia, he did not want to confine bondservants in the

32. Ibid., 2:206–10.

33. Ibid., 1:62 (quotation); McLean, *George Tucker*, 183–86; Susan J. Tracy, *In the Master's Eye: Representations of Women, Blacks, and Poor Whites in Antebellum Southern Literature* (Amherst, Mass., 1995), 48–61.

"older" states, where they would eventually outnumber whites and threaten society. Tucker believed in diffusion and looked to the day when slaves would decline in value and become a burden to their owners, who would then lead the drive for emancipation. He later supported colonization and proposed that the United States buy land west of the Rocky Mountains and colonize ex-slaves in the area. Tucker held moderate attitudes on slavery, wanting it protected but wishing somehow to reform or gradually abolish it. His divided mind appeared in his second novel. He could hardly defend the willful fracturing of slave families that he described in *Letters*, so he modified his portrayal of the slave trade. It was now something that enlightened slaveholders needed to resist. The underlying motive, however, was a justification of slave sales and an attempt to show how little the trade disrupted the lives of slaves. The evolution of Tucker's views is indicative of how southerners were learning to deal with the slave trade. They were adjusting their thinking to take into account how slaves influenced their bondage.[34]

Like Tucker, John P. Kennedy struggled to find a context for the slave trade in his writings. Kennedy's novel *Swallow Barn*, first published in 1832, reflected this ambivalent view of slavery and the separation of slave families. Although a proslavery tome in general, *Swallow Barn* had few kind words to say about the ways in which slave families were treated. Kennedy devoted a chapter to slave life and observed how a kind master frequently looked in on the slaves to make sure they were comfortable. They always happily greeted their master, who gave them gifts. There was an "air of contentment and good humor and kind family attachment" between owner and slave. Kennedy's flat treatment of the slaves robbed them of their humanity, since they were depicted as perfectly content with their lives. Even though the slaveholders were, in general, considerate and pleasant towards their slaves, there was the necessity of reform. Kennedy thought masters were liable to reproach for neglecting laws that would recognize slave marriages and protected their families. He was ashamed that he had no answer for charges that families were divided, and he called for stiff punishment to prevent the separation of husband and wife or parent and child. Slave owners who allowed the destruction of kinship ties brought more "odium" to slav-

34. *Register of Debates in Congress*, 18th Cong., 2nd sess., March 2, 1825, 1:736; McLean, *George Tucker*, 180–86; *Debates and Proceedings*, 16th Cong., 1st. sess., February 25, 1820, 1531–35.

ery "than all the rest of its imputed hardships." Preventing the destruction of families would gratify conscientious slaveholders and silence critics of slavery.[35]

Kennedy was obviously a harsh critic of family breakups and was candid enough to admit that they were prevalent, or at least widespread enough to bring infamy on the South. Although he did not mention the practice of speculation, Kennedy blamed the interstate slave trade. Calling for a reform of slavery by punishing owners who separated families would go a long way towards putting speculators out of business. Rather than allowing the sale and speculation to continue unbridled by blaming others for its existence, Kennedy would legally limit the power of slaveholders over their possessions. His musings on family separation stand in stark contrast to all later fiction that blamed slave traders rather than masters for the problem. He struggled with the same issue of property rights that bedeviled Tucker and others. That they could seriously consider such an option is testimony to the problems slave trading presented to southern society. As speculation continued to expand in power and influence, however, southerners could no longer gloss over such difficult issues. They had to find a way to explain the interstate slave trade while simultaneously defending slavery.

What is especially surprising is that southern politicians and writers seriously considered placing limits on bondage. They emphasized the relational aspects of slavery rather than unfettered property rights. Speculation challenged the concept of implied responsibilities of masters to slaves, particularly protection from adversity. A reliance on the organic nature of the master-slave relationship was more comfortable for most masters. The slave trade, and its tilt towards exploitation, intruded into this tidy dream. Those who recognized the problem wanted limits that would redress the issues raised by a growing interstate slave trade. Carefully excising speculation from slavery was the logical cure. Snuffing out the interstate slave trade would give slaves less cause for resistance, mute outside criticism, and restore the relational emphasis of masters. Such reforms, unfortunately, would be scattered and ineffective in the next decade. The interstate slave trade thrived and became an essential part of the southern culture.

Slaves, however, would not surrender, and their actions were noticed and

35. John P. Kennedy, *Swallow Barn, or a Sojourn in the Old Dominion* (1832; reprint, New York, 1856), 451–59; Charles H. Bohner, *John Pendleton Kennedy: Gentleman from Baltimore* (Baltimore, 1961), 86–87, 187–88.

celebrated, at first in the Upper South and then throughout the North. Although unsuccessful in their individual acts of resistance against the interstate slave trade, bondservants were able to provide powerful ammunition for the critics of slavery in their attacks on the peculiar institution. Anna, who tried to kill herself rather than walk in a coffle, became the central figure in an Alexander Rider etching. The image later became prominent in the American Anti-Slavery Society's broadsides and was a poignant example of one slave's humanity in the face of sheer brutality. The simple dignity of Anna and countless slaves like her was the most effective way to raise doubts about the consequences of the interstate slave trade. Their actions, particularly in Washington, led the way to making the capital a symbol of freedom for all Americans.

CHAPTER 3

The Interstate Slave Trade and the Southern Imagination: The Upper South

Patty Cannon was one of America's first criminals to gain fame for the lurid nature of her crimes. Cannon's gang of thieves, a group that included her husband and sons, abducted free African Americans, slaves with a limited time to serve, and bondservants from Delaware, Pennsylvania, New Jersey, Maryland, and the District of Columbia. Gang members reputedly used peaches to lure young black children close enough to seize them. Cannon's house was their base of operations, a dank prison where African Americans suddenly found themselves chained in the basement. The house was one of several buildings that formed a compound which supposedly straddled the state line between Maryland and Delaware and even county lines within Delaware. When authorities came near, according to one contemporary, the gang eluded them by moving across state and county lines and into another jurisdiction.[1]

Cannon and her gang were extremely successful in their endeavors. A steady string of slave traders made the trek to the compound, bought her unfortunate victims, and then dragged them to the slave markets of the Deep South. Rumors circulated that Cannon was even so bold as to rob

1. Isaac Briggs to Timothy Pickering, June 5, 1817, Select Committee . . . on the Illegal Trade in Slaves; Carol Wilson, *Freedom at Risk: The Kidnapping of Free Blacks in America, 1780–1865* (Lexington, 1994), 20–37; Hal Roth, *The Monster's Handsome Face: Patty Cannon in Fiction and Fact* (Vienna, Md., 1998); M. Sammy Miller, "Patty Cannon: Murderer and Kidnapper of Free Blacks: A Review of the Evidence," *Maryland Historical Magazine* 72 (1977): 419–23; Todd A. Herring, "Kidnapped and Sold in Natchez: The Ordeal of Aaron Cooper, a Free Black Man," *Journal of Mississippi History* 60 (1998): 341–54.

slave traders of their cash and kill them. Only when her tenant farmer accidentally dug up a chest containing the remains of a speculator did the authorities take decisive action. They searched the rest of Cannon's property and found the bones of three other persons, including a young slave. Cannon was quickly arrested and sent to jail, where she died awaiting trial. When rumors swirled about Cannon's untimely end and the eventual location of her miserable bones, she became a type of boogeyman to frighten local children.[2]

Just as Cannon's life was a confusing mixture of fact and fiction, so too did the interstate slave trade become a strange blend of the real and the imagined. The slave trade experienced solid growth in the 1820s, but observers made fantastic claims about the number of slaves who were traded. One estimate put the number at 120,000 slaves sold out of Virginia in a single year, a preposterous figure. It became easy to assume that a number of vocal critics who castigated the trade spoke for all Upper South residents. In reality, there was a wide range of attitudes about speculation. Cannon, and those like her who carried out similar crimes, contributed to the assumption that most speculators were involved in the abduction and sale of African Americans. The reverse was probably true, as the vast majority of sales involved legal rather than abducted bondspeople. Most importantly, while southerners saw the real ways in which speculation affected the slaves, many imagined that it had a greater impact on the seller. That southerners were more commonly reducing the complex interreaction between master and slave to a simple dollar amount meant they were more likely to wonder if a foreign element had crept into the relationship. Such assumptions forced residents of the Upper South to struggle with the meaning of the slave trade, and ultimately with slavery itself. When southerners looked at the white image in the white mind, many did not like what they saw.[3]

2. *Niles' Weekly Register*, May 23, 1829; Wilson, *Freedom at Risk*, 20–37; Roth, *Monster's Handsome Face*, 68–81; M. S. Miller, "Patty Cannon," 421–22.

3. Theodore D. Weld, *American Slavery as It Is: Testimony of a Thousand Witnesses* (New York, 1839), 184 (estimate); Wilson, *Freedom at Risk*, 11–13, 52; *Genius of Universal Emancipation*, August 1, 1822, 22, September 2, 1826, 413; William Birney, *James G. Birney and His Times* (New York, 1890), 57–58; Carl Degler, *The Other South: Southern Dissenters in the Nineteenth Century* (New York, 1974), 40–41; David B. Davis, *The Problem of Slavery in the Age of Revolution, 1770–1823* (Ithaca, N.Y., 1975), 209–10; H. Shelton Smith, *In His Image, But . . . : Racism in Southern Religion, 1780–1910* (Durham, 1972), 70–71; Gordon E. Finnie, "The Antislavery Movement in the Upper South before 1840," *JSH* 35 (1969): 319–42; William M. Boyd, "Southerners in the Anti-Slavery Movement, 1800–1830," *Phylon* 9 (1948): 153–63;

A primary concern that thoughtful southerners in the slave-exporting states voiced about the interstate slave trade was its tendency to destroy slave families. This criticism of speculation could be compelling. If southerners allowed traders to wantonly destroy kinship networks, then it would be difficult to assume that slavery was a benign institution. Even though most southerners normally thought of a slave family as a woman and her two children, most assumed that speculators would not hesitate to sunder even these loosely defined relationships. The Benevolent Society of Alexandria for Ameliorating and Improving the Condition of the People of Color hated how slave traders continually tore apart slave families. A Kentucky resident agreed with these sentiments and called for legislation that prohibited men from driving slaves through his state. He contrasted the rightness of slavery with the "sordid" world of selling slaves for profit. Knowing that bondservants had been severed from their families was a thought "revolting to humanity." Those who shrunk from the forced sundering of slave families thought speculation was a contagion. If it contaminated slaveowners to the extent that they would do anything for money, then it could further erode white morals. While the activity of breaking up slave families was bad, the callous attitude of masters was worse.[4]

Southern opinion, however, was not unanimous on the topic. An advertisement in an 1820 Warrenton, Virginia, paper illustrates the conflicting attitudes towards the destruction of slave families. An owner who desired to sell three likely female slaves, one of whom had a male child, stated that "No objection will be made to traders purchasing." Even though the person was willing to deal with a speculator, the specific invitation might indicate that a substantial portion of the population would not deal with traders. This advertisement may have touched off some public and private debates in the small town. Three weeks later the same paper printed the letter from "*An Inquisitive Slave-holder.*" His examination of scripture led him to believe that "buying African bondmen had the sanction of Jehovah." Most southerners would agree with his conclusion because he only addressed the issue of sale rather than speculation. Opinion on whether or not slave trading was

---

Asa E. Martin, "The Anti-Slavery Societies in Tennessee," *Tennessee Historical Magazine* 1 (1915): 269–70.

4. Kulikoff, *Agrarian Origins of American Capitalism*, 246; *Genius of Universal Emancipation*, May 19, 1827, 322; *Western Luminary*, November 3, 1831 (quotations).

acceptable was fractured enough to require the specific inclusion of speculators in advertising. Such opinions, moreover, were still taking shape as the interstate slave trade emerged as a visible part of southern life. By the late 1830s there would be no need to single out traders.[5]

Not only did private sellers feel compelled to invite traders, but public vendors did so, as well. In Alexandria, William Chapman auctioned off twenty slaves on the steps of Joseph Shumate's tavern. He carefully noted that there would be "no objection to traders purchasing at this sale." Even though speculators frequented auctions because they could buy slaves at a relatively low cost and purchase bondservants individually, these public occasions also created opportunities for citizens to shun such men. The specific inclusion of traders again revealed a divided mind regarding speculation. If traders were welcome at all auctions, Chapman would have felt no need to include them. The specific reasons for his curious phraseology were unspoken, but he may have been reacting to incidents where traders were excluded from auctions.[6]

Other advertisements, of course, put no conditions on sales and allowed anyone to buy. One anonymous owner indicated he would sell his twenty-year-old female slave with or without her infant male child. Another offered a likely fellow for sale, "Provided he is carried out of the State." The latter owner, and southerners like him, essentially invited traders to buy slaves who could not be sold to a local resident. Should the bondservant commit a heinous deed, the seller's reputation might suffer harm. Bringing slaves to the Lower South, on the other hand, insulated the seller from any repercussions should the bondservants become rebellious. Other masters offered up their slaves for sale, but usually directed interested parties to inquire of the printer. The primary benefit of this type of advertising was convenience, as the newspaper editor could screen all inquiries before interested purchasers contacted the seller directly. Thus if a slaveholder wished to avoid a speculator who possessed a bad reputation, he could easily do so. Most important, such advertisements also provided a measure of discretion to

5. *Warrenton Virginia Palladium of Liberty*, February 4, 1820 (first quotation), February 25, 1820 (remaining quotations, emphasis in original).

6. *Washington Daily National Intelligencer*, April 1, 1816 (quotation); Tadman, *Speculators and Slaves*, 113–18; Thomas David Russell, "Sale Day in Antebellum South Carolina: Slavery, Law, Economy, and Court Supervised Sales," Ph.D. diss., Stanford University, 1993.

preserve unwanted information from being subject to the prying eyes of neighbors.[7]

While such advertisements were numerous, those slaveholders who wanted to sell to a trader did not have to advertise their intentions. Speculators were ubiquitous and easy to locate. They normally stayed at the usual tavern or inn, roved the countryside in search of bargains, and visited farms in search of sellers. The slaves whose lives changed because of the traders cannot be counted, and this shadowy interstate slave trade cannot be measured. Thousands of these direct sales to speculators will remain hidden to historians. Countless residents of the Upper South took advantage of the fact that speculators preserved at least some degree of anonymity for their clients. Others had no qualms about being associated with the slave trade or speculators. Edward Hambleton of Talbot County, Maryland, for instance, made a practice of selling to speculators. He sold slaves to the various Woolfolk relatives in 1823 and 1825, and then to a different speculator in 1826.[8]

Others found that the slave trade—or at least slave movement—was beneficial and had little concern about the impact of the interstate slave trade. During the Missouri Compromise debates, Senator Alexander Smyth feared the consequences should the west be shut off from slave expansion. The more slaves are dispersed, he argued, the greater the safety for whites. Smyth also believed the corollary: that a significant concentration of slaves would lead to "probable destruction." While Smyth did not directly refer to the interstate slave trade as a benefit, his statements supported the notion that speculation could have positive consequences in reducing the proportion of slaves in the Upper South. Others were more blunt in their approval of the trade. Samuel Logan and his law partner C. Haynes contacted Joseph Meek, a speculator, in the hopes of making some extra money from slave sales. They did so even though Logan acknowledged that such participation could impair their reputation and thus hurt their law practice. They ended up recruiting another man to serve as a front for them in the buying market.

7. *Baltimore American*, April 4, 1820; *Norfolk American Beacon*, July 7, 1819 (quotation); *Baltimore American*, July 12, 1816; *Washington Daily National Intelligencer*, July 26, 1816; *Richmond Enquirer*, March 21, 1820, *Fredericksburg Virginia Herald*, July 19, 1815.

8. Talbot County Land Records, Liber 44 (August 1822 to December 1823), September 17 entry; Liber 45 (December 1823 to March 1825), March 15 entry; and Liber 46 (March 1825 to January 1827), August 5 entry, Maryland Department of Archives and History, Annapolis, Md.

The lure of money was a powerful enticement. A recent immigrant to the United States simply concluded that Richmond residents had "little regard" for auctions and the consequent fracturing of slave families.[9]

If there was a portion of the Upper South's population that embraced the interstate slave trade, there was an equally significant portion that still had its doubts. Perhaps the most that can be said about the interstate slave trade in the 1820s and early 1830s is that it engendered support as well as scorn. Edward Abdy spent several months touring the United States, and made it a point to visit Franklin and Armfield's slave pen in Alexandria. In Warrenton, Virginia, he stayed at a tavern and struck up a conversation with a doctor. When one of "Armfield's myrmidons" passed by, the doctor said no respectable person would deal with the trader. That sentiment suited the antislavery Englishman. When Abdy stopped forty miles away, in Orange Courthouse, he stayed at a hotel run by a speculator. He was surprised to learn that the man "had all the profits of the business without its odium." It seems that support for and opposition to the interstate slave trade was a mosaic that covered the Upper South, and traders could be accepted or rejected in the same locale.[10]

While selling to a trader was becoming increasingly acceptable, it was not an option that all considered. As the slave trade grew in strength, it became common amongst owners to place limitations on the sale of their slaves to prevent speculators from worming their way into the transaction. In the decade following the War of 1812, every major newspaper in the cities near the Chesapeake Bay contained advertisements to sell bondservants. An examination of them reveals that sellers used conditions to control who could buy their slaves, often excluding slave traders or planters who might transport the bondservants out of the state. Not coincidentally, the advertisements that placed limitations on sales were more frequent from September to February, the prime slave-selling season. Advertisers knew there would be more speculators in the area during these months and wanted to make sure they would not be bothered with such men. Such exclusions might be specific, such as the Fredericksburg resident who offered a twenty-three-year-old woman and her three-year-old boy for sale, bluntly

9. *Debates and Proceedings*, 16th Cong., 1st sess., January 18, 1820, 1012 (Smyth quotations); Morris Birkbeck, *Notes on a Journey in America* (1818; reprint, Ann Arbor, 1966), 20 (final quotation); Mooney, *Slavery in Tennessee*, 40–43.

10. Abdy, *Journal of a Residence*, 2:210 (first quotation), 2:215 (second quotation).

noting that "No trader need apply." Others were more subtle in registering their displeasure with the slave trade. One anonymous owner pointed out that his twenty-three-year-old house servant was "neither dishonest nor vicious" and must be sold to someone in the state. Such a requirement effectively shut slave traders out of the process.[11]

There was some of this similar sentiment in Kentucky and Tennessee, although not as much, since the slave trade from these states was not as robust. For instance, a Nashville resident offered his slave for sale, warning prospective buyers that the slave could not be carried "down the river." The same situation prevailed in Burke County, North Carolina. A historian has concluded there was no stigma attached to a master who sold a slave to his neighbor. Conversely, owners who sold bondservants to a buyer from another state were often censured, and the most objectionable act was to sell to a trader or agent who intended to carry the slaves to a distant market.[12]

Those owners who placed limitations on who could buy their slaves often specified that families must remain together. Newspaper advertisements reflected the general southern conception of a slave family as being a woman and her children. William and Hugh Pannell, for example, advertised that they would sell a woman and her three children. The Pannells, who sold a variety of items in Fredericksburg, Virginia, informed readers that the woman could not be sold out of the immediate vicinity, and required a bond and security to that end. It is highly unlikely the Pannells would go to the trouble of requiring a bond for the woman while allowing the children to be sold to someone else who could carry them to the Deep South. The underlying assumption was that they were to be sold together. Just as significant, they would remain close to all of their family. Those masters who allowed children to be separated from their mothers usually had to spell out such behavior as being within the realm of possibility. Grafton B. Duvall of Annapolis wanted to sell his slave woman and made it clear that she could

11. *Fredericksburg Virginia Herald*, January 21, 1826 (first quotation); *Baltimore American*, January 3, 1820 (second quotation); *Annapolis Maryland Gazette*, March 9, 1820; *Alexandria Phenix Gazette*, January 6, 1826; *Washington Daily National Intelligencer*, September 9, 1815; *Norfolk American Beacon*, August 8, 1816.

12. *Nashville Whig*, December 18, 1819 (quotation); *Kentucky Gazette*, June 7, 1824; Edward W. Phifer, "Slavery in Microcosm: Burke County, North Carolina," *JSH* 28 (1962): 137–65.

be purchased with or without her eight children. There were, however, few such advertisements.[13]

Bonds requiring purchasers to keep slaves in the state or locality were a consistent feature in advertisements. It was most common in Baltimore, but happened elsewhere in the Chesapeake. Charles Carroll, for instance, offered a large number of slaves for sale and required bonds that they not be taken out of the state. Those who required some type of security before selling their slaves could at least convince themselves there was a minimum of disruptions to the slaves as a result of the sale. They tried to temper the ravages of unchecked speculation by limiting the authority of the purchaser. Using bonds was a way to continue selling slaves while choking off the activities of speculators. Masters who required a security probably reasoned that bondservants who stayed in the same area could at least see their friends and relatives (provided *they* were not sold to a trader). In a few cases, owners went so far as to stipulate that their slaves not be sold to a speculator even after the owner's death. During the settlement of William Smyth's estate, for instance, the agent handling the sale was forbidden from selling the slaves to someone who would carry them out of Maryland. The fact that some owners required assurance that their slaves would not become subject to speculation is testimony to the interstate slave trade's strong and aggressive presence. It is also evidence of many whites who struggled with the effects of speculation.[14]

The decision to limit sales was a difficult one for most southerners. Charles Goldsborough of Maryland found himself "encumbered" with several slaves. He struggled with what to do. Although he had too many bondservants to support and wanted to sell a portion of them, he knew that a sale would cause "violence" and necessitate "handcuffs and chains," presumably if he sold his slaves to a speculator. Furthermore, he complained to his friend in Mississippi, selling them in Maryland would force a price one-third below market value. Despite the loss of revenue, Goldsborough convinced himself to sell slaves only in families to a cotton planter in Missis-

13. *Fredericksburg Virginia Herald*, October 20, 1817; *Norfolk American Beacon*, April 10, 1820; *Lexington Intelligencer*, May 17, 1823; *Annapolis Maryland Gazette*, June 3, 1819; *Georgetown National Messenger*, May 26, 1819.

14. *Baltimore American*, December 20, 1816 (quotation), April 1, 1822; *Easton Republican Star*, April 24, 1821; *Norfolk American Beacon*, October 20, 1817.

sippi. The net result, he felt, would be similar to the migration of a poor white family. His thinking illustrates the pretzel logic of many southerners. Even though masters may have considered themselves to be compassionate, there were definite limitations to their altruism. The most generous act would have been to free the slaves, something Goldsborough apparently never considered. Even having the decency to keep families together made him grumble about accepting a low price. Try as hard as they might, slaveholders could not stop thinking of slavery in pecuniary terms. This constant tendency to shift the center of gravity in the master-slave relationship from mutual dependence to exploitation was bothersome. Complaining about and avoiding the interstate slave trade was a way for masters to retain their faith in the goodness of slavery. Although their thoughts remained impure, the thinking went, at least they were not as bad as the speculators.[15]

Even though it is easy to criticize masters for not freeing their slaves, the fact that so many of them tried to avoid speculation reflects a struggle in southern society to understand and deal with the full implications of the slave trade. The truth remains that it would have been easier and more remunerative for owners to sell slaves to a trader than to find a private buyer for whole families. Only the wealthiest of southern citizens could afford to buy more than one slave, so it was difficult to find an individual who wanted the number and type of slaves in one family. Masters who avoided speculation made real sacrifices. James Madison, though encumbered by debt during his retirement in his home at Montpelier, refused to sell any of his slaves to a speculator. He first sold a portion of his land, but that did not provide enough income. As a last resort, he arranged for the sale of sixteen bondservants to a relative in Louisiana. Even though the transaction troubled him, Madison was able to convince himself that he shielded his slaves from the worst effects of the sale. Rather than seek the high prices of a trader, Madison stubbornly held out and tried to preserve the family structure of his slaves. In a similar fashion, Jesse H. Cobb begged Alexander Webb for "indulgence" in paying off a debt. Writing in April of 1833, he asked for time to raise and house his crop. Then he would "carry some of my blacks to the south and get your money." He asked for an extension on his loan so that he could locate "good masters" for his slaves. Should he have to sell to a speculator, Cobb feared that families would be separated and never see

15. "Governor Charles Goldsborough's Views on Slavery," *Maryland Historical Magazine* 39 (1944): 333.

each other again. He clearly linked speculation in slaves to the destruction of households, since traders would turn around and sell the slaves to the best of their advantage rather than preserve family ties. It would have been easier for Cobb to sell his bondservants to a speculator—he would not have had to travel and he would have obtained a higher price—yet the thought was distasteful to him. The men and women who deliberately avoided selling their slaves to speculators often did so to give some protection to the slave family. The trade routinely ravaged kinship ties, and those who shunned the trade knew that their slaves stood a much greater chance of not being separated if a private individual purchased them. Those owners who dealt with planters from another state seemed to draw a measure of satisfaction from their conduct. One almost seemed proud that because he avoided traders "it Took Nearly all My Property to pay My Debts." When owners decided to bypass the speculative trade, nonmonetary factors took precedence over economic motivations.[16]

There was a definite limit, though, to the compassion of the owner, and the master-slave relationship should not be romanticized. Slavery was a grim, degrading, inhumane business, and to ignore that fact is to deny reality. The level of a master's concern to keep his slave families together, moreover, varied immensely and could only operate within the bounds of the South's credit and economic system. Before James Fisher arranged to sell his slaves in family units in Louisiana, for instance, he secured the permission of his creditors. Furthermore, while owners may have made sacrifices to protect slave families, the very nature of slavery itself dictated an exploitative relationship. In reality, any such sale was bound to separate a slave from some member of his or her family, not to mention friends and familiar surroundings. Bondservants lived their lives in terms of aunts, uncles, cousins, grandparents, and friends. All sales, no matter how careful buyers tried to be, wrecked the web of the family network. Furthermore, owners were always cognizant of a slave's monetary and productive value. Perhaps the best that can be said is that even those owners who tried to preserve their slaves in family units had impure motives and substantial lim-

16. Drew R. McCoy, *Last of the Fathers: James Madison and the Republican Legacy* (New York, 1989), 255–60; Jesse H. Cobb to Alexander Webb, April 16, 1833, Jesse Cobb Letter, NCDAH (quotations); Memoir of James Norman Smith, book 2, 167, in Wallace Alexander Jones Papers, TSLA; J. J. Roane to Austin Brockenbrough, n.d., Austin Brockenbrough Papers, UV.

itations, as can be seen in the case of John Woods. He had several reasons for selling his slave Winston, whom he had purchased in North Carolina and brought to Tennessee. Woods soon realized that the slave wanted to return to his parents. The slave had served so faithfully that Woods could not bear to think of being without his trusty servant. It was, however, just such a devoted service that allowed Woods to consider rewarding Winston for all of his efforts. He explained that it was "My Duty" to reunite Winston with his family. Such an action was not to be done without regard to consequence, since Woods twice repeated he wanted a "faire price" for Winston. As with most relations between master and slave, there was a mixture of motives. Woods's attempt to reunite Winston with his family was somewhat self-serving. Although losing a trusty and obedient slave would be inconvenient, he was careful to take nothing less than the market price for his troubles. If Woods had Winston's interests truly at heart, he would have been willing to accept something less than the market value for the slave to ensure that the man could return to his family. The fact that he would sell the slave and get a good price in the bargain meant that Woods was trying to get the best of both worlds. He could convince himself he was a kind and benevolent owner while simultaneously gaining a suitable compensation for his efforts. Woods tried to reconcile the contradiction between Winston's treatment as both person and property. He succeeded, but many others failed. The slave trade heightened the tension between the desire to act in a paternalistic fashion and the need to make slavery profitable.[17]

Much hand-wringing revolved around the breakup of slave families, a criticism of speculation that was powerful because it could draw out an empathetic response. The word most frequently used to describe a slave sale or auction was "shocking." Such occasions were harrowing for the bondservants but could also be distressful for white onlookers. When slaves exerted influence over their sales, they forced whites to consider whether the sundering of family ties was worth the emotional price for all involved. These very public incidents also were an easy target for those outside of the South who opposed the peculiar institution. Family breakups eventually became a

17. John Woods to John Haywood, February 17, 1818, Ernest Haywood Collection (quotations); Sterling Neblett Papers, Account of Testimony, September 12, DU; *New Orleans Louisiana Gazette,* January 30, 1823; Thomas Lenoir to William Lenoir, April 13, 1806, Lenoir Family Papers, UNC; John Gordon to "Cott," April 17, 1819, Thomas Hardin Perkins Papers, TSLA.

mantra for the various antislavery and abolitionist groups. Such criticisms centered on what speculation did to the slave. A significant number of southerners in the Upper South, however, grew concerned about what speculation did to the master. It was this type of soul-searching that proved especially troublesome and powerful.

One of the reasons for this self-doubt was the rapid growth of kidnapping. The fact that wretches like Cannon could operate with virtual impunity tempted slave traders to combine illegal activities with their legal transactions. Abductions were especially seductive for slave traders because they turned a high profit by keeping costs to a minimum. It became a common assumption that kidnapped individuals could be found alongside slaves in the pens of Baltimore and Washington. Slave dealers in those cities were said to use stratagems to distract free African Americans, who were then "dragged by force" into the slave jails. Speculators of this ilk created confusion in the minds of many, who assumed that all traders must be crooked. The legal and illegal trade became hopelessly mixed for most people. A Baltimore resident complained that the "horrid practice of kidnapping" was far too common. He linked illegal abductions to the slave trade by describing how slaves were "chained together like oxen" and driven through the streets. It is doubtful that he saw only kidnapped slaves in the coffle. What is significant is that he automatically assumed that all speculators were involved in illegal activity.[18]

The growing number of abduction stories firmly linked slave traders with kidnappers in the public's mind. A grand jury in Baltimore, for instance, lashed out at the growth of kidnapping and noted how it attached itself to the slave trade. Not everyone who sold slaves was involved in illegal activity, obviously, but all kidnappers utilized the interstate trade since they eventually had to sell their victims. In the eyes of many observers, abductions and the legitimate sale of slaves were virtually identical and separating the two was impossible or pointless. Traders and kidnappers were both involved in the buying, selling, and movement of African Americans. The in-

18. Wilson, *Freedom at Risk*, 52; Clephane, "Slavery in the District of Columbia," 235; *Niles' Weekly Register*, July 19, 1817, 323; July Term of the Grand Jury of Baltimore, 1816, Select Committee . . . on the Illegal Traffic in Slaves (first quotation); undated *Baltimore American*, as quoted in the *Genius of Universal Emancipation*, March, 1822, 441 (remaining quotations); Steven Deyle, "The Irony of Liberty: Origins of the Domestic Slave Trade," *JER* 12 (1992): 37–62.

human and underhanded components of the illegal trade were imputed to the legal trade, making speculation even more objectionable. Kidnapping promoted lawlessness and encouraged disrespect for authority. The South was a highly stratified society, where those at the apex assumed an air of superiority. There are numerous instances where southern planters made great efforts to return free African Americans who had been kidnapped. This erosion of the moral code was a challenge to their authority. Kidnapping, most slaveholders could agree, was unnecessary and improper as it undermined the foundation of good society.[19]

Another activity that caused southerners to reevaluate the interstate slave trade was the attempts by speculators to steal or buy term slaves, that is, those with a fixed number of years to serve before becoming free. Term slavery, most commonly found in Maryland and Delaware, was a compromise within the peculiar institution. Owners benefited from having their bondservants work for several years but also eased their consciences by freeing their labor force, typically when the slaves reached thirty. Although such masters might have been trying to rid themselves of bondservants who were becoming less remunerative, they also could have sold them to a speculator. That there was less reliance on the slave trade than might be expected indicates other motives were at work. Slaves exerted pressure on the system to get decent terms for their release or self-purchase. The frequency of flight and the presence of rebellion dictated that owners used eventual emancipation as an incentive to motivate some slaves and pacify others. Speculation, in this environment, sometimes worked to undermine slavery.[20]

Most owners of term slaves specified they would sell only to a local resident, since they were well aware that purchase by a slave trader meant a trip to the Deep South. Slaves sold to the Deep South had virtually no chance to gain their freedom. Selling term slaves to speculators happened often enough, however, to draw public criticism from a grand jury in Alexandria. The panel complained of persons traveling to Virginia to buy term slaves. Such bondservants were entitled to protection "by the laws of justice and humanity." Not only was trafficking in term slaves illegal, it was immoral.

19. July Term of the Grand Jury of Baltimore, 1816, Select Committee . . . on the Illegal Traffic in Slaves; Phillips, *Freedom's Port*, 230–31.

20. Phillips, *Freedom's Port*, 45–54; Christopher Phillips, "The Roots of Quasi-Freedom: Manumission and Term Slavery in Early National Baltimore," *Southern Studies* 4 (1993): 39–66.

Those masters who sold their term slaves to a trader often risked public disfavor because they were betraying the expectations of paternalism. Condemning bondservants to a life of hard labor in the Deep South directly contradicted expectations that masters had a duty to protect their slaves.[21]

Another moral criticism of slave traders, and one that often when unspoken, was their tendency to rape female slaves. It was well known that masters were frequent sexual predators in the slave quarters. In fact, slave traders abetted such activities with a trade in "fancy girls": young, attractive women (often biracial) who became concubines. The circumstances of traders, however, provided more opportunities for exploitation. Social mores and neighborhood gossip might at least restrain some masters, but speculators had more power and fewer reasons to exercise self-control. The private lives of slave traders were scandalous. They joked about the "one-eyed man," a euphemism for their sexual organ, and bragged about how they forced sexual relations upon slaves they purchased. Franklin even mused that he would establish a slave whorehouse for the "comfort" of his agents. It was whispered in the South how Franklin, for instance, surrounded himself with "very likely mulatto girls." What was not mentioned, but was understood by all, is the sexual exploitation that Franklin was able force upon the women whom he purchased. Other traders, too, forced themselves upon female bondservants. The result was one more criticism of the interstate slave trade. It seemed to promote sexual promiscuity by putting attractive young women in the hands of lecherous old men. For white male southerners who struggled with their own attraction to their slaves, the slave trader was a convenient source of moral absolution.[22]

The assumption that slave traders were brutes who dabbled in illegal or immoral behavior closely paralleled the notion that the pecuniary nature of the trade polluted the master-slave relationship by introducing a foreign el-

21. Washington grand jury, as quoted in Tremain, *Slavery in the District of Columbia*, 49–50 (quotations); William Miner's speech in *Debates and Proceedings*, 20th Cong., 2nd sess., January 7, 1829, 177–78.

22. Isaac Franklin to Rice C. Ballard, January 9, 1832, January 29, 1833 (first quotation); January 11, 1834 (second quotation), James R. Franklin to Rice C. Ballard, March 27, 1832, all in Ballard Papers; *Succession of Isaac Franklin*, 277 (third quotation); Tucker, *Valley of the Shenandoah*, 2:208–209; Brown, *Narrative*, 47; Boney, ed., *Slave Life in Georgia*, 95; Edward E. Baptist, "'Cuffy,' 'Fancy Maids,' and 'One-Eyed Men': Rape, Commodification, and the Domestic Slave Trade in the United States," *American Historical Review* 106 (December 2001): 1637–49; Melton A. McLaurin, *Celia: A Slave* (New York, 1991).

ement: speculation. Most people raised few objections to masters who bought or sold slaves when necessity motivated such transactions. Instances of death, debt, or insolvency could usually be justified, but even then, as the case of Bushrod Washington demonstrates, there was a tacit limit to what masters should do. Their actions could be reckoned as a betrayal of their implied duty to protect the slave. With an increasingly aggressive interstate slave trade, masters who sold to speculators had difficulty convincing themselves they were acting in a paternalistic fashion that protected their bondservants to some degree. James Birney, for instance, in his attack on the interstate trade, did not condemn masters for buying or selling their slaves in good faith. He only decried the "commerce" in human beings. The notion of taking a profit from the unnecessary misfortune of others lay at the heart of this brand of opposition to the slave trade.[23]

As the interstate slave trade increased in volume, some southerners questioned whether republican government could survive. A Kentucky resident grimly noted his experience with the slave auctions on the courthouse steps, "the seat of justice." The trader who bought these particular bondservants forced one of them to carry an American flag, something the writer thought abhorrent because his forefathers "fought and bled for liberty and independence." He shrewdly linked the situation of the slaves to the symbols of justice (the courthouse), and liberty (the flag) to show how unbridled commerce trampled on the country's ideals. A Virginia resident contrasted his ability to vote with the presence of a slave coffle. He likened the power of a slaveholder to sell his slaves to an "absolute and oppressive" tyranny that was worse than any form of political despotism in the world. Just as a political system could become extreme and abusive, so too could the institution of slavery. While this Virginian did not suggest an alternative to the slave trade, he implied that there must be a way to guard against the extreme abuses of slavery. He explicitly denied that abolition was the answer. Knocking off the shackles of a slave, he thought, would be more evil than the trade itself because it would turn loose "a vagrant and a thief" who was not ready for freedom. He had no answer for the problem of the slave trade except to encourage good citizens to resist getting caught up in speculation.

23. Birney, *James G. Birney*, 57–58; Baptist, "'Cuffy,' 'Fancy Maids,' and 'One-Eyed Men,'" 1619–50.

Not only was unbridled speculation bad for the slave, but it also corrupted the master and could lead to society's collapse.[24]

That the interstate slave trade clashed with the notion of a free government was most prominent in the nation's capital. Edward Coles, a Virginian who later moved to Illinois so that he would not have to live in a slave society, winced whenever coffles marched through the streets of Washington. He described the trade as "a scene of wretched[ness] and human degradation" that undermined citizens' character. As James Madison's secretary, Coles reminded the president of the effects that such a "revolting sight" would have on foreign dignitaries. Apparently his protestations elicited no response. A few years later, when President Andrew Jackson and his cabinet marched to celebrate the French Revolution, a coffle trudged the other way. A Washington newspaper noted that "these shocking scenes" had to be prevented or Americans could no longer claim to be free. The paper wondered why there was not more indignation. Humanity, another paper explained, became paralyzed and justice was paralyzed when there was no protest against something so contrary to the nation's principles. In denying the essential humanity of the slave, the interstate trade violated the basic principles of justice upon which the nation was founded. Speculation's extreme nature could lead to corruption in slaveowners once they began to put the profit motive ahead of all others. If slave traders could induce slaveholders to trample casually on the most basic of human rights, then it was no stretch to imagine that the next threat would be a denial of justice to certain classes of whites. Individual debasement, the thinking went, would eventually lead to despotism in the political arena.[25]

The reason that republican government was imperiled was because the trade undermined individual virtue. This criticism of speculation was potentially the most powerful, since personal reputation and character were at stake. Heavy involvement in the interstate slave trade could potentially cast

24. *Paris Kentucky Western Citizen*, September 24, 1822, as quoted in Coleman Papers (first two quotations); *Lexington Virginia Intelligencer*, August 16, 1823 (final quotation).

25. Constance McLaughlin Green, *Washington: Village and Capital, 1800–1878*, 2 vol. (Princeton, 1962), 1:53; Ralph L. Ketcham, "The Dictates of Conscience: Edward Coles and Slavery," *Virginia Quarterly Review* 36 (1960): 46–62 (Coles quotations); McCoy, *Last of the Fathers*, 310–22; *Washington Spectator*, December 4, 1830, as reprinted in the *Liberator*, January 1, 1831, 1 (final quotation); *Alexandria Phenix Gazette*, June 22, 1827; Hall, *Travels in North America*, 2:141.

doubts upon a person's capacity to be a good citizen who could adequately fulfill his duties. Tangible—and loathsome—reminders of the trade seemed to indicate to many that southern society was moving in the wrong direction. Coffles especially seemed emblematic of slavery's brutality and the speculator's inhumanity. A Bourbon County, Kentucky, slaveowner could not easily understand the peculiar institution after he encountered a coffle. The sight of nearly one hundred slaves in chains and driven like animals was something that ran counter to this man's belief that the slaveowner had a duty to protect his bondservants from the worst abuses of the institution. Not only were the sights of manacled slaves offensive, but the image of an armed slave driver on horseback was particularly appalling. Eyewitnesses commonly reported seeing speculators use whips and pistols to intimidate the slaves in their coffles. If such extreme measures had to be taken, then perhaps there was something fundamentally wrong with speculation, and, by extension, slavery. A man who would treat slaves in this fashion could hardly be expected to harbor a virtuous character, according to those who disliked the trade.[26]

These misgivings with speculation assumed that cash warred against the natural tendencies of the master-slave relationship. Many slaveowners believed they had a paternalistic duty to care for and protect their slaves in some fashion. Speculation, however, ran counter to such thinking because it moved the master-slave relationship away from responsibility and towards self-indulgence. The residents of Baltimore had so much trouble squaring speculation with paternalism that the city's papers excluded advertisements headed "cash for negroes" but still arranged slave sales. The growing presence of traders' jails had become too obnoxious. Although notice of the ban appeared in 1821, the practice of excluding such advertisements started in 1820. That year most of the advertisements for slaves offered a few bondservants for sale, and a small portion requested to purchase slaves. Those notices that asked for more than one or two slaves were careful to note that such slaves were not for speculation. The editor of the *Baltimore American* knew that the sale of bondservants must continue, so he established the General Register Office, a service that bought and sold slaves on consignment. Owners paid a fee to list their bondservants with the office, and then

26. *Paris Kentucky Western Citizen*, September 24, 1822, as quoted in Coleman Papers; *Genius of Universal Emancipation*, November, 1822, 59; [Blane], *Excursion through the United States*, 226.

buyers or hirers examined the rosters of slaves. The office facilitated the matching of buyers and sellers, essentially expanding and organizing the concept of directing readers to inquire of the printer. It advertised that it had the lowest-priced slaves in town and emphasized that purchasers could always find satisfaction if they were buying or selling bondservants "*for this State only.*" All advertisements stressed that the slaves were to stay in the area rather than leave Maryland.[27]

The General Register Office was a compromise within the system of slavery. Those who used its services recognized the need for slave transactions, since they probably had "excess" slaves to sell or needed to raise some ready cash. They also wanted strict limitations on the terms of those sales. Sellers accepted the fair market value for their slaves in exchange for assurances that the buyers would not take their purchases out of Maryland. There was to be no speculation on the misfortune of others. The office tried to balance the demands of slavery's two extremes, namely tolerating the sale of bondservants while still laying down boundaries that preserved the slaves' humanity and the masters' duty. The system excluded the largest slave traders from directly using its services, since they were known by sight and would have been assumed to carry their purchases out of the state. It is possible that speculators used the office by employing a third party to pose as a local farmer and purchase slaves on their behalf, but such a ruse would not work for long. Establishing the office was one way to soften the harsh effects of speculation, since, for those who used its services, it effectively neutralized the prospect of selling to a slave trader. Those people who offered their slaves for sale through the office likely felt they were reducing the harmful effects of such transactions upon their slaves. They believed the love of money to be the root of all evil. Traders trumpeted that they would pay "cash for negroes," and it is significant that the paper banned such advertisements. This close connection between cash and the slave trade seems to have rankled Baltimore residents the most. In their view, the emphasis on money demeaned the institution of slavery and reduced the master-slave relationship to one of crass commercialism. Of course commercialism was in fact a prominent and vital component of the slave system, but few white southerners were willing to admit that fact, at least not publicly. If south-

27. *Niles' Weekly Register*, July 21, 1821, 323–24; *Genius of Universal Emancipation*, September 1821, 44–45; *Baltimore American*, December 17, 1821 (quotation, emphasis in original).

erners could rein in the amount of speculation and exclude traders, then they could still have faith in slavery's goodness. Use of the General Register Office was an attempt to dissociate slave sales from the slave trade and reassure southerners of their noble aspirations surrounding their transactions. It was a way to put a positive face on a dirty business.[28]

The system of excluding the advertisements of traders started to break down, however, as suspicious ads appeared in the Baltimore papers by late 1822. A supposed gentleman from Tennessee indicated he would pay the highest prices in cash for slaves. Another wanted several prime bondservants for his own use and promised to give cash and high prices. Such inducements were normally tools of speculators. By 1823 the effort to keep traders from using the newspapers completely collapsed. Austin Woolfolk's advertisements once again became a regular staple of the paper, and other traders soon began using the words "*Cash for Slaves*" at the beginning of their advertisements. Any attempt to limit the types of slave sales was bound to fail because it impinged on a master's power over his slaves. In a society that hungered for absolute authority over bondservants, it was difficult to accept anything that impeded this ideal. Not all owners wanted to be confined to certain conditions when selling their slaves, especially if they had bondservants who were burdensome. Just as significantly, there was a limited number of Maryland buyers who would keep slaves in the state; owners who wanted to rid themselves of their bondservants simply had limited options. The prospect of selling slaves at a high price to a trader rather than at a lower price to a neighbor was often too tempting for slaveowners to resist.[29]

Although it was short-lived, the General Register Office was indicative of efforts in the Upper South to mitigate the negative consequences of slavery. In circumscribing the alternatives and limiting the possible buyers, these owners soothed their consciences by convincing themselves that they had taken the necessary steps to make the sale more palatable to their bondservants. Much of the southern justification for slavery rested on certain obligations that masters had to their slaves, including adequate food, housing, and clothing. A significant number of slaveowners also felt the sting of conscience when separating slave families. The interstate slave trade brought this tacit obligation into public view. Placing conditions on a slave's sale was

28. Baptist, "'Cuffy,' 'Fancy Maids,' and 'One-Eyed Men,'" 1629.

29. *Baltimore American*, September 17, 1822, September 9, 1822, March 11, 1823 (quotation, emphasis in original).

one way for owners to reassert their good faith in the master-slave relationship. Many owners, moreover, were taking tangible steps to deal with the baneful effects of speculation. It was one thing to simply decry the sale of slaves but a much more serious matter to devise methods to prevent them. Such steps, however, were paltry and often meaningless to bondservants who faced the prospect of separation from all things dear to them.

In one sense, this attempt to see the humanity of bondservants put masters and slaves on the same level. A Kentucky periodical tried to underscore this point by reprinting several notices of slave auctions. Its hope, the editor explained by quoting another periodical, was to force its readers to realize that "*human beings*" were bought and sold in the land of liberty. The paper wanted to shatter the casual assumption of slaves' savagery and replace it with a deep understanding of the vulnerability of their lives. It therefore tellingly contrasted bondage and liberty, putting its argument in terms that most southerners would understand. John Randolph made much the same point, but in his own idiosyncratic style. He mocked how masters tried to ease their consciences and captured how slaveholders professed one motive but acted from another. In 1820 he placed sarcastic advertisements in two newspapers that lampooned those individuals who thought they were doing their slaves a favor by putting conditions on a sale. He asked planters to buy one thousand "prime" Virginia-born slaves from a man who was "contracting the scale of his business." Randolph exaggerated the size of the slaveholding—one thousand was preposterous in 1820 Virginia—while the use of the word "business" was a deliberate attempt to stress the proprietary nature of the master-slave relationship. He knew that the slave's prime function was to increase the holdings of the master, and as such, the pecuniary motives of slaveholders came first. Randolph's advertisement indicated that the slaves were being sold for their own accommodation, ridiculing the idea of a master putting the slaves' interest ahead of his own. "No proposals from any slave trader," he added as a parting shot, would be considered. Randolph scoffed at those planters who pretended they could ameliorate the shock of a slave sale for their slaves. He recognized that even though owners might make a distinction between selling to southern planters and selling to speculators, the slaves did not separate the two transactions because both caused pain and hardship.[30]

30. Undated *Christian Mirror*, as reprinted in *Western Luminary*, March 8, 1826, 559 (first quotation, emphasis in original); James Oakes, *Slavery and Freedom: An Interpretation of*

This early opposition to the slave trade in the Upper South rested upon the assumption of the slave's humanity. Destroying families obviously fit into this category, but so too did concerns over republicanism, virtue, and liberty. If a slave was a beast, then none of these issues would have validity. If he was human, then troubling doubts persisted. The slave occupied an ambiguous and often contradictory place in southern society, being regarded as both person and property. Slaves were treated like property when they were bought and sold, moved from place to place, and used as collateral in loans. Southern courts consistently upheld the property nature of the slave. Bondservants, however, were also human and did not always engage in behavior that suited slaveowners. Possessors of free wills, they could choose to disobey their masters (and suffer the consequences) or comply with the orders given to them. Most southerners recognized this aspect of slavery, as well. This begrudging recognition of humanity was just the minimum. Masters could also assume that slaves had feelings, had strong family ties, and were subject to the same emotions as other human beings. Doing so required a certain amount of empathy and imparted a sense of dignity to the slave. Most owners preferred not to think about the consequences of their actions upon their slaves or themselves. In the case of sale, masters could defend their decisions by telling themselves that what they did was in the best interest of the slave, or that circumstances beyond their control forced them to act. This notion of paternalism, almost a fanciful dream by the master, was one way to justify the institution of slavery. The slave trade, however, operated in direct opposition to any paternalistic pretensions. It assumed the proprietary nature of the slave and assigned a dollar amount to the master-slave relationship. Masters who had no regard for the consequences of the sale upon their slave denied the slave's essential humanity and degraded their own.

Even as many Upper South residents could almost recognize the humanity of their slaves, they came to doubt the humanity of speculators. In this view, only a man "steeled by avarice and petrified by cruelty" would remain unmoved by the shrieks of slaves who had been sold from their relatives. That slave traders denied the slaves' essential dignity was a notion that became prevalent. A resident of Loudoun County, Virginia, complained that "inhuman traders" had recently appeared in the area. Richard H. Carter of

---

the Old South (New York, 1990), 68–70; *Savannah Daily Republican*, 6 May 1820 (remaining quotations).

Rectortown, Virginia, harbored the same feelings. He wrote to George Kephart, a slave trader in Alexandria, for a favor. Kephart's agent bought a slave woman whose husband Carter owned. He wanted to buy the woman, named Mima, but already had more slaves than he wanted. Carter recognized that he was "induced to make an appeal to your humanity," and asked to pay Kephart less than market value for Mima. He fully understood that "such cannot be your usual way of doing business," but asked the trader to make an exception. Carter knew that any favoritism Kephart might show went against the strictly commercial nature of the trade. He clearly contrasted business with humanity, knowing the two could not easily coexist. It is unknown whether Carter succeeded in buying Mima at a discounted price, or even if he acquired the woman, but his motives were in stark contrast to Kephart's way of doing business. Twice Carter mentioned Kephart's "humanity," as if to stress to the slave trader that somewhere deep inside of him there was an impulse that could also see the objects of his speculation as human.[31]

Speculators faced doubts and questions, so they needed to assure a skeptical public of their veracity. Even though some traders assisted slaveowners, others tried to pass themselves off as planters. Many speculators swore that the slaves they bought were for their own use, rather than for speculation. There is the assumption in their notices that buying slaves for one's self was somehow better than buying them for resale. David Harding, a trader, tried to fool the residents of Richmond by advertising that the slaves he bought were for his own use. Woolfolk, who was too well known as a speculator to conceal his identity, tried to get good prices by indicating his desire to purchase slaves for specific cotton plantations in the Deep South. Whether such efforts were successful or not is beside the point, since traders tried to use the presence of planters in the Upper South's slave markets to their advantage. They quickly realized the possibilities of pretending to buy for a third party or themselves. It was more acceptable to sell a slave to

31. "American Convention [of] Abolition Societies, Minutes, 1828," *Journal of Negro History* 6 (1921): 328 (first quotation); Reprint of a "Letter from a gentleman" dated March 10, 1828, as quoted in *Genius of Universal Emancipation*, March 29, 1828, 75 (second quotation); Moncure D. Conway, *Testimonies Concerning Slavery* (London, 1864), 24–25 (remaining quotations); *Fredericksburg Virginia Herald*, September 29, 1818; *Easton Republican Star*, September 25, 1821; Charles Grier Sellers, "The Travail of Slavery," in *The Southerner as American*, ed. Charles Grier Sellers (Chapel Hill, 1960), 60; Baptist, "'Cuffy,' 'Fancy Maids,' and 'One-Eyed Men,'" 1633.

a private citizen than to a slave trader because the transaction was not based, southerners convinced themselves, on speculation. Without the speculative element, slaveholders purified the master-slave relationship and could believe that slavery was a benevolent institution. Gentlemen could then buy and sell slaves without concern for the consequences of their actions. Traders tried to portray themselves as part of this gentry. One suspicious advertisement called attention to the fact that a gentleman who wanted to buy slaves for his own use would give "CASH, *And the highest prices.*" The man gave no other information other than directing prospective sellers to a boardinghouse in Baltimore. Such an ad may have been placed by a planter, but the phraseology is reminiscent of a trader, especially the emphasis on cash and the highest prices. This advertiser also described himself as a "Gentleman." Planters tried to distinguish themselves from speculators by using that term, and its frequent use in the advertisements for private purchasers suggests a gulf between planters and traders. Speculators were well aware that they were not "gentlemen," even if they did make purchases on behalf of planters. A trader in Mississippi, for example, felt the sting of being ignored by a Methodist minister and knocked off the preacher's hat for "not speaking to a gentleman." This prejudice was significant enough that private citizens noticed it. Pryor McNeill observed that citizens were often forgiven of their debt to speculators because people were biased against traders. It was a rare thing, he concluded, "for a negro trader to get justice done him by a jury."[32]

The question remains, though, if speculation caused so many doubts and concerns, why was it increasing in the 1820s? Part of the answer lies in the fact that constant exposure to something provocative or controversial can deaden its impact. Contemporary critics of the interstate slave trade sensed that continual exposure to coffles dulled the senses of white southerners. The *African Observer*, a short-lived antislavery journal, thought the traffic could be reconciled once consciences became inured to the treatment of slaves as chattel. A resident of North Carolina agreed, admitting that he could tolerate everything about slavery but the "shocking separations" when

32. *Richmond Enquirer*, June 8, 1821; *Washington Daily National Intelligencer*, August 9, 1825; *Baltimore American*, February 20, 1822 (first quotation, emphasis in original), November 9, 1824; John Jones Journal, 76, manuscript in MDAH (second quotation); Pryor McNeill to Malcolm McNeill, June 10, 1825, Elizabeth Winston Collection, NCDAH (final quotation).

slaves left family and loved ones behind. When told that such scenes were inseparable from slavery itself, the man reluctantly concluded that if the slave trade could not be made better, "it must be submitted to with all its inconveniences." An Alexandria newspaper sadly noted that if southerners did nothing about speculation, they would become so accustomed to its "repulsive" features that they would no longer notice it.[33]

Such remarks contain only part of the answer. As we have seen, there was a substantial portion of the Upper South residents who were not troubled by the trade. They recognized that speculation was an effective way to reduce the number of slaves in a region that progressively required less labor. The trade was also a useful way to deal with unruly or difficult slaves. Virginia's state government even sent convict bondservants to the Deep South as part of their punishment. The slave trade served as a source of wealth for slaveowners and helped maintain a general level of prosperity. Speculation, moreover, calmed fears that a growing and restive population might rebel. Finally, many southerners, blinded by their racist society, considered slaves to be little better than animals.

Another explanation for the growth of the interstate slave trade in the face of negative public sentiment is that the expression of reservations about speculation could be therapeutic. Slaveowners did not want to consider themselves as exploiters of their chattel, but such a conclusion was hard to deny given the brutal nature of the peculiar institution. If masters could convince themselves that they made great exertions to shield their bondspeople from the particularly vile aspects of the slave trade, then they could live more easily with the idea of legal exploitation. At least they could assume they were better than others who had no regard for preserving the slave family structure. Uncomfortable with the extreme nature of slavery, these masters placed voluntary limits on their behavior. In so doing they made slavery more acceptable to themselves, since it was shorn of its most controversial aspects. These people could convince themselves they had no option but speculation. The genuine and significant longings to be rid of speculation actually strengthened slavery by making it more palatable.

33. *African Observer*, May 1827, 54; Andrews, *Domestic Slave-Trade*, 195–96 (first and second quotations); *Alexandria Phenix Gazette*, June 22, 1827 (final quotation); James S. Buckingham, *The Slave States of America*, 2 vols. (London, 1842), 1:182; "American Convention," 328; Charles Lyell, *A Second Visit to the United States of North America*, 2 vols. (New York, 1849), 2:125–26.

When citizens of the Upper South examined themselves in light of the interstate slave trade, they were divided as to what they saw. Some were not troubled by the increasing presence of speculation, auctions, and coffles. Others were. They could not embrace the interstate slave trade for fear of bringing degradation upon themselves. Their own self-regard could exist only when they avoided speculation. It took a particular feat of imagination, however, to conclude that such individual action served as insulation from a wider problem that bedeviled southern society. The white image in the white mind was not something to be proud of.

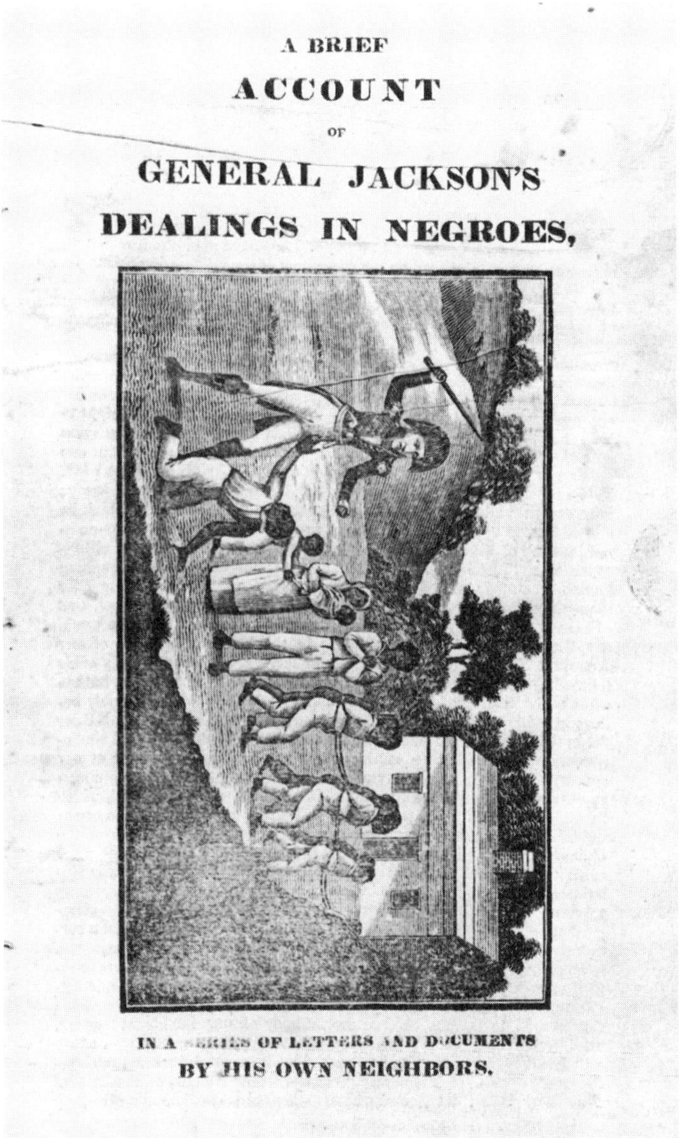

A BRIEF

ACCOUNT

OF

GENERAL JACKSON'S

DEALINGS IN NEGROES,

IN A SERIES OF LETTERS AND DOCUMENTS

BY HIS OWN NEIGHBORS.

The interstate slave trade became closely associated with public violence inflicted upon slaves. Most southerners in the Jacksonian Era did not want to be associated with speculation and the term "slave trader" became a powerful insult. In the case of Andrew Jackson, his opponents used the slave trade to imply that Jackson possessed a violent and arbitrary nature. *Courtesy of the Tennessee State Library and Archives*

By 1830 slave traders had made significant changes to their profession. Transporting slaves on sailing vessels from Baltimore or Alexandria to New Orleans was quicker and more reliable than transporting them overland. Slave traders also used coastwise transportation to hide the brutality of the interstate slave trade from southerners who found whips, guns, and shackles offensive. *Courtesy of the Library of Congress*

A Slave-Coffle passing the Capitol.

Coffles that marched past the national Capitol presented a jarring contradiction between slavery and freedom. Many southerners questioned whether the interstate slave trade undermined republican ideals and personal morality by emphasizing the pursuit of money rather than fair treatment of bondservants. *Courtesy of the Library of Congress*

The antislavery broadside depicts several facets of the internal slave trade, particularly as it manifested itself in the region near the District of Columbia. Alexandria became the base of operations for numerous speculators, who built their jails there. Traders housed slaves in these private prisons before forcing them to march south in coffles or loading them on sailing vessels bound for New Orleans. *Courtesy of the Library of Congress*

Anna, the slave depicted here, jumped from George Miller's Tavern, where she was being held prior to her movement to the Deep South in a coffle. Her actions ignited a national debate when John Randolph learned of her suicide attempt and called for the end of the internal slave trade in Washington. Slaves' individual and collective actions in resistance to speculation were powerful in shaping southern distaste for the interstate slave trade. *From Jesse Torrey,* A Portraiture of Domestic Slavery, *in the Rare Book Collection, University of North Carolina at Chapel Hill*

Isaac Franklin teamed with John Armfield to create the most powerful and successful slave-trading company in America. Franklin sold slaves in New Orleans and Natchez until the early 1830s, at which time he retired to his mansion in Tennessee. Upon his death, Franklin was one of the richest men in the United States, with one plantation in Tennessee, six in Louisiana, property in Texas, and more than 550 slaves. *Courtesy of the Belmont Mansion*

John Armfield lived in Alexandria and oversaw the purchase of slaves in Maryland and Virginia. He directed operations from Franklin and Armfield's slave jail on Duke Street. He likewise directed the activities of several agents, who roamed the countryside in search of "likely" slaves to purchase. Once the agents gathered a sufficient number of bondservants, they sent them to Alexandria to be loaded onto ships. When Armfield retired from slave trading, he purchased a hotel at Beersheba Springs, Tennessee, and operated a spa for wealthy travelers. He was also instrumental in establishing the University of the South at Sewanee, Tennessee. *Courtesy of the Belmont Mansion*

CHAPTER 4

The Interstate Slave Trade and the Southern Imagination: The Lower South

Isaac Franklin had a gruesome job to do, so he chose nighttime to conceal his actions. Several of his slaves had caught cholera on the steamboat trip from New Orleans to Natchez and later died. He buried five in the public cemetery but did not want to inter too many there, lest his business suffer. So Franklin secretly buried the rest of his victims in Natchez's washed-out ravines. He botched the job, though, and the rain soon washed away the earth to reveal a grisly scene. It was not the first time Franklin had dumped the bodies of slaves in the gullies around Natchez. Five months earlier he had jokingly confided to a friend that "the way we send out Dead negroes at night and keep Dark [i.e., silent] is a sin." Franklin's "sin" caught up to him when the scandal rocked Natchez. The coroner hastily convened an inquest, but the speculator could not give a satisfactory explanation when confronted with the evidence of his bungling attempts at a cover-up. Within two days, eighty-one of the town's citizens signed a petition that asked authorities to expel all speculators and their slaves from the city limits and to prevent the landing of slaves from New Orleans. The petition noted that some speculators had "adopted the horrible and inhuman practice of throwing the bodies of their Dead Negroes" into the city's swamps. As a result of the slaves' decomposition, the air was heavy with "obnoxious exhalations," and cholera lurked in the neighborhood. The city council soon met in special session. The audience of several hundred was in a surly mood. Council member Felix Houston set the terms of the discussion by announcing his opposition to the business of slave trading because it detracted from the city's character and standing. Another council member, William Vannerson, demanded action. He recalled how traders had introduced the scourge several times before. That evening the council unanimously passed an ordinance expelling all traders from the city's center. It applied only to those "commonly called Negro Traders," with the fine set at ten dollars per day per slave.[1]

Even before the city council's action, seven of the town's slave traders had tried to restore their damaged reputations. They appeared before a justice of the peace and swore affidavits as to how many of their slaves, if any, died from disease. Some of these speculators joined with other traders to differentiate themselves from Franklin by publishing an open letter in the local paper. In it they praised the conduct of the town's citizens and respectfully moved their slaves outside the city. The speculators and the city council were merely completing the process begun four years before when the city council banned traders from the city's center between November 15 and April 15. The town's leadership was serious about dealing with the problem this time and rigidly enforced the new ordinance. Franklin's brother James grumbled that the city council was forcing him to leave on such short notice that he might as well set up shop in the woods.[2]

The sordid story of Franklin hauling his dead slaves to the swamps of Natchez illustrates some of the ways in which speculation took shape in the

1. *Mississippi Journal and Natchez Advertiser*, April 19, 1833; Isaac Franklin to Rice C. Ballard, December 8, 1832, Ballard Papers (first quotation); City of Natchez Petitions, April 22, 1833, Record Group Natchez, Reel 47, MDAH (petition quotations); *Natchez Mississippi Gazette*, March 27, 1833; *Washington Mississippi Gazette*, May 4, 1833, as quoted in Kenneth Stampp, *The Peculiar Institution: Slavery in the Ante-Bellum South* (New York, 1956), 250; M.W.B. to Richard Watkins, July 14, 1833, Palmore Family Papers, UV; *Natchez Mississippi Journal and Natchez Advertiser*, April 26, 1833; City of Natchez Minute Books, Minute Book Number 6, 1820–1875, April 22, 1833, Record Group Natchez, Reel 2, MDAH (final quotation).

2. City of Natchez, Certificates of Negro Traders, April 22, 1833, Record Group Natchez, Reel 36, MDAH; *Natchez Mississippi Journal and Natchez Advertiser*, April 26, 1833; City of Natchez, Municipal Records, June 9, 1829; January 26, 1830, Record Group Natchez, Reel 45, MDAH; James R. Franklin to Rice C. Ballard, April 24, 1833, Ballard Papers (quotation). Traders were excluded from an area bounded by Fourth Street North, Fourth Street South, Seventh Street, and the riverfront bluff. Traders who wanted to sell slaves had to keep them out of sight, not overcrowd the rooms, make sure none was diseased, and keep the facilities clean. The amended law may have been influenced by the petition of several traders (Municipal Records, November 4, 1829, Record Group Natchez, Reel 47, MDAH).

Lower South. Residents there generally accepted the interstate slave trade—even with all its flaws—because of its importance in replenishing and augmenting the labor supply. Rather than questioning the morality or legitimacy of speculation, they sought to control it and channel it into more acceptable forms through state and local legislation. Whites in importing states prohibited speculation at various times, tried to regulate the types of slaves who crossed their borders, and kept a close eye on traders' activities. They also tended to blame speculators for a host of problems even while harboring a grudging acceptance for the businessmen's presence. Traders served as a useful outlet for public frustration. Unlike the Upper South, Deep South residents tended to have little concern over what the interstate slave trade did to slaves. No tears were shed for Franklin's dead slaves, nor did owners have second thoughts as to how speculation impacted white morals. Instead, whites were concerned that recently imported bondservants could foment rebellion, spread disease, or prove unmanageable. In the public imagination, the interstate slave trade was something to be mastered, and slaves had to be controlled.

Franklin's actions were a graphic reminder that Deep South residents had good reason to view slave traders with suspicion. It became widely believed that traders altered their slaves before putting them on the market. Speculators were known to use various techniques to make slaves appear younger, such as blacking or plucking their gray hair, and rubbing grease on their skin to make them appear more youthful. William Wells Brown, a slave who worked for a trader named Walker, helped prepare the older bondservants for market. When Walker brought his slaves down the Mississippi River, he ordered Brown to shave the men and either pluck their gray hair or color it with a blackening brush. At the completion of the process, Brown thought some of the slaves looked up to fifteen years younger. To complete the ruse, Walker taught the slaves their new ages. Since Walker transported his slaves on steamboats where they could be seen by whites, Brown tellingly explained that these operations took place in a room out of the sight of passengers, lest they discover that the trader was altering the condition of his slaves. The proof of the process's efficacy was testified to by Brown, who thought that some of the people who bought slaves from Walker had no idea they had just acquired old slaves. John Knight, writing from Natchez, affirmed Brown's experience. He complained that since traders were "generally such liars," purchasers knew virtually nothing about the slaves they bought. It was difficult to separate fact from fiction when it came to a slave's sale. Will White of Nashville traveled to Natchez to sell nine of his slaves. His frustration mounted at not being able to get as much as he had hoped for the bondservants. He told his wife that potential buyers were hesitant to commit because "a great number of deceptions have been practiced by traders."[3]

Besides altering the bodily appearance of the slaves, speculators also dressed them in new clothing. Buyers were more likely to assume that a clean, well-dressed slave would be easier to manage than one who was dirty and clad in rags. One Georgian complained of how the tidy appearance of a speculator's drove of "well dressed, good looking negroes" concealed the fact that they had been convicted of crimes and were on their way to Alabama. Southerners in the importing states generally assumed that speculators, especially itinerant traders with whom they were not familiar, concealed the true identity of slaves and would do just about anything to make money.[4]

While traders changed the outward appearance of slaves, they also tried to conceal inner qualities that might hinder a sale. The experience of Henry Bibb demonstrates how one trader erased problematic aspects of the slave's past. Bibb had twice run away from his master before the man, out of exasperation, sold him to a speculator. When prospective purchasers asked Bibb if he ever had run away before, the trader quickly answered that Bibb was a model slave who had never tried to flee. The speculator even pressured Bibb to act pious and appear to be a Christian so that someone would regard him as being docile and want to purchase him. Speculators' attempts to erase the past of the bondservants indicated that they regarded a slave's life as something malleable that had little importance. Traders tried to create a new reality that contradicted the truth. More importantly, these questionable practices contributed to the growing stereotype of slave traders. This "coaching" of slaves and the altering of their past became one of the chief complaints about traders. Buyers thought it necessary to examine slaves: look in their mouths, force them to disrobe, or have them bend down or jump up. Many observers rightly condemned these intrusions into personal dignity. The fact remains that rather than being a product of callous whites,

3. Arna Bontemps, ed., *Great Slave Narratives* (Boston, 1969), 40; John Knight to William M. Beall, March 18 1844, John Knight Papers, DU (first quotation); Will White to Eliza White, April 20, 1821, Felix Grundy Papers, TSLA (second quotation).

4. *Milledgeville Georgia Journal*, December 4, 1821.

physical examinations were a means to cope with dishonest traders. A slave's body was more truthful than a trader's tongue.[5]

Naturally a significant number of sales went bad. Dissatisfied customers frequently hauled traders into court. The legal records of the South are littered with the proceedings of citizens who were quick to look for legal assistance when they felt wronged in a slave sale. Bernard Kendig, a slave trader in New Orleans, landed in court thirteen times in ten years. Four times there was no verdict in the case, once he was found not guilty, three times he was found guilty of fraud, three times he was found to have sold defective slaves, and twice he sold stolen slaves. Lewis C. Robards of Lexington, Kentucky, also made frequent court appearances. He sold slaves who were subject to fits and had "nigger consumption" and other communicable diseases. Robards even seized and sold free blacks. Citizens of the Lower South, then, were receptive to laws outlawing the trade because they hoped to purge their state of such malefactors. The underhanded dealings of speculators almost invited legislative intervention.[6]

In Louisiana, the state with the largest market for importing slaves, warranties in the sale of slaves was the most common issue before the Louisiana Supreme Court in the fifty years prior to the Civil War. The situation became so acute that the state supported the right of redhibition through statute. In redhibition, the law specifically protected the buyer of a slave from any possible physical, moral, or mental defects of the slave. The state law forced the seller to declare any defects the bondservant possessed; silence on the subject assumed that the slave had no faults. If an undetected flaw became apparent, then the buyer could cancel the sale, return the slave, get his or her money back, or receive a refund for a portion of the slave's diminished value. Buyers of bondservants in other states had to rely on the judiciary to compensate them for any loss they suffered as the result of a sale, and Louisiana's law was a direct response to the questionable business practices of the slave traders. Instances of fraud were so widespread that the state assumed the trader was at fault, whether by omission or commission, imply-

5. Henry Bibb, *Narrative of the Life and Adventures of Henry Bibb, an American Slave* (1850; reprint, New York, 1969), 102; Greenberg, *Honor and Slavery*, 41.

6. Theodore Hunter, as quoted in Don H. Marr Jr., "Slave Trading and Slave Traders in North Carolina," master's thesis, East Carolina University, 1995, 11–12; Richard Tansey, "Bernard Kendig and the New Orleans Slave Trade," *Louisiana History* 23 (1982): 159–78; J. Winston Coleman Jr., "Lexington Slave Dealers and Their Southern Trade," *Filson Club Historical Quarterly* 12 (1938): 12–14 (quotation on p. 12).

ing that Deep South residents were comfortable in defining the master-slave relationship in commercial terms. The speculation did not rankle citizens in this area, but the willful misrepresentation of fact did.[7]

The law was most effective in combating the fraud of established speculators. It had less success in coping with the antics of itinerant traders, that is, ones without a fixed address in the importing states. They were especially bothersome because they tended to get away with more frauds. Citizens were confident they could sue an established trader or make an appeal to return a defective slave to him because they could find him after the sale. There was no guarantee, however, that a purchaser would ever see an itinerant trader again. The potential for abuse and fraud was enormous. The *New Orleans Bee* grasped this point when it made the crucial distinction between types of traders in its city. In calling for a slave-importation law that kept out the worst slaves, it sought protection against nonresident sellers who cared nothing for local residents. Such men, a Spartanburg, South Carolina, grand jury agreed, were dangerous to the state's safety. Most people thought this class of speculators bought the cheap and seemingly ubiquitous questionable slaves. They bought slaves at rock-bottom prices so they could make absurd profits through deception. Southerners feared that itinerant dealers of this type introduced the worst slaves imaginable. Such bondservants would eventually "corrupt the entire mass of our colored population." Louisiana considered a law against itinerant traders in 1831, about six months before the Nat Turner rebellion in Virginia. Isaac Franklin, an established trader who was not a Louisiana resident, was "Foilled and bedeviled" when he heard the news. He confessed he was at a loss and feared for his economic future. Franklin accused the legislature of trying to close down the trade and pledged to use his influence to thwart passage of the measure. The "depressed" speculator confided that he might have to become a citizen of Louisiana. Fortunately for Franklin, the measure did not become law.[8]

The distrust of itinerant traders coexisted with the vague notion that residents of the Upper South were trying to jettison the worst of their slaves.

7. Judith Kelleher Schafer, *Slavery, the Civil Law, and the Supreme Court of Louisiana* (Baton Rouge, 1994), 129–31.

8. *New Orleans Bee*, December 29, 1820; Spartanburg grand jury, as quoted in H. M. Henry, *The Police Control of the Slave in South Carolina* (Emory, Va., 1914), 106; *Milledgeville Georgia Journal*, October 13, 1818, December 4, 1821 (first quotation); Isaac Franklin to Rice C. Ballard, February 20 (second quotation), February 28, 1831 (final quotations), Ballard Papers.

Deep South citizens could assume such because they would probably have done the same thing. Other than for debt or some calamitous circumstance, the sale of a slave who was, on the surface at least, contented and a good worker made little sense. One Georgian described the slaves found in a trader's coffles as "incendiaries, poisoners and murderers" who had somehow escaped conviction. A Louisiana resident whined that citizens of Virginia and Maryland were ungrateful and unappreciative of the risks his neighbors took when they bought the "most dangerous" Upper South slaves. He asked the legislature to put a stop to slave speculation in the state. Maryland residents, a Natchez newspaper thought, viewed the slave trader as a benefactor because he bought the "rogues and vagabonds" and sent them south. Other residents in the Deep South thought it made perfect sense to assume that slaveholders in other states would usually sell their worst slaves to "unprincipled" speculators. In this manner they would gradually rid themselves of the most difficult part of the population. A Washington paper, in observing that Mississippi complained about convict slaves, admitted there was no doubt that the worst of its slaves had long been subject to the trade. With a bit of unconcealed glee, it noted that the process was good riddance for Virginia and Maryland, but not for Mississippi.[9]

These musings on the interstate slave trade provide a significant glimpse into the manner in which Deep South residents regarded their slaves. They were more forthright in assuming that slavery was an exploitative relationship and were unconcerned with providing excuses or rationales for it. The interstate slave trade was not a distressful issue because southerners in the Deep South faced the problem of exploitation and essentially shrugged it off. They had a more jaundiced view of slaves and slavery. For them, it was a grim and difficult institution. Instead of wringing their hands and worrying about the excesses of slavery, they embraced many of the negative facets of the peculiar institution. One might either condemn their callousness or praise their forthrightness.

Residents of the Deep South had good reason to accept the interstate slave trade with significant reservations. They harbored strong fears about

9. *Milledgeville Georgia Journal*, December 4, 1816 (first quotation); *New Orleans Courier*, January 13, 1831 (second quotation); undated *Natchez Ariel*, as quoted in *Genius of Universal Emancipation*, July 4, 1827, 7 (third quotation); *Milledgeville Georgia Journal*, October 13, 1818 (fourth quotation); *Niles' Weekly Register*, September 14, 1822, 18, December 1, 1827, 211.

kidnapped freemen who might be in shackles. Rumors circulated that Georgia slave owners unknowingly bought abducted blacks. Those who considered the matter wondered why the citizens of Georgia would permit abducted slaves to enter their state. Such slaves were likely to seek liberty "at any cost, and at every sacrifice," and their example would make it difficult to preserve order. The underlying fear of those who gave any thought to the illegal traffic in freemen and apprentices was that the entire system of slavery would become unstable through the efforts of a few troublemakers, both white and black. Whites broke the law and introduced a black element that was too closely associated with liberty. Slaveholders worried that abducted freemen would contaminate those slaves who, their owners thought, were content with their lives and who did not need to know about such dangerous ideas as freedom or independence. The fear of kidnapped freemen was confined mainly to Georgia, since the kidnapping trade peaked around 1820. As fewer traders resorted to kidnapping, those states that received the bulk of the slaves were less concerned with the problem.[10]

While the kidnapped freemen found in slave traders' coffles could infect slaves with ideas of liberty, it was common to assume that speculators trafficked in diseased bondservants. The prospect of sick slaves struck fear into the hearts of owners, since an epidemic could cripple a planter's workforce. Those who dealt with speculators had to be careful in all respects. James A. Tait, a planter in Alabama, believed that speculators often had diseased slaves and instructed his overseer not to allow any traders or their slaves on the property. Tait later fired the man for negligence, noting in his memoranda book that his former employee permitted a coffle with sick slaves to spend the night on the plantation. Four of Tait's slaves "took the cough" and died.[11]

Even more than coffles, traders' jails were often breeding grounds for diseases of all types. Cities of the Lower South constantly faced epidemics, and the packing together of slaves in close quarters was a recipe for disaster. Natchez and New Orleans, the two largest slave markets, constantly battled with the slave traders over the issue of infected bondservants. We have seen how Natchez handled the problem, and New Orleans took similar steps at

10. *Milledgeville Georgia Journal*, August 12, 1817, September 1, 1818, December 4, 1821; *Niles' Weekly Register*, July 19, 1817, 323 (quotation).

11. Memoranda Book of James Tait, Tait Collection, Auburn University Archives, Auburn University.

about the same time. After numerous complaints from citizens, the city council passed an ordinance prohibiting the exposition or sale of slaves in the city's center because of the high risk of an epidemic. When this law proved inadequate, the council banned "negro dealers" from housing their slaves within the incorporated city limits. Although passed in late November 1834, the law was only in place from January through April of 1835. Austin Woolfolk successfully presented a petition to the city council that allowed slave pens below Esplanade Street. By 1840 the city had successfully negotiated a truce with the slave dealers. The council passed an ordinance requiring a license for slave depots and specified that such structures must be built of brick, be two stories high, and "kept constantly clean and properly ventilated." Additionally, if an infectious disease broke out in such a place, the speculator must notify the mayor within twenty-four hours. Deep South residents sought control over an unstable situation and wanted to minimize risk.[12]

Even though such laws might have been burdensome to traders, the prospect of facing epidemics was even worse. The loss of slaves to disease was obviously a blow to their income, but it also hurt their reputations. Franklin had to deal with so many epidemics that he would not listen to the complaints of one of his business associates. He laughed when his friend complained about losing two slaves and pointed out that he had forty or fifty sick and had lost four in forty-eight hours. Franklin feared that the only way he could do business next season would be to purchase sparingly at reduced prices. He knew too well that if he, like others, was linked to disease, he would have a difficult time drumming up business. Competition for purchasers was intense during epidemics because buyers were scarce. Traders knew that it was in their best interest to take the necessary steps to ensure that their slaves were healthy, or at least distance their operations from sickly slaves. One speculator felt the pinch when a smallpox epidemic broke out in Natchez amongst the imported slaves. He told his wife that the disease crippled his business because it prevented the "country people" from

12. *New Orleans Louisiana Courier*, March 30, 1829, as quoted in *Western Luminary*, June 3, 1829, 377; *A Digest of the Ordinances, Resolutions, By-laws and Regulations of the Corporation of New-Orleans, and a Collection of the Laws of the Legislature relative to the said City* (New Orleans, 1836), 139–41 (first quotation); *A Digest of the Ordinances and Resolutions of the General Council of the City of New-Orleans* (New Orleans, 1845), 28 (second quotation); *New Orleans Louisiana Courier*, April 7, 1835.

coming to town and buying bondservants. It forced him to vaccinate his slaves and move them to the country in the hopes of preventing them from becoming infected. Franklin's brother, James, simply said about Natchez during an epidemic, "I never wanted to leave any place so bad as I do want to leave this damn hole."[13]

Slaveholders of the Deep South harbored more fears of contagion than just those involving liberty and disease. The omnipresent fear was rebellion, and on this score it was the activities of the slaves themselves that went a long way towards shaping attitudes towards speculation. The great shock was, of course, the Nat Turner rebellion. It scared southerners in all areas, and their attitudes toward the slave trade are revealed by the hysteria in the rebellion's aftermath. One Virginian confided that he could no longer look at his favorite slaves "with any degree of complacency." Where he saw loyalty before, now he only detected an attitude of "trickery, murder & bloodshed." The owner thought his slaves used smiles to conceal thoughts of "I only wait for an opportunity to embrace my hands in yours & your innocent childrens [*sic*] blood." Such thoughts amongst those close to the uprising are understandable. What is not so clear is why citizens who were not even remotely close to the area had such extreme reactions. Their responses revealed the clefts in the society of the importing states even as it exposed a deep distrust of speculators. There was an "almost frenzied legislative activity" throughout the South as legislators passed another round of laws designed to repress the activity of free blacks, control the activities of slaves, prevent the introduction of more bondservants, and thwart slave traders. Deep South residents had already feared being swamped by bondservants, but now they assumed that Virginia slaveholders would jettison all of their troublemakers.[14]

The slave-importing states had already dabbled with antitrader legislation, and the impulse to prevent speculation passed like a wave over the importing states. Indeed, the growth of the trade can be measured by the

13. Isaac Franklin to Rice C. Ballard, March 30, 1834, Ballard Papers; Alfred Royal Wynne to Almire Wynne, March 8, 1831, Wynne Family Papers, Box 18, Folder 1, TSLA (first quotation); James R. Franklin to Rice C. Ballard, May 7, November 14, 1833, February 2, 1834 (second quotation), Ballard Papers.

14. Robert P. Walker to George Blow, September 24, 1831, Blow Family Papers, VHS (first three quotations); Herbert Aptheker, *Nat Turner's Slave Rebellion* (New York, 1966), 74 (final quotation); Judith K. Schafer, "The Immediate Impact of Nat Turner's Insurrection on New Orleans," *Louisiana History* 21 (1980): 361–76.

response of the states that received the majority of the bondservants. Both Georgia and South Carolina prohibited slave traders from bringing slaves into the states in 1817. As the bulk of the slave trade shifted to the emerging Southwest, those states tried to close their borders as well. In 1826 Louisiana prohibited anyone from bringing slaves into the state with the intent to sell or hire them, while Alabama enacted a similar provision the next year. Mississippi was a slightly different case. The framers of Mississippi's first constitution incorporated a provision empowering the legislature to prevent slave traders from doing business in Mississippi, but legislators tried to regulate the slave trade instead. An 1819 law required a tax of $20 for each slave brought in for sale or as merchandise. Slaves convicted of murder, burglary, arson, rape, or grand larceny could not cross the border, and state residents were exempt from the tax unless they brought the slaves from Louisiana or Alabama. Six years later the legislature imposed a two and a half percent tax on any "auctioneer, or transient merchant, or vendor of merchandize or slaves." Like the earlier tax on slaves, the law was an attempt to discourage transient traders from selling slaves in Mississippi; but it was also a means of combating the state's deficit.[15]

All of these early laws against the slave trade lasted only a few years before being repealed. It was only the intense threat of a massive slave rebellion that scared southerners into action again. Louisiana responded first to Turner. Governor A. B. Roman argued that the people of Louisiana reaped fewer benefits from the trade than they expected, especially given the low quality of slaves they purchased. Roman described how the "cupidity of the negro traders" induced them to purchase bondservants of questionable character. He feared that speculators would stoop so low as to buy rebellious slaves right out of Virginia jails. Rumors swirled about the evil nature of Chesapeake slaves. It became accepted as truth that a number of bondservants involved in the uprising were pardoned and ordered to be transported out of the state. Nervous residents lamented that the rebels would soon set

15. *Milledgeville Georgia Journal,* January 1, 1817; *Savannah Republican,* January 11, 1817; *Baton Rouge State Gazette,* March 31, 1826; *Woodville Republican,* May 12, 1827; *Natchez Mississippi State Gazette,* March 1, 1818; *Acts passed at the first Session of the second General Assembly of the State of Mississippi* (Natchez, 1819), 4–7; *Laws of the State of Mississippi,* 8th sess. (Jackson, 1825), 123 (quotation); Winbourne Magruder Drake, "The Framing of Mississippi's First Constitution," *Journal of Mississippi History* 29 (1967): 321–22; Alfred H. Stone, "The Early Slave Laws of Mississippi," *Publication of the Mississippi Historical Society for 1899,* 135; Charles Sackett Sydnor, *Slavery in Mississippi* (New York, 1933), 162.

foot on the banks of the Mississippi. Another bit of malicious gossip reported that a Richmond resident noted with satisfaction that the slaves in the Southampton area were "*thinning by sales for distant markets.*" Seasoned slave trader Franklin knew that some form of prohibitory legislation was forthcoming. He was so convinced that something would be done that he frankly declared, "I am much at a loss how to act should no law be passed." Even though Franklin did not welcome another ban on the trade, he knew that the probability of a restriction depressed prices.[16]

Serendipitously, Governor Roman had already called a special legislative session for the purpose of electing a new senator. He kept up the pressure for a new law when the session opened. The governor dismissed the idea that insubordinate slaves had crossed Louisiana's borders, but reminded the legislature of its duty to adopt prudent measures to keep undesirable slaves out of the state. He told legislators that a large number of slaves from Virginia had been tried for involvement in the revolt and were condemned for deportation. Louisiana had the right to refuse such "wretches" in order to preserve its public tranquility. Roman did not have to do much lobbying. The legislature easily enacted a law that prohibited the interstate slave trade. Immigrants could bring in slaves for their own use, but neither they nor Louisiana residents could purchase slaves in Mississippi, Alabama, Florida, or the Arkansas Territory. This provision, although easily evaded, was an effort to make up for the lack of legislation in the neighboring states.[17]

Other states besides Louisiana got caught up in the antitrader fervor. Georgia, a state that imported few slaves by this time, passed a nonimportation law anyway. In neighboring Alabama, Governor John Gayle exhorted the Deep South states to put up a united front against Virginia. He noted how speculators bought slaves "of bad character" at low prices and then peddled them to innocent farmers, thus spreading the contagion of rebel-

16. *New Orleans Courier*, October 1, 1831 (first quotation); *New Orleans Advertiser*, October 14, 1831; undated *Richmond Compiler*, as quoted in undated *Lexington Kentucky Reporter*, as quoted in *Western Luminary*, November 6, 1831 (second quotation, emphasis in original); *New Orleans Louisiana Advertiser*, October 21, 1831; Isaac Franklin to Rice C. Ballard, October 26, 1831, Ballard Papers (final quotation).

17. *Louisiana Senate Journal*, Extra 10th sess., 1831 (Baton Rouge, 1831), 1–2 (quotation), 8; *New Orleans Louisiana Advertiser*, November 15, 19, 1831; *New Orleans Courier*, November 16, 19, 1831; *New Orleans Bee*, November 19, 1831; Joe Gray Taylor, *Negro Slavery in Louisiana* (Baton Rouge, 1963), 42; Schafer, "Immediate Impact," 367–68; Stephenson, *Isaac Franklin*, 75. The law lasted until its repeal in January of 1834.

lion. Scenes similar to the Nat Turner rebellion might be repeated in Alabama, Gayle predicted, if the states of the Deep South did not prevent the "mischief" inherent in allowing the entry of slaves of every imaginable description. The discovery of a slave who had been kicked out of North Carolina for distributing David Walker's *Appeal* only served to increase fears in the state. Caught up in the frenzy, the legislature quickly passed a bill that was intended to put slave traders out of business. The law was part of a larger effort to control the slave and free blacks. While it prohibited the entry of slaves except those accompanying citizens and immigrants, it also had numerous provisions regarding free persons of color. They could not enter the state, while those already in Alabama were prohibited from learning how to read and write, gathering in groups greater than five without permission, and from talking to a gathering of slaves without permission. The next session, when passions cooled, the legislature repealed the clauses pertaining to the importation of slaves, making it legal for speculators to bring in slaves once again, but did not touch the provisions regarding free blacks.[18]

Mississippi, true to form, responded differently from the other importing states even though it had the same attitudes. Similar types of rumors circulated through the state, as evidenced by a report in the *Natchez Gazette.* It warned that Virginia was teeming with Negro traders who were purchasing slaves who had been "directly or indirectly engaged in the work of murder." These malcontents would soon arrive in Mississippi. Instead of enacting legislation like its neighbors, however, the state changed its constitution. The new document prohibited the introduction of slaves as merchandise after May 1, 1833. A bill to enact enforcement legislation failed to pass in the ensuing legislative session, leaving Mississippi in the anomalous position of prohibiting the slave trade but having no means of enforcing the constitution. The situation was a way to encourage compliance without forcing citizens to submit to draconian legislation. The lawmakers reasoned that a

18. Ruth Scarborough, *Opposition to Slavery in Georgia prior to 1860* (Nashville, 1933), 119–20; *Journal of the Senate of the State of Alabama,* 13th sess. (Tuscaloosa, 1832), 56–57 (quotations); *Mobile Commercial Register,* December 14, 1831; James F. McKee to the Police of Mobile, November 3, 1831, and David Crawford to Gov. John Gayle Jr., November 18, 1831, Governor's Papers (1831–1835), Gayle, Container SG 5628, Folder 1, Alabama Department of Archives and History; *Alabama Senate Journal,* 13th sess., 103, 134–35, 14th sess., 6, 25, 37; *Mobile Commercial Register,* January 15, 1832, November 17, 24, 1832; *Huntsville Southern Advocate,* January 28, 1832, March 16, 1833; Sellers, *Slavery in Alabama,* 175.

strict law would favor the rich, who could send their agents to Virginia or Maryland. The poor, who wanted only one or two slaves, could not afford such an expense and would have to "submit to the extortions of the wealthy, or rest content with what they have." Thus a loose and weak law was supposedly more just. Mississippi's citizens voted to repeal the slave-trading amendment in 1833, but county officials did not follow proper form in tallying the votes, and thus the constitution remained intact. The legislature refused to amend the constitution, and a bill for another referendum failed. Even as it ignored the will of the people, the Mississippi legislature increased the bond for transient merchants and imposed a two and one-half percent tax on sales by slave traders. The state, then, prohibited slave trading in the constitution but taxed it by legislation.[19]

It might seem odd that residents tried to deny themselves the very thing that they knew was necessary for the expansion of their society. Most residents of the Lower South recognized that the importation of slaves was vital to support the expansion of the plantation system. A Louisiana resident who refused to believe that his state was in such low repute that it was considered the "Botany-Bay, the Australasia for the discarded villainy of the other states," recited a litany of reasons why the Deep South needed the interstate slave trade: there was no replacement for them; with the exception of a few great slaveholders, the rest of the state needed slaves to convert unproductive land to fertile acreage; common maladies like eating dirt conspired to ensure a high mortality among the slaves and kept their prices high; prohibiting the entry of slaves would deter migrants to the state, thus depressing land prices; and any such law would be unconstitutional. Much of his reasoning was accurate, so it seems curious that southerners would enact legislation that was contrary to these ends.[20]

This pattern of legislation shows that citizens of the Deep South generally accepted the interstate slave trade with reservations and did their best to control the abuses—whether real or perceived—of traders. They wanted

19. James R. Franklin to Jordan M. Saunders, January 2, 1833, Burford Papers; *Natchez Gazette*, October 5, 1831, as quoted in Stampp, *Peculiar Institution*, 254 (first quotation); Sydnor, *Slavery in Mississippi*, 163; Winbourne Magruder Drake, "The Mississippi Constitutional Convention of 1832," *JSH* 23 (1957): 366; Andrew Fede, "Legal Protection for Slave Buyers in the U.S. South: A Caveat Concerning Caveat Emptor," *American Journal of Legal History* 31 (1987): 351–52; *Natchez Courier*, January 25, August 23, 1833 (second quotation); Sydnor, *Slavery in Mississippi*, 163–64.

20. *New Orleans Advertiser*, October 21, 1831 (quotation).

new bondservants to be docile because they feared a substantial increase in the black population. While the slave trade was the most efficient way to move slaves to the importing states, many southerners remained unconvinced of its true nature. They did not trust speculators to buy "good" slaves, expected traders to deceive them, and were uncertain how the slaves themselves would react to the whole process. Reservations in the Deep South were confined to the type of slaves imported or the possible negative impact on other slaves. Perhaps it was easier to justify the purchase of slaves rather than their sale. After all, the slaveowner who purchased more bondservants could argue that he was fulfilling his duty to the slaves. Instead of abandoning them at a sale, he was adopting them into his household.

The spotty statutes sent a mixed message to speculators. Some paid no attention to the laws, but others were more careful and did not automatically evade them. Their reactions and activities serve as a rough measure of whether or not prohibitory legislation was effective. Some of the largest slave traders complied, at least initially, with the Louisiana bans. One strategy involved diverting their operations to Natchez, a market that was just as profitable as New Orleans. Following Louisiana's initial importation ban, Austin Woolfolk concentrated his efforts on selling slaves in Natchez. He told his Louisiana customers that they should act now to supply themselves, since the prohibitory legislation would go into effect within three months. As advertised, Woolfolk began sending his slave shipments to Natchez. Whoever filled out the customs manifests for Woolfolk crossed out the words "for the purpose of being sold or disposed of as Slaves, or to be held to Service or Labor" and wrote "to be held to Service or Labor" and "to be shipped aboard a steamboat for Natchez in the State of Mississippi." Seven of Woolfolk's shipments in 1826 and 1827 went to Natchez in this manner. He directed Louisiana residents to go to Purnely Tavern in Natchez, where he had large numbers of Virginia-born slaves for sale. Franklin, for his part, mulled over whether or not to establish a floating slave mart at the mouth of the Mississippi River. There he could sell bondservants outside of Louisiana's borders and then the planters would introduce them into the state, in accordance with the letter of the law.[21]

21. *New Orleans Louisiana Advertiser*, March 21, 1826; Slave shipments with arrival dates of December 5, 1826, February 6, May 11, May 31, November 22, December 7, 1827, New Orleans Inward Slave Manifests (quotations); *New Orleans Louisiana Courier*, January 13, 1827; John Armfield to Jordan M. Saunders, December 11, 1831, Burford Papers; Richard McMillan, "A Journey of Lost Souls: New Orleans to Natchez Slave Trade of 1840," *Gulf Coast Historical Review* 13 (1998): 49–59.

Likewise, Louisiana's 1831 ban and the Turner scare influenced the behavior of Franklin, the greatest speculator of the day. He worked quickly to liquidate his operation before the ban took effect, selling an astounding 270 slaves in a month. After he sold out, Franklin executed no bills of sale in New Orleans until the law's repeal. He was not the only speculator to stop doing business in the Crescent City. A visitor to New Orleans saw steamboats crowded with slaves glide past the city and continue up the Mississippi to Natchez. That market, he learned, became inundated with bondservants. Up to three hundred slaves awaited sale in Natchez in the months following the Louisiana ban. Traders diverted so many slaves there that prices dropped noticeably. Paul Pascal, who normally traded in New Orleans, grudgingly admitted to a colleague that times had changed. The law and Nat Turner's rebellion had inhibited demand. He told his supplier in Norfolk that, despite the decreased supply, "Niggers do not bring any price at this moment." Speculators had up to three hundred bondservants awaiting sale, but did not put them out on the market because of the low prices. They simply could not recoup their investment. When the situation in Mississippi became problematic because of legislation, Franklin considered moving his base of operations to Memphis.[22]

Citizens in the exporting states knew quite well that trading bans affected slave prices, and they kept a close eye on legislation. In the Chesapeake, the area from which the bulk of the slaves came, the Georgia law drew attention. A Baltimore paper reprinted the law's provisions, and a notice of both the Georgia and South Carolina legislation appeared in a Washington paper. Publications in Washington, Alexandria, Lexington, and Baltimore printed notices when Louisiana prohibited traders in 1826. According to a Virginian, the law's enactment dropped the value of slaves in the Old Dominion by 25 percent two hours after its passage was known in Richmond. When Louisiana prohibited the trade following Nat Turner's rebellion, newspapers in North Carolina, Georgia, and Virginia printed comments on the law. Thus even while citizens in the different sections of the South reacted differently to speculation, they were beginning to realize that the slave trade bound them together.[23]

22. James R. Franklin to Rice C. Ballard, January 18, October 29, 1832, Ballard Papers; Stephenson, *Isaac Franklin*, 76; Ingraham, *South-West by a Yankee*, 1:106–7; Paul Pascal to Bernard Raux, December 24, 1831 (translation from the French), Pascal Papers, Houghton Library, Harvard University (quotation).

23. *Baltimore American*, January 16, 1817; *Niles' Weekly Register*, February 15, 1817; *Niles' Weekly Register*, May 20, 1826, 262–63; *Alexandria Phenix Gazette*, March 31, 1826; *Lexington*

Even though it is clear that the importation bans influenced prices and prompted speculators to change their practices, the laws often went unheeded and unenforced. Armfield thought Louisiana's law might not work as intended and would instead prevent planters from traveling north to buy slaves. The speculator was giddy at the prospect, since it would drive up prices in Virginia and Maryland. Where others saw Alabama's law as being effective, William Beverley scoffed at it. He wrote his father that the law prohibiting the activities of speculators was a dead letter and officials were loath to enforce it. The situation in Louisiana was similar. Although the rate dwindled, speculators still imported slaves into New Orleans following Louisiana's two bans, and some speculators even advertised in the newspapers. While open defiance was one strategy, another was to find clever ways to evade the laws. One common complaint about prohibitory legislation was that it contained too many loopholes by which the speculators found a "mode of creeping out" of any penalties. A method was for traders to pose as immigrants and hire out their slaves for the term of eighty or ninety years. As for the Georgia law, slave traders like Woolfolk and Joseph Wood brought slaves to the state's borders and waited for residents to cross into South Carolina before consummating a sale. By this means traders obeyed the law's letter but not its spirit, since the practical effect was merely to shift the point of sale to another location without excising the trader from the transaction. The purchaser then legally brought slaves into the state, since they were for his own use.[24]

Laws requiring certificates of good character for slaves were similarly ineffective. One Louisiana man bought twelve slaves who had been convicted in Maryland but pardoned on condition of their transportation out of the state. Such slaves obviously should have been prohibited from entering

---

Intelligencer, May 25, 1826; *Genius of Universal Emancipation*, July 29, 1826, 382; Speech of Abel Upshur at the 1829 Virginia Convention, as quoted in Harriet Beecher Stowe, *The Key to Uncle Tom's Cabin* (1854; reprint, Salem, N.H., 1987), 289; Abdy, *Journal of a Residence*, 2:249; *Milledgeville Southern Recorder*, October 27, 1831; *Raleigh Register and North Carolina Gazette*, October 27, 1831; *Richmond Enquirer*, December 2, December 6, 1831.

24. John Armfield to Jordan M. Saunders, December 11, 1831, Burford Papers; William Beverley to Robert Beverley, January 10, 1833, Beverley Family Papers, VHS; *New Orleans Louisiana Advertiser*, October 3, 1826; *Augusta Herald*, December 9, 1816, as quoted in the *Charleston Courier*, December 15, 1817 (quotation); *Milledgeville Georgia Journal*, August 12, 1817; advertisement of Joseph Wood, as quoted in William Jay, *A View of the Action of the Federal Government in behalf of Slavery* (New York, 1839), 78; *Liberator*, April 21, 1832, 62.

Louisiana, but were not. That he could get away with his actions was a testament that justice was "often both lame and blind in Louisiana." A Baton Rouge paper expressed indignation at the fact that speculators publicly announced their willingness to purchase slaves who lacked the necessary certificates. When needed, however, the certificates mysteriously appeared. Bacon Tait, a Richmond slave trader, could have solved any mysteries for the newspaper. Tait tutored a fellow speculator on the finer points of evading a Mississippi law requiring the certificates. He dismissed the paperwork as a hassle, but advised his friend Paul Pascal to have the certificates on hand to prevent any difficulties. Tait graciously provided a copy of the certificate in which the signers swore that the slaves were not guilty of any felonies, including murder, burglary, or arson. Armfield, for his part, had another strategy. He told fellow slave trader Rice Ballard that he purchased preprinted forms that left spaces for the purchaser's name and the slave's price. Armfield then took the forms to a justice of the peace who signed them and had his clerk testify that the speculator was "a Hell of a fellow." The miserly Armfield anticipated there would be no difficulty getting the receipts printed, but resented having to pay printing costs. Regarding the laws of all types, one trader simply said they presented "no important difficulty."[25]

He was correct because traders knew quite well that it was difficult to keep track of which slaves entered a state. Many of the laws asked citizens and traders to register with the local court system or the justice of the peace. Besides being onerous, such activity was ineffective. Lack of desire for strong government intervention and the rural nature of the South combined to ensure that compliance was irregular. Itinerant traders were involved in much of the interstate slave trade, and keeping track of their transactions was next to impossible. Those who wished to avoid registering their slaves or wanted to import them illegally usually could do so with impunity. Furthermore, slave traders could pass through a "closed" state on their way to an "open" state. When they entered the "closed" state they were initially complying with the law, but while on the march they could easily sell slaves.

25. *New Orleans Mercantile Advertiser*, December 29, 1826, as quoted in *Woodville Republican*, January 8, 1827 (first quotation); *Baton Rouge Gazette*, October 15, 1831; Bacon Tait to Nathaniel Courier, October 4, 1832, Pascal Papers; John Armfield to Rice C. Ballard, January 26, 1832, Ballard Papers (second quotation); *African Observer*, May 1827, 54 (final quotation). For examples of the preprinted forms, see Folder 5, "Entry of Slaves into Concordia Parish, Louisiana, 1826–1831," Natchez Trace Slavery Collection, University of Texas.

Additionally, the provisions that allowed immigrants to bring in slaves for their own use provided a cover for slave traders who claimed they were moving to the state. Even those traders who operated primarily in the urban areas could easily sell slaves, as there existed no desire to clamp down on scofflaws and no effective police agency to enforce the laws. Most often the legislation became a burden for those it was intended to help.[26]

Another reason slave traders could evade the laws stemmed from the fact that it was virtually impossible to distinguish between the different types of slave migration in the South. A Georgia newspaper noted there was no possible way to differentiate between traders and migrating citizens. Migrants who brought slaves with them or planters who bought bondservants in the Upper South were engaged in activities that elided with the trade. Citizens who migrated with their slaves, however, carefully separated themselves from speculators even though their activity was virtually indistinguishable on a practical level. The laws that singled out traders for exclusion upheld the fiction that the slave trade was completely disconnected from bondservants who migrated with their masters. The ubiquity of southern legislation shows just how eager southerners were to draw a fictional line between themselves and traders. Slaveowners liked to think that they were, somehow, more enlightened than speculators. Masters believed they treated their slaves better than traders did—and thus were different. Owners, moreover, thought they dealt with "better" slaves. They wanted to believe that they could differentiate between "good" and "bad" slaves. The creation of a wall between themselves and traders was one way to reassure themselves that they could continue to control their bondservants. Legislation prohibiting speculation was a comfortable fiction that supported the fallacy that slaves could be kept in a state of subjection.[27]

Most importantly, the demand for slaves was too intense for the southern states to suppress the trade for any lengthy period. The domestic slave trade was an effective means of readjusting the South's labor supply. As long as Deep South residents continued to expand their holdings, they would require bondservants. Speculation was simply too vital to be suppressed for any significant length of time. Legislation occurred in spasmodic bursts, and it usually took a year or two for citizens to recover from the hangover and demand repeal. Thomas Dew knew that the nonimportation laws were

26. Hall, *Travels in North America*, 2:219–20; Ingraham, *South-West by a Yankee*, 1:181.

27. *Milledgeville Georgia Journal*, October 23, 1830.

more sound than fury. He observed that as long as the demand for slaves existed, "the supply will be furnished in some way or other." Dew thought that the price of slaves in Virginia rose instead of fell after Louisiana enacted its 1832 law. He attributed the increase to the large volume of southern purchasers in the state. They looked for bargains, since Virginians were frightened and wanted to get rid of all their slaves. He correctly predicted that the storm would blow over and Louisiana would no longer be in a position to deny itself what it needed to sustain its agricultural system. One slave trader in Louisiana knew he only had to ride out the storm of protest against speculators. He confidently predicted that residents would come to their senses and demand repeal. When that happened, "the Niggers will augment in price."[28]

If the laws were so "utterly inefficient," then it is curious why all of the states that imported slaves wrestled with whether or not to forbid the activities of speculators, and only Mississippi did not enact legislation designed to thwart traders' activities. Lawmakers in the Deep South knew that other legislatures tried, and failed, to cope with the issues surrounding the importation of slaves. It is puzzling why they would enact measures that were proven to be ineffective and then leave some of them on the books for years. There were a variety of motives that gave rise to the laws, and it was only when several factors combined that states tried to regulate the interstate slave trade. A latent opposition to the slave trade and traders existed in the South, but some leading issue had to gain credence before legislation became a reality. Deep South citizens wanted to have it both ways. They depended on the trade for growth but feared the abuses associated with it. They accepted, for the most part, the proprietary nature of servitude and did not fear what the commercial relations would do to their society. The fact that slaves were still human agents was the heart of the trouble. Rebellion and disobedience were all too human. Most of the laws associated with speculation were directly connected to abuses associated with speculation—abuses that traders used to smother any semblance of humanity in their slaves. Misgivings about the slave trade in the Deep South, then, were directly tied to the activities of the slaves themselves.[29]

28. Thomas R. Dew, "Review of the Debate in the Virginia Legislature of 1831 and 1832," as reprinted in *The Pro-Slavery Argument as maintained by the Most Distinguished Writers of the Southern States* (Philadelphia, 1853), 361 (first quotation); Paul Pascal to Bernard Raux, December 24, 1831 (translation from the French), Pascal Papers (second quotation).

29. Hall, *Travels in North America*, 2:219.

Slaveholders in the Deep South did not intend the legislation against the slave trade to drive speculators out of business or to abolish the importation of bondservants. The legislation, at its core, was designed to control the slaves. Residents of the importing states worried that they were trading money for the potential of rebellion. They desperately sought to find some way to restrain a people whom they knew to be dissatisfied, restless, cunning, and resilient. The volume of slaves arriving in New Orleans, a local resident commented, only contributed to the growing disparity between the black and white populations. Slave ships carried "a living cargo of vice and crime" that would soon be "disgorged upon our shores." The probable result was too terrible to mention. The Turner uprising only accelerated these fears. Governor Roman tried to quell concerns that rogue slaves had crossed Louisiana's border even as he steered the state in a different direction. He argued that Louisiana had already received too many slaves who were the "scum" of Virginia's population. The only way to reduce the danger was by prohibiting the entry of all slaves into the state except those brought in by bona fide immigrants.[30]

The influx of bondservants, especially those found in traders' coffles, fed into these assumptions about the likelihood of a rebellion. Even though southerners usually overestimated the potential for revolt, there were enough unsuccessful revolts and individual acts of resistance to nurture the idea a massive slave rebellion. A Georgia resident grimly admonished his fellow citizens to remember Gabriel's rebellion and a similar revolt in Camden, South Carolina. The fact that the 200 voters in his county lived amidst 7,000 slaves was a cause for concern. Matters would only get worse, since a reported 13,000 slaves crossed the Yadkin River in the last three months and up to 50,000 entered the state in the last year. The preposterous estimate and the apocalyptic rhetoric reveal more about the writer's state of mind than about the slave trade itself. A wild importation figure such as this reflected the fear of a slave population that was growing exponentially and a white population that was virtually stagnant. Even as owners bought more slaves in order to expand their holdings, they also feared that the very slaves they imported would rise up and destroy white civilization. A. L. C. Ma-

30. Undated *New Orleans Louisiana Advertiser*, as quoted in *Genius of Universal Emancipation*, January 22, 1830, 155 (first quotation); *New Orleans Courier*, January 7 (second quotation), November 16, 1831; *Senate Journal of the tenth extra session* (New Orleans, 1832), 3 (third quotation).

gruder carefully recorded his thoughts on the subject in a leather book, evidently preparing for a debate on the potential of barring slave traders in Mississippi. The growth of the "pestiferous" slave population was due mainly to the demand of "lazy, slothful persons" who delight to spend their time in idleness. Their selfishness would eventually cause "an overflow" of slaves and lead to an insurrection. If Mississippi did not act, a slave rebellion was the likely result. There were just too many "evil consequences" to allow speculators a free hand to import slaves.[31]

For southerners who worried about the potential of a slave revolt, Haiti or Santo Domingo was an unforgettable example that seemed to haunt them at every turn. In fighting for the bill to outlaw the entry of slaves into South Carolina, John O'Neale described the horrors of that revolution. A grand jury in Putnam County, Georgia, held similar beliefs. In an official statement it argued that the entry of too many slaves would cause the state to become like the "ensanguined fields of St. Domingo." Two years later a Georgia citizen repeated the slogan to argue that slaves were a "*domestic enemy*" and should not be allowed to grow in force. Similarly, Magruder feared that an influx of bondservants might give rise to an insurrection like the one in Santo Domingo that would lead to "the expulsion of all the whites."[32]

Those who cited Haiti's example may or may not have wanted to prohibit the activities of slave traders, since reference to it was not necessary to persuade others that slave traders were potentially dangerous for the South. The notion that speculators bought and sold undesirable slaves was firmly fixed in the heads of most southerners. Thus, it was not just the addition of more slaves that scared these southerners, but the purchase of the wrong kind of slaves. A grand jury in Putnam County made just this point. It labeled the introduction of slaves into Georgia by slave traders a "demoralizing tendency" that had dangerous consequences. No evidence was needed to support the assertion that speculators brought in the worst possible slaves, "*corrupting those already among us, and ready at all times for insurrection*

31. Clement Eaton, *The Freedom-of-Thought Struggle in the Old South* (Durham, N.C., 1940), 89–96, 116; *Milledgeville Georgia Journal*, December 4, 1816; A. L. C. Magruder, untitled manuscript, March 19, 1828, James T. Magruder Papers, MDAH (quotations).

32. "Memoir of John O'Neall," 63, John O'Neale Papers, DU; *Milledgeville Georgia Journal*, November 6, 1816 (first quotation), September 29, 1818 (second quotation; emphasis in original); Magruder, untitled manuscript, April 19, 1828, John T. Magruder Papers (final quotation); Eaton, *Freedom-of-Thought*, 89

and crime." A Natchez judge was concerned that slaves entering Mississippi brought a multitude of evils. Slaves in traders' coffles, then, could become a convenient scapegoat for all types of unrest in the Lower South. Whites knew that the threat of rebellion was omnipresent but refused to believe that their own slaves had the potential to revolt. It was the imported slaves who were the troublemakers. This convenient fiction helped nervous masters to sleep at night by thinking they could isolate those slaves who would destroy their regime. One southerner summed up this idea when he complained that slaves from the Upper South might one day cause his state to be plunged into a war of extermination. Slave traders had the worst kind of slaves imaginable for sale, and these malcontents would only "scatter firebrands among the combustibles."[33]

That many southerners assumed a thriving slave trade increased the risks of a rebellion reveals much about their underlying attitudes toward the peculiar institution. They recognized the exploitative nature of slavery and made no apology for it. Rather than fretting over the blatant commercialism of the slave trade, most residents of the Deep South viewed speculation as a natural and necessary consequence of slavery. They feared, however, that traders would abuse the system. Speculators could easily exploit their position as middlemen by purchasing inferior slaves and then selling them at high prices. Deep South residents were all too familiar with myriad deceptive practices found in their slave markets. Like their brethren in the Upper South, they made a firm distinction between speculation and private citizens buying or selling slaves, or even migrating with them. The latter actions were no problem because planters could exercise sound judgment in choosing slaves. Speculators did present a real difficulty, though. Their greed automatically led them to abuse the commercial system, or so most southerners thought. Viewed in this way, corruption engendered by speculation endangered society, but in a different way than found in the Upper South. Instead of undermining masters' morals, the trade brought in an unstable population that could overthrow white society. The fear in the Upper South was a slow, quiet corrosion of good society; the fear in the Lower South was a quick and violent upheaval. No matter where one lived, however, it was necessary to come to terms with the perceived flaws of the peculiar institution.

33. *Milledgeville Georgia Journal,* November 16, 1816 (first and second quotations, emphasis in original), October 13, 1818 (third quotation); *New Orleans Mercantile Advertiser,* December 29, 1826, as quoted in *Woodville Republican,* January 8, 1827.

Legislators recognized that they had to take some sort of action to quiet public concerns. To that end, they tried to filter out undesirable bondservants by differentiating between the activities of private citizens and speculators. Like their counterparts in the Upper South, residents of the Lower South tried to make a careful distinction between the slaves purchased by private citizens and those who were found in slave traders' coffles. An observer of the Georgia law thought that just as many slaves entered his state but that they were, somehow, better slaves. He complained that speculators "*frequently* purchase slaves of the worst characters, because they can get them cheap." What the writer failed to note was that Georgia citizens who traveled to the South Carolina border bought slaves from speculators. It is hard to imagine how this process improved the "character" of the slaves; whether consummating the sale in South Carolina or in Georgia, slave traders still were instrumental in the transaction. At any rate, the importance of the legislation against slave traders is that citizens *felt* better about the types of slaves who came into their states.[34]

The legislation was a means of reassurance that the future of slavery was secure. In reality there was no essential difference between slaves purchased by citizens or traders, so it appears that whites projected their worst assumptions of slavery on the slave trade and tried to ease their fears by passing legislation that could not, or would not, be enforced. They feared being overwhelmed by slaves but wanted to preserve the fiction that they had taken action to ensure the stability of their society. Slave-importation bans, particularly those that excluded traders, were a comfortable fiction by nervous whites who felt increasingly outnumbered.

Despite concerns about rebellion, residents of the Deep South tolerated and ultimately embraced the interstate slave trade because they had no other choice. Their continued expansion and vitality depended on a fresh supply of bondservants. Speculators saw the need and worked vigorously to meet it. Citizens, however, did not always view speculators' efforts with favor. They groped for easy answers to a complex situation and lashed out at speculators for causing problems of their own doing. They did not want to face the fact that they themselves were to blame for the currency drain and the rapid growth of the slave population. Epidemics, moreover, defied any rational explanation, but it was convenient to blame speculators for importing sick slaves. Traders gained a reputation for shady business dealings.

34. *Milledgeville Georgia Journal,* November 10, 1818 (quotation, emphasis in original).

The pronouncements against the trade and the traders reflect southern fears. Striking at the interstate trade was a means of defusing the tensions of slavery. Instead of taking definite action to limit the growth of the slave population, or being serious about limiting the types of imported slaves, southerners used ceremonial solutions against speculators. The Deep South's inability and unwillingness to deal forthrightly with the interstate slave trade led to distorted perceptions of speculation. Citizens were increasingly willing to rely on simple stereotypes of traders and slaves rather than look realistically at the trade's consequences.

Residents of the Lower South, moreover, reacted differently from their counterparts in the exporting states. Instead of being fearful of how speculation affected white morals, Deep South citizens were concerned with how the large increase of bondservants would impact their society. They had no qualms with the dual nature of slaves being person and property; they embraced it. Residents of the exporting states betrayed their fears about the ill effects speculation had on the slave and the owner. Lower South residents were just the opposite: rather than being concerned with how speculation affected the slaves, they were concerned with how slaves affected society. In either case, residents throughout the South looked to slave traders to explain away the problems of slavery or reconcile the inherent problems associated with the peculiar institution.

CHAPTER 5

Profits and Piety

John Hartwell Cocke was a prosperous slaveholder in Fluvanna County, Virginia, who owned Bremo Plantation. When thinking about slavery, Cocke's mind could not find rest. He considered the institution to be a "curse upon our Land." It is not that he feared a rebellion or thought that slavery inefficiently allocated labor. Instead, Cocke wrestled with the moral dimensions of the institution. He understood his dependence on slavery even while reluctantly admitting that it clashed with his Christian faith. Cocke and his wife, Louisa, were evangelical Protestants who had difficulty reconciling the teachings of the New Testament with the ownership of human beings. They thought slavery was a corrosive agent that undermined the basis of good society, since it ran counter to the development of Christian character in both whites and blacks. Instead of sitting by idly, the Cockes worked to ameliorate slavery where they could and even entertained ideas that someday the institution would be abolished.[1]

John Cocke hoped ultimately to free his slaves, but emancipation required careful planning and gradual implementation. He believed that only domestic slaves and skilled workers were capable of making intelligent and enlightened decisions if freed. The other bondservants, who formed a "separate Caste," must be readied for emancipation, especially since God would one day remove slavery. Cocke arranged for local artisans to instruct his slaves in the mechanical trades and hired northern women as tutors to teach

1. Unsigned, undirected letter of John Hartwell Cocke Sr., December 1833, Cocke Family Papers, UV.

reading and writing. While John concentrated on the practical aspects of the slaves' education, Louisa saw to the spiritual component. She taught Bible classes to their bondservants and oversaw their Christian education. Not only would the slaves be productive when freed, but they would also be virtuous. The Cockes used Bremo as a training ground for freedom.[2]

Their attitudes had limits, however, and John Cocke could not envision ex-slaves living harmoniously next to their former masters. He thought an African colony was a providential idea. Like many other enthusiasts of colonization, Cocke did not rigorously apply logic to his schemes and believed the government could fund the endeavor with its surplus revenue. With the weight of God and government on its side, colonization was the perfect answer, and Cocke could not understand why any slaveholder would not support the idea. He wrote that once colonization secured adequate funding, the slaves would be carried away as naturally "as water flows down to the Ocean." While colonization might be irresistible to the slaveholder, Cocke recognized that not all slaves would consent to the scheme. Deportation to Africa would sever family ties, hence another reason for the slow preparation of bondservants. Given enough time, slaves would eventually recognize the benefits of colonization and agree to it even if it meant leaving behind kin. The Cockes and others like them were, in essence, trying to break through what they saw as the grime of slavery and recast their slaves as copies of themselves. Slaves must be rescued from the intellectual and moral retardation imposed by the peculiar institution. At the same time, they must be sheltered from the withering effects of slavery's worst abuses.[3]

John and Louisa Cocke were certainly too sanguine about colonization and held condescending views of their slaves. Even so, they also recognized the essential humanity of the bondservants and endeavored to treat them in accordance with biblical principles. They were sensitive to the destruction of slave families, as evidenced by their attitudes towards the slave trade. Both husband and wife saw the trade as one of the worst consequences of slavery because it destroyed the basic spiritual unit of society, the family.

2. Undirected letter of John Hartwell Cocke, September 23, 1831, Cocke Family Papers (quotation); Louis B. Gimelli, "Louisa Maxwell Cocke: An Evangelical Plantation Mistress in the Antebellum South," *JER* 9 (1989): 53–71; Martin Boyd Coyner, "John Hartwell Cocke of Bremo: Agriculture and Slavery in the Ante-Bellum South" (Ph.D. diss., University of Virginia, 1961).

3. Undirected letter of John Hartwell Cocke Sr., September 23, 1831, Cocke Family Papers.

Without a stable slave community, the Cockes could not adequately train their people. Moral development began in the home, and a ravaged family unit was a poor foundation for Christian growth. Selling slaves indiscriminately also set a bad example on the plantation and undermined the Cockes' efforts to model spiritual values for their bondservants. John explained to a friend that the "deep depravity of the slave trade" ran counter to his faith. He not only disagreed with speculation, but took active steps to counteract it. Cocke intervened during the sale of his brother-in-law's slaves and arranged the transaction through a commission merchant rather than a speculator. When Cocke's brother-in-law complained of his low profit, the commission merchant testily responded that it was the best possible price unless the slaves were sold to traders. In this case, Cocke prevailed upon his brother-in-law to accept a lower price in order to prevent the slaves from falling into a trader's clutches. He recognized the necessity of sale but wanted to blunt its impact as much as possible. In the final analysis, though, Cocke allowed the bondservants to become subjects of speculation, as he could have purchased the slaves himself or made some arrangement to keep them off the market.[4]

Cocke also tried to shield his own slaves from the trade. The smooth operation of Bremo, however, bounded his humanitarian principle. When faced with dissension or sale, Cocke chose the latter but still spared his slaves from the most harmful effects of speculation. The continued disobedience of a few slaves led Cocke to sell them lest the rest of his workforce catch the contagion of impudence. He sold bondservants to close friends whom he knew would treat them properly. Louisa hated such occasions. She confided to her diary that she was "a good deal disturbed" because John recently sold some slaves to Alabama on account of their disobedience. Louisa understood the deep pain associated with the slave trade and worked to protect her slaves from it. On more than one occasion she was unsuccessful, showing that the principles of faith had their limits and even those owners with good intentions could not always act upon their scruples. For John Cocke, there was no question that speculation in slaves was wrong, but he

4. John H. Cocke to Ralph Gurley, March 31, 1833, American Colonization Society Papers, Library of Congress, as quoted in Alison Goodyear Freehling, *Drift toward Dissolution: The Virginia Slavery Debate of 1831–1832* (Baton Rouge, 1982), 224 (quotation); Bernard Peyton to John Hartwell Cocke, February 20, 1828, Cocke Family Papers.

also had to preserve his livelihood. He believed in the essential dignity of his slaves, noting that slavery caused them to "sink" and ignorance kept them hobbled. Cocke did sell his slaves on occasion, but not for profit or gain. Instead he sold his bondservants out of necessity, in order to maintain strict discipline on his plantation, and sacrificed money in the process. No doubt Cocke could have obtained a better price had he dealt with a speculator, but he put his slaves' feelings ahead of his desire for extra cash. He also tried to prevent the pangs of a guilty conscience. However much Cocke might agonize over selling his slaves, though, he ultimately treated them as property.[5]

The Cockes' attitudes towards slavery and the slave trade rested on the bedrock of their Christian faith. John Cocke considered American plantations to be the most fertile ground for missionaries. Christian doctrine was necessary to correct the wrongs among the "domestic heathen" in the middle and southern states. He was unlike most of his fellow slaveowners in that he made an essential distinction between slavery and the slave. It was the institution of slavery that degraded the slaves, and, ultimately, whites as well. Others pointed to bondservants themselves as the trouble, essentially believing that Africans were destined to be slaves and that slavery itself was something that must be tolerated and protected. Cocke's thinking led him to believe that owners should not treat their slaves as beasts of burden and callously sell them for gain. For evangelical Christians like Cocke, it was the unbridled commerce in slaves that caused much discomfort. The interstate slave trade epitomized this blatant disregard for the basic dignity of the slave. But as Cocke's situation demonstrates, the line between selling slaves for disciplinary reasons and selling them for gain was often blurred. While Cocke could claim he wrestled with what was proper, he doubtless made money from the sale. To those outside the plantation, it probably mattered little why Cocke sold the slaves, since many thought one reason was as good as the next. Most important, the results for the slaves were the same no matter which explanation Cocke used to justify his actions. The slaves were separated from their families just as they would have been had Cocke been deliberately dabbling in the slave market. Evangelical Christians, while they might find fault with speculation, often ended up participating in the very

5. Coyner, "John Hartwell Cocke," 83; Louisa Cocke Diary, January 16, 1824, Cocke Family Papers (first quotation); unsigned, undirected letter of John Hartwell Cocke Sr., December 1833, Cocke Family Papers (second quotation).

thing they abhorred. They found their situation exacerbated by the fact that they could find no effective remedy for what they saw as a deadly poison.[6]

Individual Christians and southern evangelical churches, as the example of the Cockes shows, struggled with the slave trade. A grudging acceptance of slavery in the eighteenth century grew into specific denunciations of slave trading. Congregations disciplined members who took part in speculation in order to purify the church. Most of the qualms about the trade dealt with violations of Christ's teaching or the fear that speculation in slaves would corrupt the master by encouraging him to pursue riches rather than holiness. Until about 1830, southern evangelical religion was an effective force that shielded the slave from the master's excesses. The situation changed, however, as the churches began to actively defend slavery. Denunciations of the trade's injustice gave way to an emphasis on slavery's goodness no matter the consequences for the slave. Masters' authority over their bondservants approached an absolute right that should not be interfered with or questioned.

Evangelicals' fundamental distaste for the interstate slave trade stemmed from an equivocal attitude towards slavery and concern over the effects of speculation. Revolutionary rhetoric about freedom, furthermore, combined with the powerful message of the New Testament to ensure that slavery was not universally accepted by Christians as a beneficial institution. In the eighteenth century, the southern evangelical denominations—Methodist, Presbyterian, and Baptist—were morally neutral about slavery. In the main, they subscribed to the belief that slavery was neither good nor bad but masters could put it to positive or negative uses. While good slaveholders could redeem slavery, evil ones could abuse it. Evangelicals feared that too many whites became overly concerned about money at the expense of their spiritual affairs, making making them grow callous toward the suffering of individuals. Thoughtful slaveowners knew that as slavery exploited blacks and destroyed their family lives, it could also undermine the morals of whites. There was a vague sentiment amongst evangelicals to either free the slaves or ameliorate their condition, and there was moderate support for prohibiting ministers from owning bondservants. Evangelicals tended to criticize slavery in the abstract, point out its evils, and emphasize that slaves were

6. Unsigned, undirected letter of John Hartwell Cocke Sr., December 1833, Cocke Family Papers.

persons precious to God. There was, though, no concerted or determined effort by the evangelical denominations to destroy the peculiar institution.[7]

The situation was further complicated by the fact that the Bible was open to dispute regarding slavery. It could be used to defend or attack servitude. For instance, the Israelites held slaves and the apostle Paul instructed slaves to obey their masters. Sympathetic clergy used these examples and others to justify slavery and protect it from attack. They shored up their arguments by imploring masters to enforce the Bible's commandments as they impacted slavery. Many southern Christians also believed in the utility of slavery to keep the races separate and as a means of social organization. While slavery was not uniformly positive in their eyes, it was necessary. Those who opposed slavery, though, used other scripture to their advantage. The operation of the Golden Rule, teaching to do unto others as you would have them do unto you, could undermine the basis of a slave society. Few people would willingly consent to being enslaved. Even if the Bible justified slavery, the Golden Rule militated against a harsh treatment of slaves. Most Christians assumed masters had a duty to treat their slaves with more than a modicum of decency lest they face heavenly sanction.[8]

The nebulous opposition to slavery translated into different actions by the three evangelical denominations. The Baptists of the eighteenth century officially condemned slavery as a moral evil and cautioned members about its ill effects. They took no effective steps, however, to ensure its demise within the denomination. At a time when the interstate trade was of minor significance, especially in comparison to the African trade, the Baptists left it up to the local churches to take their own steps to root out commerce in slaves. A 1793 report of the Virginia Baptist General Committee seems to be typical of the attitude amongst many Baptist churches. It described slavery as neither a moral nor a religious issue and thus not a legitimate topic of discussion. Slavery, the conference decided, was firmly established in the country and was a purely political matter addressed in the political realm.

7. Donald G. Mathews, *Religion in the Old South* (Chicago, 1977), 66–69; John B. Boles, introduction to *Masters and Slaves in the House of the Lord: Race and Religion in the American South, 1740–1870*, ed. John B. Boles (Lexington, Ky., 1988), 8–9; James D. Essig, *The Bonds of Wickedness: American Evangelicals against Slavery, 1770–1808* (Philadelphia, 1982), 26–52; John P. Daly, *When Slavery Was Called Freedom: Evangelicalism, Proslavery, and the Causes of the Civil War* (Lexington, Ky., 2002), 31–36.

8. Anne C. Loveland, *Southern Evangelicals and the Social Order, 1800–1860* (Baton Rouge, 1980), 206–9.

The church, in other words, should not become entangled in the issue. Like the Baptists, the Presbyterians made tepid moves against slavery. In 1787 the denomination's ruling synod, fearing that slaves might be dangerous to the community, recommended that church members prepare their slaves for freedom and take steps to bring about abolition. There was no mention of the church's stance regarding the sale of bondservants. In 1818 the Presbyterian General Assembly used even stronger language to condemn slavery itself, calling it a "gross violation" of natural and divine law that was inconsistent with divine character.[9]

Unlike the other two denominations, the Methodists took direct action in the eighteenth century to deal with slavery within the church. The denomination that would become the biggest in the antebellum South proclaimed in 1784 that it should find some method to "extirpate this abomination from among us." It voted to expel members who did not take steps to emancipate their slaves within a year, although individuals who lived in states that did not allow manumission were exempt from the rule. Delegates also decided to banish members who bought or sold slaves, except to liberate them. Although not specifically noted, the rule applied to both the foreign and domestic slave trades, although it appears to be intended more for the importation of Africans. The foreign trade was the most important source of new slaves at this time, and if the church could prevent its members from acquiring new slaves, then it was more likely to eliminate bondage. These rules, though, were so unpopular that they were suspended the next year. Five years later the church asked members as a "general rule" to refrain from buying or selling slaves. In 1796 the General Conference voted to permit slaveholders to join the church and allowed members to buy slaves as long as they notified their local church. A committee would then determine the number of years the slave had to work before paying off his or her purchase price. Methodists could not, however, sell slaves, presumably to protect all parties involved from the ravages of the trade. The general intent was to stop the spread of slavery within the Methodist denomination and ultimately render it extinct, although such an outcome was highly unlikely. The net result was a compromise with slavery even as

9. Alice D. Adams, *The Neglected Period of Anti-Slavery in America* (Boston, 1908), 100; W. Harrison Daniel, "Virginia Baptists and the Negro in the Antebellum Era," *Journal of Negro History* 56 (1971), 1; *Religious Intelligencer*, June 27, 1818, 58 (quotation); *Niles' Weekly Register*, supplement to vol. 16 (1819), 153–55; H. S. Smith, *In His Image, But . . .*, 47–58.

the Methodists desired to eliminate the abuses associated with the indiscriminate sale of slaves. Methodists continued to struggle with the commerce in slaves, as the 1804 General Conference exempted members from Georgia and the Carolinas from the rule regarding the purchase and sale of slaves. These three states were the primary areas for the importation of Africans, so their exemption made the rule virtually useless. By the time the African trade was outlawed in 1808, the individual conferences could set their own rules regarding speculation, but conferences in those states that imported the bulk of the slaves did not bar members from buying or selling slaves. The Methodist church stopped trying to regulate the trade and concentrated its efforts on the moral suasion of its members.[10]

Part of the reason for the softening of the Methodists' stance, and that of the other denominations as well, was the spread of the plantation system throughout the South. The churches competed for membership, and one way to attract potential members who owned slaves was to remain silent on the issue. Resistance to slavery moved out of the official church debates and into local congregations and individual consciences. Southern churches no longer offered any effective resistance to slavery. Much of the antislavery clergy left for Ohio, Indiana, and Illinois because their views increasingly came into conflict with the opinions of their members, and their departure made it even more difficult for the churches to mount any effective resistance to slavery. The only true opposition to the peculiar institution remained in the Upper South, where there was less dependence on slave labor.[11]

As opposition to slavery itself dwindled, the evangelical churches reexamined their relationships with the peculiar institution. They realized that

10. Lewis M. Purifoy, "The Methodist Anti-Slavery Tradition, 1784–1844," *Methodist History* 4 (1966): 4 (quotations); H. S. Smith, *In His Image, But . . .*, 38–47; Arthur Dickens Thomas Jr., "The Second Great Awakening in Virginia and Slavery Reform, 1785–1837" (Th.D. diss., Union Theological Seminary, Richmond, Va., 1981), 78–79; Donald G. Mathews, *Slavery and Methodism: A Chapter in American Morality, 1780–1845* (Princeton, 1965), 69–70; Emory S. Bucke, ed., *The History of American Methodism*, 2 vols. (New York, 1964), 2:13; Lucius C. Matlack, *The History of American Slavery and Methodism, from 1780 to 1849, and History of the Wesleyan Methodist Connection of America* (1849; reprint, Freeport, N.Y., 1971), 31–34.

11. Christine Leigh Heyrman, *Southern Cross: The Beginnings of the Bible Belt* (New York, 1997), 92–95, 155; H. S. Smith, *In His Image, But . . .*, 69–76; Merton Dillon, *Slavery Attacked: Southern Slaves and Their Allies, 1619–1865* (Baton Rouge, 1990), 110; Mathews, *Religion in the Old South*, 75–79.

overthrowing the social order by abolishing slavery would not work, so antislavery members tried to blunt the harsh impact of the peculiar institution. In this fashion, Baptists, Methodists, and Presbyterians wanted to influence the behavior of individual slaveholders rather than make sweeping changes in their society. These denominations hoped to persuade masters to reconsider the treatment of their slaves, especially living arrangements, housing, food, punishment, religious instruction, and the threat of sale. Using scripture as a guide for action would "promote the moral welfare of the whole plantation." Antislavery Christians found strange bedfellows in their proslavery counterparts who hoped to bolster slavery by reforming its abuses. They reasoned that removing the most objectionable features would make it more difficult to undermine the institution as a whole. Such efforts, though, needed the cooperation of slaveowners, and their commitment varied. Some wanted no interference in their affairs. Those owners who seriously believed in the tenets of spiritual dominion over their slaves, however, saw the institution as beneficial to the bondservants because it provided them with an introduction to civilization. The slave quarters was potentially a mission field for the master.[12]

These different ideas were played out in the life of John Jones. Before accepting the call to the ministry, Jones felt it was good to own slaves. After his conversion, he came to hate slavery and thought that most of his fellow evangelicals saw it as a "great social, political, and moral evil." Like many churchgoers, Jones endured slavery for the present but looked to the day when it would ultimately be extinguished. The attitude of evangelicals like Jones, who hoped for slavery's eventual end but took no decisive steps to bring it about, was typical. Their rhetoric was concerned with fixing their eyes on the heavenly kingdom rather than on earthly affairs. As a result, they were more likely to tolerate the evil of slavery and work to lessen the harsh impact of the peculiar institution. Instead of trying to reshape society

12. Bertram Wyatt-Brown, "Modernizing Southern Slavery: The Proslavery Argument Reinterpreted," in *Region, Race, and Reconstruction: Essays in Honor of C. Vann Woodward,* ed. J. Morgan Kousser and James M. McPherson (New York, 1982), 34 (quotation); Mathews, *Religion in the Old South,* 75; Randy J. Sparks, "Mississippi's Apostle of Slavery: James Smylie and the Biblical Defense of Slavery," *Journal of Mississippi History* 51 (1989): 96; Oakes, *Ruling Race,* 96–100; Joyce E. Chaplin, "Slavery and the Principle of Humanity: A Modern Idea in the Early Lower South," *Journal of Social History* 24 (1990): 299; Rose, "Domestication of Domestic Slavery," 18–36; Kenneth Moore Startup, *The Root of All Evil: The Protestant Clergy and the Economic Mind of the Old South* (Athens, 1997), 69–74.

to fit their conception of Christianity, they did the reverse. They modified their faith to fit peculiar aspects of their situation. Evangelicals tried to make the more objectionable features of their society less problematic for Christians, and even those who did not believe. The churches tended to accommodate the social system rather than change it. It was their sense of moral stewardship and their belief that they could reform slaveholders that led them to accept what many regarded as sin.[13]

Even as the plantation system spread and slaveholders filled the church pews, the Second Great Awakening swept through the South and gave impetus to the growth of the evangelical churches. Converts flocked to the Methodist, Presbyterian, and Baptist churches in record numbers. By 1850 these three denominations had grown to such an extent that they composed over nine-tenths of the churches in the South, with a membership of about one-seventh of the population. Affiliation was only part of their influence, since ministers regularly preached to congregations up to four times the size of the enrolled membership. The evangelical denominations, then, had widespread power in the South at a time when church attendance was a customary feature of life. Most slaveowners in the South belonged, at least nominally, to one of the evangelical denominations. This new religious enthusiasm happened, coincidentally, at the same time as the great expansion in slavery and the interstate slave trade. Even while the hierarchical nature of southern society tended to reproduce itself within the church, there still was an undercurrent of egalitarianism. All white people, whether they owned slaves or not, could join the church provided they made the necessary declaration of faith, although not all men would have the same amount of influence once inside its doors. Much of the early-nineteenth-century preaching stressed the equality of man before God, in that all people were sinners regardless of station in life. This leveling influence, combined with the democratic structure of the expanding churches, tended to attract the poorer segments of the population, especially nonslaveholders. More important, the egalitarian current of evangelicalism operated against the idea of racial inequality and allowed African Americans to be church members. In Mississippi, for example, evangelical churches routinely baptized African Americans and gave them the right hand of Christian fellowship, but also

13. John Jones, as quoted in Randy J. Sparks, *On Jordan's Stormy Banks: Evangelicalism in Mississippi, 1773–1876* (Athens, 1994), 67; Albert J. Raboteau, *Slave Religion: The "Invisible Institution" in the Antebellum South* (New York, 1978), 186–87.

made sure they sat in their own section in the back of the church. Baptists, in particular, sought out blacks for church membership. In Virginia, black and white Baptists worshipped together throughout the eighteenth century and up until 1860. The criteria for membership were the same for both races, as were the disciplinary rules, although slaves might suffer church discipline for running away from their masters or for being disobedient. Blacks could legally preach to congregations until 1832, when the outburst of legislation following the Nat Turner rebellion prohibited black preachers. Although practices varied widely, slaves commonly participated in the church life of the evangelical denominations in the South. Social interaction did not lead to social equity, and whites controlled the power structure of the churches. Having said that, it is significant that the egalitarian bent of Christian doctrine ensured that evangelicals would be more likely than other southerners to regard slaves as human rather than as some type of beast. This belief made Christians more sensitive to preserving slave families.[14]

The presence of African American members was a visible reminder that early church doctrine emphasized slaves as being persons precious to God. This idea created burdens for masters who assumed the role of moral guardian for their bondservants. The Virginia Conference of the Methodist Church ordered owners to instruct their slaves in the principles and duties of religion. Teaching slaves to read and write was illegal in most southern states, but earnest masters assumed responsibility for their slaves' religious instruction or delegated it to their wives or trusted slave preachers. Reflective owners extended their efforts into the moral lives of their slaves. They tried to improve the living conditions in the quarters. Other owners raised money for the American Colonization Society or sent their slaves to Africa. The idea of guardianship was extended to include almost any aspect of a slave's life and gave masters an excuse to meddle wherever they pleased.[15]

14. John B. Boles, *The Great Revival, 1787–1805: The Origins of the Southern Evangelical Mind* (Lexington, Ky., 1972); C. C. Goen, *Broken Churches, Broken Nation: Denominational Schisms and the Coming of the American Civil War* (Macon, Ga., 1985), 54–57; Oakes, *Ruling Race*, 96–100; Sparks, *Jordan's Stormy Banks*, 60; Mathews, *Religion in the Old South*, 66–69; Boles, introduction to *Masters and Slaves in the House of the Lord*, 8–12; W. Harrison Daniel, "Virginia Baptists and the Negro in the Early Republic," *Virginia Magazine of History and Biography* 80 (1972): 60–62; Daniel, "Virginia Baptists in the Antebellum Era," 1–7; Raboteau, *Slave Religion*, 101–2.

15. William W. Sweet, *Virginia Methodism: A History* (Richmond, 1955), 200.

Of particular concern for masters who presumed the mantle of trusteeship was discipline, punishment, and sale. Evangelical religion, when viewed in this way, provided principles that were subversive to the complete authority of the master over his slaves. Those who owned other human beings, after all, would eventually be accountable to their heavenly master. The prospect of a divine judgment could persuade owners to reconsider harsh treatment of slaves. This idea was especially noticeable when the slave was a Christian and when the interstate slave trade was involved. Presbyterians went further than the other two evangelical denominations in protecting slaves who belonged to the church. In 1822 the Presbyterian General Assembly used strong language to prevent a master from selling a slave who was in good standing in a local church. The offender was to be suspended from church membership until he repented and made some reparation to the slave. The Hanover, Virginia, Presbytery reaffirmed the stance of the national church when it mandated that any of its members who sold a slave who was also a church member should be disciplined until the seller repented. Here the church denounced the slave trade in general and, amazingly, extended special protection to slaves who were members of a local congregation. Insulating a slave from sale was virtually unthinkable and a serious erosion of the rights which slaveholders presumed. Bondservants who converted and then joined the church would have special status that limited masters' abilities to attend to their affairs.[16]

A Tennessee widow ran into just such a problem. She planned to move to Alabama, but had to make arrangements for her slaves. The woman, who belonged to a Presbyterian church, wanted to sell a female slave and her two children. The slave's husband lived in the same city but had a different owner. When the woman applied for a certificate of good standing from the church in order to be admitted to another Presbyterian congregation in Alabama, she was denied. Since the slaves were members of her church, the elders thought it wrong to grant the request unless she made arrangements not to separate the woman and the children from the father. The husband's

16. *Abolition Intelligencer and Missionary Magazine*, July 1822, 36; *Religious Remembrancer*, June 20, 1818, 171; *Religious Intelligencer*, June 27, 1818, 60; West, *Politics of Revelation and Reason*, 82; Barbara Layenette Green, "The Slavery Debate in Missouri, 1831–1855" (Ph.D. diss., University of Missouri, Columbia, 1980), 110–11; Dillon, *Slavery Attacked*, 97–100; Mathews, *Religion in the Old South*, 28–30, 40–41, 68–71; Thomas, "Second Great Awakening," 148.

owner made a reasonable offer for the three slaves, but the widow refused. She then sold the female slave to a "most wicked man" and moved to Alabama with the children. The woman was "of course" suspended from the church. While this episode demonstrates that evangelical churches took action against speculation, it also shows that church discipline was ineffective for those members who did not feel compelled to remain in good standing. They chose personal autonomy over group affiliation.[17]

Even though the Presbyterian church was the only one specifically to bar its members from selling one another, evangelicals in the other denominations often fell into line. A minister from Prince George, Maryland, was particularly troubled by what transpired when he was out of town. Ned, a "very reputable black communicant," frequently attended prayer meetings, much to his master's chagrin. The owner flogged Ned for his diligence and then sold him to a speculator for continued disobedience. The minister could not comprehend the action, especially since it came on the sabbath. Ned did not complain when the irons were riveted on his wrists, but cried and said, "Jesus suffered more." The minister implored his fellow Christians to come to their senses and look at the treatment of slaves. He wondered if God would send a lightning bolt of wrath to chasten the nation. The minister probably had qualms about slavery before the incident, but the callous sale of Ned sent him firmly into the antislavery camp. The actions of Ned and others like him show how slaves actively shaped how Christians viewed the interstate slave trade and slavery itself. When he behaved better than his master, in a way that was fully in accord with Christian principles, he proved that slaves could understand and apply the gospel.[18]

Even though religious enthusiasm directly challenged speculation, most southern clergy supported slavery. They made a conscious distinction between ownership and abuse of it. Jeremiah Jeter, a Presbyterian minister and slaveowner in eastern Virginia, wondered what to do with his slaves. He wanted to be rid of his bondservants, but the laws of Virginia forbade emancipation. None of his slaves wanted to go to Liberia, and he was not willing to force them into exile. The best course of action, he decided, was to sell them or give them away. Again, the slaves protested, and Jeter did not carry out his scheme. Failing to dispose of his bondservants, Jeter concluded it was his "solemn obligation" to keep them and be a conscientious master.

17. Undated *Maryville Trumpeter*, as reprinted in the *Liberator*, May 9, 1835, 73.

18. *Religious Remembrancer*, October 26, 1816, 33–34.

He justified his inaction by arguing that free blacks were usually worse off than whites. Although Jeter's writing may be an exercise in self-justification, he seemed to be truly troubled with slavery. His preaching reflected his sense of personal confusion. Instead of emphasizing the goodness of slavery or illuminating whites on the scriptural basis of the institution, he stressed the responsibility of masters to their slaves. Jeter revealed much about his own attitudes when he wrote that the "prevalent opinion" of the 1820s was that slavery was a great responsibility that was fraught with "economical, social, political, and moral" evils. Most people, he thought, expected slavery to be abolished in the foreseeable future. Jeter himself harbored a slight hope that eventually slavery would be peaceably removed but remained paralyzed while the peculiar institution gained strength.[19]

Divided minds like Jeter's were not unusual for the time, since most evangelicals had a conditional acceptance of slavery. Even though they tolerated the presence of the peculiar institution, they could not abandon the vague idea that it was, somehow, wrong and needed to be reformed, controlled, or possibly eliminated. They tried to make the system of slavery itself seem moral by ameliorating the blatant violations of God's law. Moreover, they looked at the peculiar institution through the lens of responsibility, or privilege. If Christians abused their position by heartlessly selling bondservants, then they invited God's retribution. This sense of stewardship had dominion over all aspects of the master-slave relationship. Evangelicals thought it their Christian duty to prevent, as much as possible, many of the abuses that were too often associated with slavery. Excessive labor, extreme punishment, and the withholding of necessary food and clothing were the most common targets. Thomas S. Clay prepared a pamphlet for the Georgia Presbytery on how masters could improve the moral condition of their slaves. He first noted that bondservants learn from the "experience of judicious, humane planters." Owners must buttress their personal lives with procedures that promoted religious instruction, moral excellence, temperance, stable family unions, and plantation discipline. One catechism stressed the need for masters to provide adequate clothing, abundant food, medicine, and proper care for the old or infirm. These notions were not just intended to help the slaves, but the masters, as well. Evangelicals stressed the need to live a life of self-discipline and self-denial. To over-

19. Jeremiah Jeter, *The Recollections of a Long Life* (Richmond, 1891), 68 (quotations); Loveland, *Southern Evangelicals*, 187.

indulge in anything invited spiritual examination. Evangelicals wanted to convince themselves that controlling their evil desire to exploit slaves through speculation was a spiritual experience. If cleanliness was not next to holiness, then perhaps self-denial was.[20]

If evangelicals were serious about bringing civilization and morality to their slaves, then the wanton operation of the interstate slave trade was a poor message to send to bondservants or to critics of slavery. The family unit was the building block of society, and to endanger it was to threaten the basis of community. A thriving interstate slave trade, most evangelicals thought, sabotaged efforts to teach slaves the virtues of white society. Even though much of the southern perception of slavery involved the exclusion of slaves from many rights and privileges, most evangelical Christians would not begrudge slaves the opportunity to have a family life. The *Western Luminary*, a publication of the Presbyterian Church, lamented the suffering associated with the slave trade. Speculation broke up families through "heathenish commerce in the blood, and sinews of human beings." The thought of such suffering should ignite a passion in Christians to put an end to such madness. A publication intended to serve as a guide for Christian slaveholders made much the same point. It stressed the need to "*keep families together.*" Isham Harrison had already taken these lessons to heart. When his brother James sent forty-nine slaves from South Carolina to Alabama for sale, it was hard on Isham. Several years later the devout Isham praised his brother for embracing Christianity even while confessing that he had always regretted the sale of the bondservants. When Isham had the opportunity to buy some slaves for himself, he tried to cushion the blow by purchasing a family. Even though Isham said he paid $200 too much for the slaves, he admitted it was worth something to see slave families reunited. That Isham was so bothered by his brother's actions is telling. A devout Christian faith could make a man sensitive enough to anguish over the notion that someone else was being eaten by the canker of speculation. Another evangelical as-

20. Bertram Wyatt-Brown, *The Shaping of Southern Culture: Honor, Grace, and War, 1760s–1890s* (Chapel Hill, 2001), 85; Mathews, *Religion in the Old South*, 75–79; Chaplin, "Slavery and the Principle of Humanity," 299–315; Loveland, *Southern Evangelicals*, 209; Startup, *Root of all Evil*, 70–71; Thomas S. Clay, *Detail of a Plan for the Moral Improvement of Negroes on Plantations* (n.p., 1833), 3 (quotation); Charles Colcock Jones, *A Catechism of Scripture Doctrine and Practice, for Families and Sabbath Schools, Designed also for the Oral Instruction of Colored Persons* (Savannah, 1837), as quoted in Mason Crum, *Gullah: Negro Life in the Carolina Sea Islands* (Durham, N.C., 1940), 204; Daly, *When Slavery Was Called Freedom*, 36–41.

serted that a Christian country should be distinguished by its belief that all men love one another. He doubted that such an ideal penetrated the slave markets and wondered if any slave driver had the label "Whatsoever ye would that men should do to you do ye even so to them" inscribed on his whip.[21]

The fact that southern society did not recognize slave marriages as legally binding did not deter evangelicals from ascribing some degree of moral equivalency to slave unions. J. D. Paxton, a Presbyterian minister, expressed the attitude of many when he wrote that the forced separation of husbands from wives, and children from parents, was "at variance with natural religion." Such absences meant that husbands could not protect their wives, wives could not be obedient to their husbands, and neither could provide for their children. For Paxton, the interstate slave trade destroyed the integrity of the slave family and eroded the Christian basis of slavery. It did not matter to him whether the state recognized such marriages as valid, since God's natural law was more important. In a similar fashion, separation between parent and child could be especially poignant and was hardly evidence that slavery improved the life of the enslaved. The members of the Glen's Creek, Kentucky, Methodist Church were especially troubled by the actions of William Garnett, one of their own. Some members accused Garnett of selling his slave woman and child down the river. The church voted to strike him from the membership roll in order to teach him a lesson about the worldly depravity of speculation. Garnett returned to fellowship once he made amends.[22]

It was the interstate slave trade, the evangelical churches realized, that caused most of the family separations. Philip A. Bolling, a Virginia evangelical, recognized the connection between the two. During the Virginia slavery debates, he defended slavery itself but said no one could justify the traffic in human beings. If men would read their Bibles and take the Golden

21. *Western Luminary*, November 23, 1831 (first quotation); Jones, *Catechism of Scripture*, as quoted in Crum, *Gullah*, 204 (second quotation, emphasis in original); Isham Harrison to James Harrison, March 8, 1836, James T. Harrison Papers, UNC; *Western Luminary*, January 19, 1831, 322 (final quotation); Mitchell Snay, *Gospel of Disunion: Religion and Separatism in the Antebellum South* (New York, 1993), 95–98; Loveland, *Southern Evangelicals*, 209–10.

22. J. D. Paxton, *Letters on Slavery; Addressed to the Cumberland Congregation, Virginia* (Lexington, Ky., 1833), 56 (quotation); Minutes of the Glen's Creek Methodist Church, as quoted in Walter B. Posey, *The Baptist Church in the Lower Mississippi Valley, 1776–1845* (Lexington, Ky., 1957), 94.

Rule to heart, he lectured his colleagues, then the slave trade would disappear. A Presbyterian divine had a similar argument. He attacked the slave trade as one of the "palpable evils" connected with slavery and was shocked that his brethren were caught up in a traffic that put prices on souls. It was incomprehensible to him that traders chased only after money and threw away their scruples in the process. The result was an offense to the Lord. John Early, who preached at a Methodist camp meeting in Portsmouth, Virginia, called the slave speculator "among the blackest of characters." When a trader's wife stopped Early after the service and said she was offended by him, he apologized for injuring her feelings but was more sorry that she had a speculator for a husband.[23]

Although the separation of slave families was bothersome to evangelicals, the commercial aspect of slave trading was even more alarming. The two were interconnected, since it was the speculative nature of slave sales that usually destroyed black families. Evangelicals feared that the rampant growth of slave speculation—with all of its potential for profit—would seduce church members into worshipping money rather than God. An evangelical who sold slaves to a speculator was assumed to be doing it for the wrong reasons. In 1823, for instance, the Goshen Association, a Baptist group centered in Fredericksburg, Virginia, dealt with the issue of trafficking in slaves. It used the "strongest terms" to denounce speculation as "unchristian" and not to be tolerated. The association stressed the business nature of the trade as the most objectionable feature rather than emphasizing the harmful aspects upon the slave family. The mere pursuit of wealth was selfish and something not to be excused because it was diametrically opposed to the spirit of Christianity. It is not that the church was antimoney, but it was against speculation, especially when it wreaked such devastation on the lives of slaves. Such naked pursuit of wealth clouded the eyes of the true believer and caused him to take his concentration off of spiritual matters. The *Western Luminary* made its position clear. Speculators merely acted for "*gold—sordid gold,*—for the sake of heaping up that unrighteous mammon." Masters shared culpability with speculators and could not be excused for their actions.[24]

23. Bolling, as quoted in Thomas, "Second Great Awakening," 414–15; F. R. Cossitt, *The Life and Times of Rev. Finis Ewing*, 3rd ed. (Louisville, 1853), 273 (first quotation); Early, as quoted in Thomas, "Second Great Awakening," 32–33 (second quotation).

24. Goshen Association Minutes, 6, Library of Virginia, Richmond (first quotation); *Western Luminary*, November 23, 1831 (second quotation, emphasis in original); Startup, *Root of all Evil*, 43–44, 68.

The problematic influences of greed spilled over into the pages of the *Religious Herald*, a publication with a wide circulation amongst Virginia Baptists. A reader wondered if it was wrong for a Christian to buy or sell slaves from a speculator. He answered his own question by announcing that it was "improper" to censure members in such circumstances. The *Herald* noted that it had previously received questions of a similar nature, but could not pass on this challenge to its authority. It blasted the reader's attitude with a long and detailed indictment of the slave trade. It was a "manifest impropriety" for a Christian to engage in slave trafficking. Speculation, the paper noted, was generally held in disrepute, and those who engaged in it usually lost standing in the community. Since the term "negro-buyer" was often used in reproach, the Christian should avoid association with the trade, since it would dishonor "the cause of Christ." Baptists "generally" agreed that it degraded the church and was incompatible with the spirit of the gospel. Slave trading had a "hardening tendency" and frequently led to association with gamblers and others riddled with vice. The only conclusion believers should draw was that it would be "wholly impracticable" to maintain a Christian character in a traffic that was concerned with the pursuit of mammon. It followed that speculation should be made a subject for church discipline, since a congregation that harbored a slave trader could not retain a vibrant faith. Since the public had decided that the traffic was discreditable, then the church could not disregard public opinion with impunity. The *Herald*'s statement condemned the trade in the strongest terms possible, on religious, social, and moral grounds. While it pointed out the effects that the trade had on the slave, it was more concerned with the effects on the church and the white community. Christians had a duty to be separate from the evil in the world, and speculation could bring only bad results. Believers who dabbled with the interstate slave trade were playing with fire. The lust for money could scorch the master and burn the slave.[25]

Owners, then, could not take their duties lightly and should strive to remain uncorrupted by the potential for evil that lay in the slaveholding relationship. There lurked about all kinds of opportunity for immoral thoughts and actions. The slaveholder who began to put the pursuit of money ahead of spiritual affairs would be tempted to use the money from slave sales to gratify fleshly desires. Personal comfort would take precedence over slaves' familial relations. Complacency could then stand in the way of spiritual

25. *Religious Herald*, April 15, 1836.

growth. It was this side of speculation in slaves, the desire to make money in order to pursue a type of hedonism, that seemed to bother evangelicals the most. Slaveholders who believed in this idea sought to act in accordance with the principles of humanity and justice. Any who made "merchandize of their fellow-creatures" engaged in a "flagrant violation of duty." Elijah Eagleston, pastor of the Presbyterian church in Madisonville, Tennessee, took quick action to root out what he saw as evil in his midst. He secured the expulsion of two of his most prominent members after they sold slaves because of the high market prices. This thirst for money could spread and poison the entire congregation.[26]

In contrast to a type of heedless speculation, most Christians understood the necessity to sell slaves in hard economic times or at the settlement of an estate. One religious writer articulated the distinction by condemning the "indiscriminate" sale of slaves as immoral, while recognizing that there were occasions where such transactions sprang from "motives of humanity." Where owners acted as humans, they realized that slaves had legitimate claims on their "sympathies." The result would be that slaves would be treated with a measure of regard for their feelings. Speculation involved the naked pursuit of profit and came from the exploitation of the slaves. In this way, it was a twofold evil—corrupting the speculator and demeaning the slave. The former was a more serious issue than the latter. Christians who avoided the interstate slave trade were trying to make peace with their own hearts rather than do right by their slaves. It is almost as if they needed some type of tangible measure of piety. Evangelicals could then hope that virtuous actions in this area would spill over into the rest of their lives. Proper personal conduct could lead to a wider societal reform, in this case the institution of slavery. Evangelical Christians sought to improve southern culture by policing their individual actions when it came to sale and speculation.[27]

This gnawing sense of the slave trade's evil can be found in evangelical sermons. The Reverend Finis Ewing consistently preached against the "traffic in human flesh," referring to the disruptive effects on the slave family. He noted that too many masters cared only about a high sales price. The worldly desire for riches crowded in and led owners into temptation, leading to debasement of both master and slave. God was displeased with the

26. *Western Luminary*, November 23, 1831 (quotations); Ernest T. Thompson, *Presbyterians in the South*, vol. 1, *1607–1861* (Richmond, 1963), 345.

27. *Abolition Intelligencer and Missionary Magazine*, June 1822, 18–22 (quotations on 18).

situation, Ewing surmised, and doubtless heard the cries of those who were separated from their families. Paxton also called the slave trade an "evil" that ought to convince people to reform slavery or abandon it altogether. He pointed out that most southerners had seen the trade, whether at a courthouse or in a coffle along the road, and realized that speculation involved vast sums of money. Paxton knew that the love of money was the root of all evil, so the high profits of the trade led to the blatant disregard of the slaves' families. "No passion is more unfeeling than avarice," he concluded. In speaking to Christians, Paxton asked any who had "hearts to feel for a fellow creature's woes and a fellow creature's wrongs" to work to prevent such scenes from occurring in the future.[28]

While such attitudes were agreeable to most southern evangelicals—it was hard to argue in favor of exploitation for personal gain—the growth of the interstate slave trade in the 1820s and beyond challenged the church's relationship with slavery. A thriving trade brought the harsher features of slavery to light and forced evangelicals to reconsider their support for the peculiar institution. They desperately groped for a way to reduce speculation while simultaneously affirming their support for slavery. The three evangelical denominations took different approaches, with the Presbyterians taking national action, the Baptists making local efforts, and the Methodists hewing to a middle way. None of them met with much success.

In 1815 the Presbyterian General Assembly officially condemned slave speculation. This national meeting of church representatives denounced the "transfer of slaves by way of traffic" as antithetical to Christianity's message. The Assembly recommended that churches use "prudent" measures to stamp out "such shameful and unrighteous conduct." Three years later the same body asked individual churches to "discountenance" the separation of slave families: Such actions undermined the sanctity of the family and should trigger church discipline or censure. In what was probably an attempt to avoid making difficult decisions, the Assembly did not elaborate what punishment would be suitable for those who engaged in speculation.[29]

28. Cossitt, *Finis Ewing*, 273 (Ewing quotation); Caleb Perry Patterson, *The Negro in Tennessee, 1790–1865* (1922; reprint, New York, 1968), 131–32; Paxton, *Letters on Slavery*, 134–35 (Paxton quotations).

29. Thompson, *Presbyterians in the South*, 328 (first, second, and third quotations); H. S. Smith, *In His Image, But . . .*, 59; *Religious Remembrancer*, June 20, 1818, 171 (final quotation); *Religious Intelligencer*, June 27, 1818, 60; *Abolition Intelligencer and Missionary Magazine*, July 1822, 36; *Niles' Weekly Register*, supplement to vol. 16 (1819), 153–55.

Part of the Assembly's reluctance to take decisive action might have been conditioned by the difficulty in discerning a seller's motives. The fact that a sale did not always amount to speculation bedeviled all of the denominations. The Concord, Kentucky, Presbyterian Church excluded John Moore from church privileges for selling a boy slave at an auction. An outraged Moore appealed this decision to the Presbytery of West Lexington, which reversed the decision. The appellate presbytery expressed its "decided disapprobation" of slave auctions but could find no scripture that directly applied to the situation. Determined to ferret out the evil in its midst, the church appealed the decision to the synod, which seemed at a loss as to what to do next. After originally reversing the presbytery's decision, the synod remanded the case to the session for more information. Specifically, the synod wanted to know whether Moore took "due pains" to sell the boy at a private sale before resorting to an auction. The evasion of the synod illustrates a crucial problem in dealing with those who sold slaves: determining motive. If Moore tried to find a private buyer, then it could be argued that he wanted the sale to be as least disruptive on the slave as possible, since the slave would remain near his family. The use of an auctioneer, on the other hand, presumably signaled Moore's desire to profit on the transaction at the expense of the slave. Sale to a stranger likely meant exile for the slave and a higher profit for the seller. The churches could not always discern an owner's motives, so action usually became the basis of judgment. Since the sale of slaves was integral to southern society, the churches faced an intractable problem.[30]

Unlike the Presbyterians, the national church body of the Baptists made no official pronouncement on the trade. Instead the national body left it up to the church associations or the individual congregations to set their own policies when it came to the buying and selling of slaves. Although the Baptist church was traditionally decentralized, church leaders may have also assumed that local congregations were in a better position to separate attitude and action. The Baptists, however, fared no better than the Presbyterians. Their reactions varied from artful dodging to hard-line pronouncements. One association, when mulling over what to do when there was a forcible separation of slaves, advised churches to "act discretionally." The Dover Association, on the other hand, ruled in 1816 that its members who engaged in the slave traffic should be thrown out of the church. Expulsion of this

30. Thompson, *Presbyterians in the South*, 327–28.

type was the strongest form of discipline available to the church. Likewise, the Chowan Association, a group comprising eighteen churches in four counties of North Carolina, faced the problem two years later. A query, or formal question, was put to the association asking if it was consistent for a Christian to buy slaves in order to sell them to speculators. The association did not mince words in its reply, describing such an action as "shocking" because it was "at open war with the spirit of the gospel." The answer to whether a Christian should sell slaves to a speculator was an emphatic *no* in this case.[31]

Like the Baptists, the Methodists as a national body ceased to regulate the interstate slave trade. Certain portions of the church, though, continued to operate as a brake on the growing commerce. In 1813 the Virginia Conference agreed that if any of its members were found guilty of speculating in slaves, they were to be expelled. Four years later the conference clarified the matter by affirming the principle that Methodists should buy or sell slaves only to keep husbands, wives, parents, and children together. Slave trading was, according to the church, another form of "immorality." Church members could own slaves and buy and sell them as long as they did so for humanitarian reasons. What constituted benevolence was open to debate, and the eventual result was a permissive attitude regarding the speculation in slaves. For instance, two elders of a Virginia church faced charges of buying and selling slaves, but the Conference considered some ameliorating circumstances and acquitted them. Most likely they were able to demonstrate their good intentions in the transaction, although the justification of one sale over another suggests a significant loophole.[32]

Tennessee Methodists tried to simplify the matter by specifically excluding members who bought or sold slaves for speculative profit. This stance remained the official position of the Methodist churches in Tennessee. Although this rule and others might have attracted African American converts to the Methodist Church in Tennessee, as time passed the matter was for-

31. Daniel, "Virginia Baptists in the Early Republic," 62–64; Reuben E. Alley, *A History of Baptists in Virginia* (Richmond, n.d.), 149 (first quotation); James A. Delke, *History of the North Carolina Chowan Baptist Association, 1806–1881* (Raleigh, 1882), 80 (remaining quotations); George W. Purefoy, *A History of the Sandy Creek Baptist Association from Its Organization in* A.D. 1758, to A.D. 1858 (New York, 1859), 163–64.

32. Sweet, *Virginia Methodism*, 200; William W. Bennett, *Memorials of Methodism in Virginia, from Its Introduction into the State, in the Year 1772 to the Year 1829* (Richmond, 1871), 641 (quotation); Thomas, "Second Great Awakening," 80.

gotten. The Western Conference of the Methodist Church had a similar policy. Embracing the states of Tennessee and Kentucky, it called upon its members to cease their involvement in the slave trade. Such westerners were not to "sell or buy a slave unjustly, inhumanly, or covetously." Methodists were not asked to stop all transactions, merely the ones that were contrary to God's law. The rule appears to be just as much for the slaveholder as for the slave, since it was designed to protect the owner from the temptations of the world. While a dampened enthusiasm for the slave trade would certainly uphold the sanctity of the slave family, it would also keep the owner from falling into the trap of pursuing worldly gain at the expense of heavenly business. Suspected members were judged at the quarterly meeting and those who fell short of the standard were expelled. This loosely drawn provision proved too permissive, since justice, humanity, and covetousness were subject to various interpretations. The result was an ineffectual standard that was difficult to enforce.[33]

Even though evangelical denominations and church associations failed to establish clear policies in dealing with the trade, Christians worked individually to reduce speculation's impact. Mary Blackford, a devout Christian, lived in Fredericksburg, Virginia. She was outraged when the slave-trading firm of Smith and Finnall bought a house in her neighborhood by "deceiving" the owner's son. They started converting the structure into a jail by building a sixteen-foot-high brick wall to keep slaves in and curious stares out. Blackford organized resistance to the "Bastille," but no one could afford to buy the property. Then, a "generous, kind-hearted Yankee" interceded and bought the house at an exorbitant price. Blackford had the infinite pleasure of seeing the wall pulled down and the iron grating taken out of the windows. While Blackford's opposition to the trade may seem extreme, she was motivated by her religious beliefs and the desire to keep undesirables, both slaves and speculators, out of the area.[34]

Evangelicals may have taken strength from the denunciations of the slave trade they read in religious publications. The *Western Luminary* had no

33. Goodstein, "Black History on the Nashville Frontier," 416; Charles B. Swaney, *Episcopal Methodism and Slavery: With Sidelights on Ecclesiastical Politics* (1926; reprint, New York, 1969), 6 (quotation); Patterson, *Negro in Tennessee*, 108–13.

34. L. Minor Blackford, *Mine Eyes have seen the Glory: The Story of a Virginia Lady Mary Berkeley Minor Blackford 1802–1896 who taught her sons to hate Slavery and to love the Union*, ed. F. Nash Boney (Cambridge, Mass., 1954), 39–42.

sympathy for the speculators Edward and Howard Stone when they were murdered by slaves. Calling the attack the "*Awful Judgment of Heaven upon Slave-Traders,*" the *Luminary* implied that the "inhuman and merciless" actions of the speculators justified their being bludgeoned to death and weighted down with stones to sink to the bottom of the Ohio River. Following the incident, the paper printed a reader's letter from two years earlier that detailed the horrible practices of Edward Stone, implying that his brutality excused the actions of the slaves. The letter closed with the ominous line, "*Heaven will curse that man who engages in such traffic, and the government that protects him in it.*" Instead of calling for the apprehension of the slaves, who were still at large, the publication urged the legislature of Kentucky to end slave trading. The sharp words drew no protest from readers. The *Christian Advocate*, a publication affiliated with the Methodist Church, attributed the grisly death of the slave traders to the "*Shocking effects of Slave-trading*" and reprinted much of the *Luminary*'s information. These Christian publications did not condemn the actions of the slaves, despite the obvious threat that such a massacre entailed to white hegemony. The fear of slave revolt was constant in the South, and the *Luminary*'s words gave no comfort to skittish whites. There was almost an implied sanction to the deed, as if the evil actions of the traders needlessly provoked the slaves into armed rebellion.[35]

The coverage of the religious publications is in stark contrast to that of secular newspapers. A paper in nearby Louisville described the "horrid crime" and "shocking deed" in great detail. It described the "plundering" of the boat and the "timely vigilance" of citizens in rounding up the slaves. Another labeled the deed a "DREADFUL MASSACRE!!!!" and described how one of the slaves defended his master to the end. At least the bondservants were arrested, convicted, and sentenced to hanging, the article stated. The *Kentucky Reporter*'s account of the incident sought to instill sympathy for the "unfortunate victims." Such reactions were in line with what one might expect from white society: shock that whites were murdered, no sympathy for the slaves, and a call for retribution. No matter how awful the actions of the traders, the slaves were not justified in their actions because they engaged in the ultimate form of disobedience. That these attitudes were noticeably

35. *Western Luminary*, October 4, 1826, 108 (emphasis in original); *Christian Advocate*, October 21, 1826, 27 (emphasis in original).

absent from religious publications shows the difficulty that evangelicals had in reconciling the trade to their Christian beliefs.[36]

As time wore on, evangelicals found it increasingly difficult to condemn the slave trade and remain loyal to slavery. The abolitionist campaign in the 1830s helped convince southern churches to swing around to slavery's defense. Some of the most biting criticism of the peculiar institution came from northern churches and northern Christians. These attacks came on a broad front, including political, moral, and religious grounds. Abolitionists used scripture to indict slaveholders and southerners in general. The Presbyterian Synod of Cincinnati was especially vocal in pushing for deliberate and concrete action that would put slavery on the road to extinction. Among other things, it resolved that the buying or selling of slaves for profit was a "heinous sin and scandal." Since such sins prevailed "to an alarming extent" in the nation and the church, the synod called for a day of prayer and fasting to help slaves. Such prayers were as much for the petitioners as they were for the slaves, since the church was trying to deliver the country from God's wrath. The Chillicothe, Ohio, Presbytery adopted a similar statement. The northerners, though, subtly shifted the debate to an emphasis on the slaves' basic humanity and away from the vile effects of speculation. They naturally related to the efforts by bondservants to assert their individuality. By moving the argument away from speculation, northern Christians accidentally made it easier for double-minded southern evangelicals to accept the interstate slave trade. They focused less attention on how speculation affected themselves and concentrated on the issue of family destruction. In so doing, they could readily adopt the growing presumption that evil slave traders—and not innocent southern citizens—were responsible for slavery's abuses. The northern denunciations of slavery, moreover, broke no new ground; southern evangelical churches had been saying the same thing for years. What changed was the accusations coming from individuals outside the slave regime. Instead of being a valid topic for discussion and reform, the interstate slave trade was an embarrassing eyesore.[37]

36. *Louisville Gazette*, September 22, 1826, as quoted in *Genius of Universal Emancipation*, October 14, 1826, 33; *Lexington Kentucky Gazette*, September 29, October 27, 1826; *Lexington Kentucky Reporter*, September 25, 1826; *Woodville Republican*, October 14, 1826; *Milledgeville Southern Recorder*, October 24, 1826.

37. For Cincinnati, see *Western Luminary*, December 1, 1830, 290; for Chillicothe, see Walter B. Posey, "The Slavery Question in the Presbyterian Church in the Old Southwest," *JSH* 15 (1949): 322 (quotation); and H. S. Smith, *In His Image, But . . .*, 81.

Southern clergy raced to their Bibles to prove that God's word upheld the peculiar institution, and as a result, the church became the "bulwark" of slavery from the 1830s. Synods, presbyterians, associations, and conferences began issuing statements that the Bible sanctioned slavery. Eventually the southern proslavery argument united religion and morality with slavery, investing the sectional conflict with a profound religious significance. Once the southern clergy began to defend the peculiar institution at all costs, southerners with qualms about slavery could no longer speak out, for fear of being branded as disloyal. Nor could they risk questioning an objectionable portion of slavery such as the slave trade. For example, in 1835 a minority report of the Synod of Kentucky leaked out that blasted the slave trade. The report described the trade as especially odious because it caused a slave to be treated "like a beast of the field" while being transported "in chains, like a felon." Such actions were a "flagrant violation of every principle of mercy, justice, and humanity." The resulting instability of slave family life produced licentiousness, since there was no guarantee of a permanent family. While the separation of slave families was hateful, "cupidity" was often worse, since it corrupted those who sold slaves. The writers asked preachers to read the lengthy address to their congregations, although it is unlikely that preachers did so. Northern antislavery activists obtained a copy and used it as an indictment of southern society, reprinting it widely. In fact, the most provocative portion could be found in the leading antislavery tomes of the day. Once northerners started using the report to attack slavery, southern moderates were discredited; any condemnation of the slave trade made them look like abolitionists. The committee's report just worsened the situation and encouraged those who would oppose the slave trade to remain silent on the issue.[38]

In such a divisive atmosphere it could hardly be expected that the national church structures could survive. They did not. The Presbyterian Church was the first to buckle under the strain. When antislavery advocates within the church pushed for a statement on slavery in 1836, the General

38. Snay, *Gospel of Disunion*, 53 (first quotation); Goen, *Broken Churches*, 66–67; Loveland, *Southern Evangelicals*, 194–96; Committee of the Synod of Kentucky, *An Address to the Presbytery of Kentucky, Proposing a Plan for the Instruction and Emancipation of Their Slaves* (Cincinnati, 1835), remaining quotations on 5, 12; Weld, *American Slavery as It Is*, 67; Jay, *Miscellaneous Writings*, 259; John G. Palfrey, *The Inter-State Slave Trade: Anti-Slavery Tract No. 5, 1855*, reprinted in *Anti-Slavery Tracts, Series I, Numbers 1–20, 1855–1856* (New York, 1970), 6; Daly, *When Slavery Was Called Freedom*, 57–72.

Assembly ruled that it was a legal matter and not the province of the church. The following year, the church divided. In 1845 the Baptist Church split along sectional lines due, in large part, to the slavery issue. The Methodist Church, too, fell victim to agitation over slavery. A report of the Tennessee Methodist Conference in 1836 called slavery an "evil" but one that was subject only to civil authority. The church could do nothing except "require kindness" on the part of owners towards their slaves. As a result, the "indiscriminate" traffic in slaves was cruel, criminal, and subject to church discipline. Just what constituted the indiscriminate traffic in slaves was not defined and went unenforced. Owners could now justify nearly any transaction involving slaves. When the issue reappeared in the 1840 General Conference, northern delegates fought to ban slave sales. Southerners resisted and the resulting agitation split the denomination within four years.[39]

Once the southern churches began to defend slavery aggressively, evangelicals found it much easier to excuse the actions of slaveholders. Most looked for ways to justify slavery and explain its ill effects rather than seeking to question its objectionable aspects. They began to explain away the slave trade rather than decry its negative effects. James Smylie, for instance, refuted the allegations of the Chillicothe Presbytery. The Mississippi minister stressed that masters were patriarchal leaders of their slave families who had specific duties for their slaves. In this case, since most slaveholders were "honest[,] scrupulous and conscientious," slavery itself was not sinful. When masters acted as Christians, the result was beneficial to the slaves, who received food, clothing, medical attention, and religious instruction. The slave trade, he also explained, was a natural part of slavery. Smylie noted that Abraham bought slaves and treated them well. Joseph's sale to slave traders showed that the practice was common in biblical days. The fact that Abraham prospered and Joseph rose to high rank in Egypt was enough for Smylie to conclude that God sanctioned the slave trade. Smylie was not the only Presbyterian minister to defend the interstate slave trade. George Junkin argued that the Bible clearly condoned slave sales. He pointed to the

39. Posey, "Slavery Question," 322; H. S. Smith, *In His Image, But . . .*, 81; David T. Bailey, *Shadow on the Church: Southwestern Evangelical Religion and the Issue of Slavery, 1783–1860* (Ithaca, N.Y., 1985), 241–44; Snay, *Gospel of Disunion*, 131–38; Posey, *Baptist Church*, 97–98; *Liberator*, April 9, 1836, 57 (quotations); Lewis Purifoy, "The Southern Methodist Church and the Proslavery Argument," *JSH* (1966): 352; Bucke, ed., *History of American Methodism*, 2:17–18.

example of Moses, but also noted how the Hebrews bought servants from "heathens" and held them in perpetual servitude. In this way, God used righteous masters to teach salvation to their slaves. The implication of Junkin's reasoning was not only that Christians should hold slaves, but that they were justified in buying more because it could be construed as a missionary activity. This notion fit in well with the emerging idea that masters had an organic duty to protect their slaves from the negative aspects of slavery. Masters could thus do as they pleased with their slaves because the philosophy was flexible enough to pardon just about any sin.[40]

The popular *Religious Herald* even dropped its opposition and fell in line with the shift in opinion when it defended the slave trade. In 1848 a reader wondered if it was proper to be a slave trader if he conducted his business "on principles of humanity." Two decades earlier, such a question would have been dismissed because most Christians assumed that speculation by its very nature opposed compassion. In the turbulent decade of the 1840s, however, the paper was compelled to tackle the issue. It answered that no general rule could be laid down because each case must be decided on its own merits. The church normally excluded speculators from fellowship, but the paper realized that auctioneers and general agents often had to "dispose" of slaves as well. There could be no overall judgment of slave traders because scripture was silent on the matter. All cases must be decided on their own merits, "as exceptions from ordinary rules." The paper, in essence, accepted the presence of the slave trade in southern society when it offered no more resistance to it. Baptists had come to recognize that speculation, while troublesome, was not an issue that deserved much attention or debate because it was a normal course of southern society. To question the trade would be to open the door to an even broader examination of slavery, something that zealous antislavery northerners were only too willing to undertake.[41]

While the Baptists proved able to sharply change course, it was the southern Methodist Church that did the most dramatic turnabout. Its General Conference in effect sanctioned the domestic slave trade without spe-

40. James Smylie, *Review of a Letter, from the Presbytery of Chillicothe, to the Presbytery of Mississippi, on the subject of Slavery* (Woodville, Miss., 1836), 4 (first quotation), 16–19; Sparks, "Mississippi's Apostle of Slavery," 95; George Junkin, *The Integrity of Our National Union vs. Abolitionism* (Cincinnati, 1843), 30–31, 37–39, 43 (second quotation).

41. *Religious Herald*, April 27, 1848.

cifically mentioning it. When the church split, the southern wing kept the 1789 General Rule of the *Discipline* that forbade the buying and selling of slaves. Attempts to repeal it in 1846 and 1850 were unsuccessful, but the 1854 Conference interpreted the clause as meaning the African trade. Since the domestic trade had no legislative strictures associated with it, the implication was that it was not off limits for Methodists. Two years later the Conference decided the rule was "ambiguous" and could be used to undermine slavery. Since the church had no right to "meddle" with slavery, the rule was expunged. The general attitude of the Methodist Church towards the slave trade went from antagonism, to tepid opposition, to noninterference, to support.[42]

By 1840 then, most southern evangelicals came to accept the slave trade as a regular and necessary part of southern society. In the 1820s it was still possible to think that slavery might just someday go away, and options such as colonization were still seriously discussed. Once colonization was proved impractical, most people realized that there was no quick resolution of the problem and a "marked change" in public opinion came over the South. Doubts about the peculiar institution faded, according to the Reverend Jeremiah Jeter. He noticed that southern evangelicals no longer questioned the permanence of slavery, but actively worked to defend it. By the same token, they dropped any opposition to the interstate slave trade, and some even defended it. Evangelicals, moreover, became silent when it came to denouncing the trade as encouraging a love of money. They could do so by excusing the motives of slaveholders. As we shall see, it came to be generally accepted in the South that slave traders, or at least traders of a specific type, were to blame for speculation and not the owner. An emerging belief system exonerated owners for any culpability in selling their slaves to speculators. With masters no longer responsible for the slave trade's abuses, the church did not have to hold them accountable for speculation.[43]

As the church became the vanguard of the proslavery movement, it was necessary to prevent any quibbling over the problems concerning the interstate trade. Slavery in all its forms must be protected, and that meant the

42. Charles Elliott, *History of the Great Secession from the Methodist Episcopal Church in the Year 1845* (Cincinnati, 1855), 824; Loveland, *Southern Evangelicals*, 204 (quotations); Ronald T. Takaki, *A Pro-Slavery Crusade: The Agitation to Reopen the African Slave Trade* (New York, 1971), 136–39; Swaney, *Episcopal Methodism*, 246–47.

43. Jeter, *Recollections*, 68 (quotation); Loveland, *Southern Evangelicals*, 187.

church must drop any qualms it had concerning the buying and selling of slaves. The churches increasingly looked at slavery itself as a civil matter and separated it from the spiritual realm. Methodists, for instance, modified their views so that the church should not interfere with civil relations, thus ensuring that the presence of slavery was no longer open for debate. The separation of the sacred from the secular meant an acceptance of the slave trade and the resulting belief that doubts about speculative activity were misguided. Once the southern churches dropped all effective resistance to speculation, the slave lost his most influential advocate. Individual masters were less likely to be held accountable for the ravages of the slave trade because doing so would open up the entire system for criticism. As abolitionist pressure on the South increased, evangelicals ceased their criticism of slavery, since such attacks could be construed as disloyal. The church fell silent on the issue of speculation, and like much of the rest of southern society, looked for some other way to explain the presence of the interstate slave trade.

CHAPTER 6

The Trade Transformed

Long before Andrew Jackson became president, the means and manner by which he conducted his personal life left him open for scathing personal attacks. Old Hickory's fiery disposition and his penchant for creating controversy made him a political target. One event that later came back to trouble him happened in 1811 after he had entered into a partnership with Horace Green and Joseph Coleman. The three men intended to make some quick money by transporting commodities from Nashville to Natchez. In 1810 they had profited from the sale of cotton and tobacco and then bought slaves from Richard Epperson the next year. They paid $10,500 for the slaves, $2,500 of which was paid immediately with the rest payable in two six-month installments. What happened next is unclear, but Jackson somehow became responsible for the entire debt. He traveled to Natchez to get the slaves, brought them back to Nashville, and sold them to pay off the loan. This transaction only came to light because Boyd McNairy, a candidate for elector in Tennessee, acquired several of Jackson's bank books and released their contents. In 1828 he teamed with Andrew Erwin, a longtime opponent of Jackson, to publish a particularly noxious pamphlet that accused Old Hickory of "buying and selling slaves for profit."[1]

1. *National Journal*, May 1828, as quoted in Abdy, *Journal of a Residence*, 2:153–54 (quotation). The information for this and following paragraphs is taken from [Andrew Erwin], *A Brief Account of General Jackson's Dealings in Negroes, in a Series of Letters and Documents by his own Neighbors* (n.p., [1828]); [Andrew Erwin], *Gen. Jackson's Negro Speculations, and his Traffic in Human Flesh, examined and established by Positive Proof* (n.p., [1828]); [Andrew Erwin], *Supplement to Andrew Jackson's Negro Speculations* (n.p., [1828]); *National Banner and Nashville*

McNairy and Erwin's accusations were timed, of course, to have maximum political effect during the 1828 presidential campaign. The widening circle of eligible voters opened the door to more sensational methods of influencing public opinion. Instead of addressing genteel arguments to a few voters, newspaper editors made wide-ranging ad hominem arguments to stir up interest in the election. Personal attacks abounded in the 1828 campaign, with Andrew Jackson's supporters accusing John Quincy Adams of installing a billiard table in the White House, of being an aristocrat, and of pimping for the Russian tsar while ambassador. Adams's supporters responded by calling Jackson a "vain ignorant old man, a duellist, murderer, traitor, or traitor's traitor, cruel negro-trader, villainous intriguer, liar, scoundrel, blasphemer, + what not." Being called a slave trader was a powerful insult both inside and outside the South. It is a wonder that Jackson did not end up dueling or brawling with Erwin or McNairy over this assault on his honor.[2]

Jackson's defenders disputed the charges of slave trading. They claimed he had no knowledge of the slave purchase, never intended to speculate on any bondservants, and served only as security in case his associates defaulted on their payments. They pointed to the fact that Jackson was listed last in paperwork as proof of his tertiary involvement. Jackson's opponents scoffed at that defense. They accused him of buying out the interest of Coleman and Green so that he could take sole possession of the slaves and pocket all the profits. Erwin collected the evidence and published it in a series of pamphlets that were a pastiche of newspaper clippings and virulent personal attacks.

More revealing than the two sides' stories is the rhetoric used to describe slave traders. Jackson's opponents thought that his actions disqualified him from the nation's highest office. Erwin accused Jackson of dissembling in an attempt to avoid being assigned "the character of a negro trader." He connected speculation in slaves with other immoral activities such as slander,

---

Whig, August 5, 1828; *Nashville Republican and State Gazette*, August 8, 1828; Robert V. Remini, *Andrew Jackson and the Course of American Empire, 1787–1821* (New York, 1977), 162–64; James Parton, *Life of Andrew Jackson*, 2 vols. (Boston, 1860) 1:353–60.

2. Calderhead, "Role of the Professional Slave Trader," 205–206; A. W. Putnam to Peter Force, September 14, 1828, in Emil Edward Hurja Collection, Peter Force Materials, Box 8, Folder 25, TSLA (quotation); Robert V. Remini, *Andrew Jackson and the Course of American Freedom, 1822–1832* (New York, 1981), 116–42; Sellers, *Market Revolution*, 298; Norma Basch, "Marriage, Morals, and Politics in the Election of 1828," *Journal of American History* 80 (1993): 890–918.

hypocritical behavior, disrespect for the law, torture of slaves, and prevarication. Erwin was not alone. In appealing to the "public morals" of the nation, the *Frederick Political Examiner* believed Jackson "disgraced himself" because he was seen with a "*drove of negroes.*" Any man who would "trade in *human flesh* for gain" could not be trusted. Jackson's critics were careful not to object to the possession of slaves or even their sale; instead they emphasized the deliberate speculation. If Jackson would exploit the slaves without a second thought, his critics reasoned, then he was unfit to govern. These charges were closely related to the belief that Jackson was a tyrant who could not be trusted with the reins of government. After all, if he acted so reprehensibly towards his slaves, his opponents shuddered to think what he might do while in office. They accused him, in essence, of being devoid of honor.[3]

Honor was a central tenet of southern society. It depended on reputation and the esteem of the community. Although a private concept, honor rested on public perception and was assumed to be a reflection of a person's true character. A challenge to an individual's honor, then, was a way to call into question his essential nature. Southerners were quick to defend any assaults upon their character, and so honor was a means to uphold the particular moral code of the South. In this case, southerners used the honor code to exclude and dishonor blacks in what historians have described as a "herrenvolk democracy." The notion that any white person, no matter his station, was superior to an African American person served as a unifying principle in the South. The concept of honor, however, could also function as a means of protection for slaves in a variety of circumstances. Masters were expected to possess a modicum of respect for slaves' basic human rights. Such respect, of course, was to be manifested in the public realm rather than in the private one, thus allowing and even encouraging private exploitation of bondservants. In public, at least, southerners were uncomfortable with the open degradation of slaves brought on by the interstate slave trade. Speculation laid bare the contradiction between the unrealistic assumptions of a paternalistic honor code and the blunt reality of slavery.[4]

3. Greenberg, *Honor and Slavery;* [Erwin], *Brief Account*, 15–18 (first quotation on 17); [Erwin], *Supplement*, 1–8; undated *Frederick Political Examiner*, as reprinted in *Genius of Universal Emancipation*, June 21, 1828, 139 (remaining quotations, emphasis in original).

4. Wyatt-Brown, *Southern Honor;* Greenberg, *Honor and Slavery;* Oakes, *Slavery and Freedom*, 14–16; George M. Fredrickson, *The Black Image in the White Mind: The Debate on Afro-American Character and Destiny, 1817–1914* (New York, 1971), 61–71; George M. Fredrickson, *The Arrogance of Race: Historical Perspectives on Slavery, Racism, and Social Inequality* (Mid-

This uncomfortable intrusion of reality can be seen in a political cartoon designed to attack Jackson in the 1828 campaign in Kentucky. The cover of one of Erwin's pamphlets about Jackson as a slave trader showed Old Hickory, in an exaggerated military uniform, beating a slave with a stick, while other bondservants trudged away in a coffle. A common way to challenge honor in the South was to point out the difference between a person's public persona and his real life and actions. In this case, Erwin accused Jackson of projecting a paternalistic shell to conceal his evil deeds. Since honor and power were intimately related, Jackson's lack of honor disqualified him from holding power.[5]

Jackson's defenders were dismayed with the label of slave trader. The charge was an "infamous falsehood" and an "odious" accusation made for purely political purposes, according to the *Nashville Republican and State Gazette.* Jackson had no choice but to go to Natchez to get the slaves because, being an honorable man, he wanted to pay his debts. He did so out of compulsion, he claimed, and "not with a view of *profit.*" The paper made a distinction that most southerners would have understood: Jackson did not act selfishly to make money, but rather he defended his reputation and his honor. The difference between a private citizen and a slave trader was that the former was relying on just motives, whereas the latter was acting from personal gain and the love of money. "Wilberforce" made this distinction even clearer in his defense of Jackson. He noted that the "serious" charge of slave trading came late in the election so that a full refutation of it would be difficult. This accusation was "justly odious" and entailed more than the "mere owning and employing of slaves." Anyone who would destroy bondservants' lives in order to profit from the master-slave relationship was a "monster in human shape." Jackson, whose slaves "venerated and almost idolized" him, never intended to sell bondservants for profit in a "distant market." Instead, he brought them back to Nashville where they would be treated kindly. Jackson, in other words, was doing the slaves a favor by shielding them from the whims of speculation. "Wilberforce" successfully turned the argument inside out. If Old Hickory intended to speculate in slaves, then he would have kept them in Natchez and sold them there. That Jackson escorted the bondservants back to Nashville was convincing evidence that he spared them from the degradation of the slave market. Jack-

---

dletown, Conn., 1988), 138–41; Ariela J. Gross, *Double Character: Slavery and Mastery in the Antebellum Southern Courtroom* (Princeton, 2000), 47–71.

5. [Erwin], *Brief Account,* cover; Greenberg, *Honor and Slavery.*

son thus was a hero because he rescued the bondservants from being sold down the river.[6]

"Wilberforce's" vigorous defense of Jackson the slave trader proved effective. Old Hickory did not become known as a slave trader, because most people thought he was selling the slaves from personal rather than speculative motives. It made no sense for a professional slave trader to bring the slaves from Natchez to Nashville. Had Jackson wanted to obtain the best price for the slaves, he would have sold them in Natchez. One of Jackson's strong supporters in Mississippi wrote his colleague in Washington that those with "reasonable minds" knew that there was not enough evidence to make the allegations stick in the South. He acknowledged, however, that the accusations "must strike a death blow to his prospects among the religious, moral & respectable & intelligent people of the northern states." He might have added that the people of the northern states were unable to understand the fine distinctions between a private citizen selling a slave and a speculator who made his living from such transactions. They assumed that anyone who sold slaves could be lumped in with speculators because it was impossible, or pointless, to differentiate between attitudes and actions.[7]

The issue of Jackson being a speculator demonstrates how the evolving interstate slave trade soon made the term "slave trader" an insult in the South. As a speculative market thrived, more and more white southerners distanced themselves from the commerce. In response, speculators took great pains to overcome negative associations with the trade's brutal elements: coffles, chains, jails, armed guards, escapes, and self-mutilations. Such sights disgusted most northerners and foreigners visiting the South, as well as a growing number of southerners. Traders sometimes made compromises with slaves, such as inducements to behave properly, even as they made crucial changes to their business to make it more palatable for southerners. To convince a skeptical public that the slave trade was beneficial to the South and that slaves were grateful for its existence, speculators softened

6. *Nashville Republican and State Gazette*, August 8, 1828 (first, second, third, fourth quotations, emphasis in original); *National Banner and Nashville Whig*, August 5, 1828 (remaining quotations); *Lexington Kentucky Gazette*, August 29, November 7, 1828; *Lexington Kentucky Reporter*, October 1, 1828.

7. A. W. Putnam to Peter Force, September 14, 1828, in Emil Edward Hurja Collection, Peter Force Materials, Box 28, Folder 25 (quotations); *Raleigh Star and North Carolina State Gazette*, September 4, 1828; *Natchez Ariel*, May 10, 1828; *Woodville Republican*, October 28, 1828.

some of its harsh features. They established routines and practices for the interstate slave trade that made it a normal and accepted part of the southern economy and culture. Speculators especially cultivated the stereotype that there were different kinds of slave traders, namely, good and bad ones. In this scenario, the "bad" traders became responsible for the worst features of speculation, while the "good" traders merely facilitated the exchange of bondservants, serving as benign middlemen in a trade that brought benefits to whites and blacks.

Traders used many techniques to improve the image of their business. They cleaned up and expanded their private jails, lessening their dependence on public jails, the use of which was a particularly odious practice in the Upper South. Bondservants could wait for weeks in crowded jails, drawing significant protest from local citizens. Locating the slave pens on private property away from the city meant that whites had less exposure to the sights, sounds, and smells of coffles. Setting up a depot for the collection of slaves also meant that traders could be readily located. By 1830 slave pens had gained enough notoriety that they became a tourist attraction for curious foreigners and opponents of slavery who wanted to examine them firsthand.[8]

The movement of slaves out of public places and into private jails enabled speculators to conceal the worst actions and glaring abuses of the slave trade, thus making it more palatable to southerners. Their credo seemed to be "out of sight, out of mind." Now traders could move their coffles at night, since they were not dependent on the schedule of the local sheriff. Many speculators made it a habit to start their southward trek long after most people were in bed. Woolfolk, who transported the majority of his slaves in the coastwise trade, waited until after dusk to move his bondservants from his pen to the ship. A curious observer learned that the trader did so to prevent Baltimore's residents from seeing the horror of coffles. Woolfolk was not the only trader to hide the seamier side of speculation. Since the trade was offensive to a "large portion of the community," according to a group opposed to slavery, it was difficult to obtain "details" of it. Speculation was also

8. July Term of the Grand Jury of Baltimore, 1816, Select Committee . . . on the Illegal Traffic in Slaves; undated *Baltimore American,* as quoted in the *Genius of Universal Emancipation,* March 1822, 441–42, March 1834, 39–40; Bancroft, *Slave Trading,* 23–24; Abdy, *Journal of a Residence,* 2:179–80; Andrews, *Domestic Slave-Trade,* 135–143; Joseph Sturge, *A Visit to the United States in 1841* (London, 1842), 85.

partially concealed in the nation's capital. J. M. McKim visited slave jails in the District of Columbia and found out to his "horror" that the slaves were "awakened *at night* to set out on their southern journey." This movement of slaves at night was also a boon to those speculators who sold persons who had been kidnapped. These traders hurried free persons off in the night in the midst of slave coffles so that the victims could not protest to any spectators. The great irony is that as speculation became more ubiquitous, slave traders worked hard to make it invisible. This emphasis on stealth made it easier for southerners to deny the existence of a large interstate slave trade.[9]

Just as traders hid the objectionable sight of coffles from the public, they also tried to dissociate themselves from competitors who engaged in questionable business practices. Woolfolk worked hard to establish a reputation for fair business dealings. He was so effective that even a critic of slavery admitted that Woolfolk conducted himself so that there was "never any suspicion of unfairness" in his mode of acquiring slaves. Woolfolk was a savvy trader and knew that men who stayed in the trade for any length of time could not get away with shady dealings. Bacon Tait, an established speculator, advised George Kephart, who was just entering the business as one of Franklin and Armfield's agents, that "Trash and defective" slaves were "never permanently profitable." Tait drew a sharp contrast between short-term profits and long-term results. In advising Kephart to avoid questionable slaves, he noted that even if they were profitable, such sales "often recoil upon the vendor." Traders, then, knew they had to behave with a certain measure of propriety in order to establish a positive reputation.[10]

Traders consistently educated the public about the utility of speculation. The steady stream of visitors to Franklin and Armfield's pen in Alexandria provided the firm with the opportunity to proselytize the unbeliever. Since Franklin handled business in New Orleans and Natchez, Armfield did most of the entertaining in Alexandria. He never missed an opportunity to in-

9. Andrews, *Domestic Slave-Trade*, 80 (first and second quotations); *Liberator*, April 20, 1838 (remaining quotations, emphasis in original), March 11, 1836, 61; *Genius of Universal Emancipation*, January 2, 1827, 109; Blassingame, ed., *Slave Testimony*, 504; Joseph Allen to Theodore Parker, January 25, 1848, Theodore Parker Papers, Massachusetts Historical Society, Boston; Deposition of Francis Scott Key, April 22, 1816, Select Committee . . . on the Illegal Traffic in Slaves. Key's legal career and activism against slavery has been overshadowed by his authorship of the poem that became the words for the national anthem.

10. Andrews, *Domestic Slave-Trade*, 80 (first quotation); Conway, *Testimonies Concerning Slavery*, 22 (remaining quotations).

struct his guests on the values of both slavery and the interstate slave trade. In addition to using his "fine personal appearance" and "engaging and graceful manners" to win over skeptics, Armfield skillfully designed the visitors' experience at the slave jail to emphasize the basic decency of slave trading. On one such visit, the serious and the curious waited in a well-furnished room where they could sip wine. After a few pleasantries, which one guest thought was a way to buy time for workers to clean up the facility, visitors entered the jail itself, where numerous rooms held the slaves. All the chambers were clean and had fires to warm the slaves. Armfield had at least two intentions: to demonstrate how humane the slave trade could be, and to prove that speculators' nasty reputation was undeserved. He strove to persuade skeptics that he and, by implication, other traders treated slaves with decency. Franklin rivaled his junior partner in presenting the best possible interpretation of a dreadful business. A visitor to Franklin's office in Natchez could not quite comprehend what he saw. He described the slave trader as a "man of gentlemanly address." Franklin and the city's other slave traders were "not the ferocious, Captain Kidd looking fellows" he had imagined.[11]

While visitors sat in the parlors of slave pens and sipped wine, the speculators had ample opportunity to review the benefits of their business. Traders actively sought to create a positive image for the interstate slave trade. One strategy was to promote the idea that they did the South a favor by removing difficult slaves. Woolfolk, for instance, frequently mentioned how he did Maryland residents a favor by purchasing difficult slaves. Such an idea had its limits, of course, since these slaves had to go somewhere and those states that imported them sometimes felt as though they were dumping grounds for malcontents. Upper South residents did begin to understand the utility of the slave trade, as an incident with Benjamin Lundy demonstrates. Lundy, an agitator for the abolition of slavery, published one of the earliest periodicals dedicated to the overthrow of the peculiar institution, the *Genius of Universal Emancipation.* Although he began publication in Greenville, Tennessee, he moved his operation to Baltimore to expand his readership and influence. Once in Baltimore, Lundy came across Woolfolk and was chagrined at the quick growth of his slave-trading operations. Lundy remained unconvinced by the trader's talk and blasted him as a

11. Andrews, *Domestic Slave-Trade,* 136 (first and second quotations); Ingraham, *South-West by a Yankee,* 2:245 (remaining quotations); Abdy, *Journal of a Residence,* 2:179; Brown, *Narrative of William Wells Brown,* 53.

"monster in human shape" and a "soul seller." The thin-skinned Woolfolk detested the descriptions because, besides being personal insults, they associated him with the worst portions of the trade. When the two men met on a Baltimore street in 1827, their encounter quickly degenerated into an argument and a shoving match. Woolfolk threw the much smaller Lundy to the ground and beat him about the head before several bystanders intervened. Lundy charged Woolfolk with assault, to which the trader pleaded guilty. The judge found Lundy's extreme rhetoric distasteful, noting that the terms "slave trader" and "soul seller" were offensive. Rather than concluding the obvious—that Woolfolk *was* a slave trader—he ruled that Lundy provoked Woolfolk with abusive language. In issuing a one-dollar fine, the judge called the interstate slave trade an economic benefit to Maryland that "removed a great many rogues and vagabonds who were a nuisance in the state."[12]

Even as Woolfolk aggressively defended himself, Armfield calmly handled all challenges to his character and business practices. An English visitor, concerned about the mistreatment and physical abuse of slaves, bluntly asked about the methods of discipline employed in the jail. Armfield assured him that no dungeon or thumbscrews existed in his slave pen. Although Armfield may have answered the question literally, it is clear that slave traders used various methods of physical punishment to coerce slaves. Likewise, Hope Slatter, when challenged about the evil consequences of the slave trade, replied that the law permitted speculation. He added that he was willing "to have the system abolished" if suitably compensated for his loss. Besides, Slatter concluded correctly, "dealing in slaves was not worse than slaveholding." These traders were able to present the slave trade in a positive light. Rather than being roughnecks on horseback who rudely escorted gangs of shackled slaves, they were sophisticated professionals who performed a vital service.[13]

The context in which a person encountered a slave trader, moreover, made a difference, and that is why traders worked hard to control their

12. *Genius of Universal Emancipation*, August 26, 1826, 406, January 20, 1827, 25–26, February 24, 1827, 142–43, March 31, 1827, 174; Dillon, *Benjamin Lundy*, 104–20 (quotations); Henry Mayer, *All on Fire: William Lloyd Garrison and the Abolition of Slavery* (New York, 1998), 76; Calderhead, "Role of the Professional Slave Trader," 205–206.

13. Abdy, *Journal of a Residence*, 2:180; Fredrika Bremer, *Homes of the New World: Impressions of America*, trans. Mary Howitt, 2 vols. (New York, 1854), 2:533–35; Sturge, *Visit to the United States*, 31–32 (quotations).

image. George Featherstonhaugh, an English geologist, traveled across the United States in 1834. He met a man who overwhelmed him with a "farrago of bad grammar." The individual was a "compound of everything vulgar and revolting, and totally without education." When the man left, Featherstonhaugh asked his stagecoach driver about the barbarian. The driver responded that it was John Armfield, the celebrated slave trader. Featherstonhaugh concluded that Armfield's "abominable vocation" was the key to his manners and expressions. He was only partly correct. Armfield's occupation was vital to Featherstonhaugh's perception, not Armfield's personality. Featherstonhaugh's extremely negative portrayal of Armfield starkly contrasted with those by visitors to Franklin and Armfield's slave pen. The Englishman had recently encountered his first slave coffle and was certainly no friend of slavery. Many of those who praised Armfield, however, were also abolitionists who had no reason to find good qualities in the man. The primary difference was the context in which Armfield appeared. In his slave pen he was able to pose as a charming and suave gentleman. On the road, since Featherstonhaugh immediately associated Armfield with a slave coffle, he seemed to be rude, uncivilized, and totally devoid of all honor. As we have seen, moreover, the larger traders employed agents to handle the nastier portions of the business. In doing so, men like Woolfolk, Franklin, and Armfield could appear to be untainted by the trade's excesses. Agents, while necessary for business, also served as a layer of protection from specific objections to the trade. Armfield, in private correspondence, snickered at how the Louisiana trade ban caused two "Land pirats" to get stuck with one hundred slaves they could not sell. The sneering reference to "Land pirats" was a way to distinguish himself from traders who had to escort their slaves to Louisiana. Slave trader Seraphim Cucullu shared the same attitude as Armfield. The irony here is that Armfield was in the same business as his two unfortunate colleagues. When asked about a slave sold in his name, he replied contemptuously, "See those gentlemen, I have nothing to do with that," pointing to the men he hired to sell the slaves on commission. Established traders worked to create a gulf between themselves and the legions of roving agents. The latter labored just as assiduously to span the divide. Speculators wanted to be regarded as useful businessmen rather than as money-grubbing traders.[14]

14. Featherstonhaugh, *Excursion through the Slave States*, 46 (description of Armfield); Seraphim Cucullu as quoted in Walter L. Johnson, "Masters and Slaves in the Market of

Theodore Dwight Weld was one person who looked at slavery from the outside and was perceptive enough to realize that there was a difference between an established slave trader and one who was an agent or an itinerant dealer. Weld mocked this idea, though, for he thought slavery indelibly stained all who touched it. He noticed how "some 'gentleman of property and standing' and of a 'good family'" embarked in speculation by paying "soul drivers" to move slave coffles to the Lower South. Even though such a person was responsible for the forced migration of slaves, he did not "lose caste." Weld listed several prominent southerners connected with the slave trade, noting that a member of the Kentucky Senate accompanied a coffle, "Not as the *driver*, for that would be vulgar drudgery, beneath a gentleman, but as a nabob in state, ordering his understrappers." Weld sarcastically added that the "wholesale soul-seller doubtless despises the retail 'soul-drivers' who give him their custom." Even though Weld mocked the idea that there was any difference between slave traders, he recognized that many southerners ascribed to the belief. He was familiar enough with slavery to know that speculators successfully used various methods to put some distance between themselves and the trade.[15]

Weld elaborated on his theory a few years later when he collaborated with James Thome on another attack on slavery. This time he pointed out the difference between soul-drivers, slave traders, and speculators. Weld placed them into two classes, one of which had the large "factories" in Alexandria, Baltimore, Norfolk, Richmond, and Petersburg. Traders who stayed at their headquarters and sent out agents to gather slaves could put a kindly façade on their involvement in the inhuman portions of speculation. These men of large capital "conduct the traffic on the broadest scale." They held an "honorable rank among the heavy capitalists and extensive merchants of our southern cities" and moved in the highest social circles. The other class of slave traders consisted of the "agents and pimps" of the first group. They were "constantly scouring the breeding states" for slaves to put on ships or in coffles. Those who drove coffles or could not afford to employ underlings were also in this category. Such men were "doubtless horribly base wretches of vile origin, and viler lives." Speculators like Franklin, Armfield, and Woolfolk could be accepted in southern society because they did not *appear*

Slavery and the New Orleans Trade, 1804–1864" (Ph.D. diss., Princeton University, 1995), 35.

15. Weld, *American Slavery as It Is*, 174 (emphasis in original).

to be slave traders. They seemed to be professionals who merely facilitated the transfer of slaves from one individual to another. It was the use of agents or employees of such men who suffered the indignities associated with being labeled a trader. Naturally it was the ambition of most of the small scale traders to join the ranks of their larger fellows. Not only was it financially rewarding, it was socially more acceptable. Even the example of Andrew Jackson attests to the belief in a type of slave-trading hierarchy. Jackson's friends did their best to minimize his personal contact with the slaves. His opponents did the opposite; they emphasized his close affiliation with coffles, even using a picture as a visual reminder. It was as if the continual exposure to bondspeople and cash nexus of speculation was a contaminating agent to those who dealt with both simultaneously.[16]

Besides conducting a public relations campaign and using agents as a buffer from criticism, the large traders also distanced themselves from the illegal kidnapping of slaves. Joshua Leavitt, who campaigned actively against slavery, visited Franklin and Armfield's pen in an effort to study the slave trade firsthand. He asked Armfield if any slaves sold in the interstate trade were kidnapped. Leavitt likely hoped to amass ammunition for use in attacking slavery and the interstate trade. Armfield was too clever to fall into the trap, so he did not deny that abductions happened. He quickly pointed out that every business was "cursed with mean fellows," subtly distancing himself from the illegal portion of the trade and from smaller speculators. Armfield went on to assure his visitor that he had done everything in his power to prevent such things. He explained that he and Franklin conducted their business affairs "in such a way that gentlemen who traded with their house should always know whom they dealt with." Leavitt then tried to ambush Armfield by producing evidence that two men on one of the firm's ships had been sold improperly. Although he must have been shocked, Armfield kept his composure. Such a predicament might have undermined the trader's claim to strict business practices against buying kidnapped slaves. In looking closely at the matter, Armfield admitted a mistake in the purchase of the men, took them off the ship, and sent them back to Maryland. Leavitt may have found evidence for his accusations, but Armfield successfully defended his personal honesty. The speculator was willing to sacrifice the profit on two men to preserve the firm's reputation.[17]

16. Weld and Thome, *Slavery and the Internal Slave Trade*, 67–68 (quotations); Edmund L. Drago, ed., *Broke by the War: Letters of a Slave Trader* (Columbia, S.C., 1991).

17. *Genius of Universal Emancipation*, March 1834, 39–41.

Armfield was not the only slave trader who claimed he prevented the kidnapping of slaves. Woolfolk reputedly turned in traders who bought kidnapped slaves. Two visitors to Slatter's slave pen in Baltimore brought an activist against slave kidnapping. Slatter heartily endorsed the man's activities. The guests then confronted Slatter about two of his slaves who were actually free men. When challenged about their status, he swore out a complaint against the sellers and had the men released. Slatter, being a keen businessman, hoped to insulate himself from the suspicion of illegal activity while also trying to get his money back from a fraudulent sale. James McFall tried to separate himself from any association with the kidnapping trade when he advertised that all his sales were "executed conformable to law, accompanied with *legal vouchers, guarantees, &c.*" Likewise, Samuel Dawson would buy only slaves of "sound Property and good titles." Advertisements of this nature served two purposes. They deterred shady transactions even while being an effective means of public relations. Whether or not speculators actually intended to adhere to their promises was questionable. They did, however, want to convince a skeptical public that they would. Southerners needed to be convinced that traders conducted their business with probity.[18]

Another way traders restored their tarnished image was to pretend to keep slave families together. Armfield patiently explained to his guests that his firm went to great pains to prevent family separations. Slatter also tried to convince people that he did not break up families. He made the fanciful claim that slaves came to him and asked to be purchased so that they could go to a good master who would respect the integrity of their household. Slatter told visitors that slaves in his care were "treated kindly." Stories circulated that Woolfolk's slaves gathered around him in a display of affection "and even the little children manifest the most eager solicitude to share in his affections." Such an attitude on the part of slaves would have shocked Frederick Douglass had it been true. He equated all slave traders with the name Woolfolk and understood all too well that being put on the open market was equivalent to a death sentence. That bondspeople treated specula-

18. *Genuis of Universal Emancipation*, August 26, 1826, 406; Sturge, *Visit to the United States*, 31; undated *Baltimore Sun*, as quoted in *Liberator*, November 17, 1837, 185; *New Orleans Louisiana Advertiser*, January 10, 1834 (first quotation, emphasis in original); *Fredericksburg Virginia Herald*, April 19, 1826 (second quotation); *Washington Daily National Intelligencer*, May 7, 1816; *Baltimore American*, June 14, 1825.

tors as some type of celebrity is absurd, but what is almost as surprising is the notion that southerners would entertain it as a possibility. Traders used these fairy tales to make the argument that they somehow did not impinge on the paternalistic expectations of southerners.[19]

Although undoubtedly traders overemphasized their decency and sophistication, at least Franklin and Armfield changed their buying practices to blunt criticism of the trade. Statistical evidence shows that Armfield, who handled the purchases in Alexandria, bought more slaves in family units after 1834. The percentage of slaves in family units rose from just over 7 percent in 1828–29 to nearly ten times that figure in 1835. Armfield explained the reasons for the change to Leavitt. The speculator said he recently purchased about twenty children who were under ten years of age. He bought them all from one estate and pledged to keep them together. Armfield tried to convince his visitor that they would "fetch a higher price in market" if sold together. In reality, the value of slaves dropped if they were sold in family units because purchasers frequently had to buy slaves they did not want and were able to negotiate a lower price. Thus, on the face of it, Armfield was deceiving his visitor. What is important, though, is that he recognized the long-term benefit of persuading the public of his good intentions. Once word spread that Franklin and Armfield bought slave families, they would be in a better position to bargain with planters who were reluctant to part with their slaves for fear they were exiling the bondservants to a fate worse than death. Armfield promised Leavitt that he "never" sold slaves "so as to separate husband and wife, or mother and child." He neglected to mention that his partner normally handled the sales, so the number of slaves he actually sold was negligible. Armfield, as the director of the firm's slave-buying efforts in the Chesapeake, was able to put enough distance between himself and speculation that his reputation remained intact.[20]

Other slave traders went to extreme lengths to show they did not separate families. When Joseph Ingraham visited a slave pen in Natchez, a planter offered a high price for a slave girl but did not want to purchase her

19. Sturge, *Visit to the United States*, 31 (first quotation); Andrews, *Domestic Slave-Trade*, 81 (second quotation); Preston, *Young Frederick Douglass*, 76.

20. Sweig, "Northern Virginia Slavery," 220–23; Donald M. Sweig, "Reassessing the Human Dimensions of the Interstate Slave Trade," *Prologue* 12 (1980): 5–21; *Genius of Universal Emancipation*, March 1834, 39 (quotations); Tadman, *Speculators and Slaves*, 52–55.

sister. The trader refused to make the sale because, as he explained, "when their mother died I promised her I would not part them." It is likely the speculator was playing the part of a benevolent despot rather than truly seeking to honor a pledge he made to the mother. The thought of a trader actually refusing money because of a promise made to a deceased slave was ludicrous. What was most important to him in this instance was the appearance of preserving families. He probably hoped his visitor would make favorable comments about the slave market. Once the northern visitor left, there would be ample time to find buyers for the two girls. Some traders, though, seem to have sensed that they could not convince a skeptical public they kept families together. One left himself a way out of his contention that he preserved slave ties. He often broke up families because "his business is to purchase, and he must take such as are in the market!" In other words, forces beyond his control were to blame for family separations.[21]

Slave traders who claimed to protect the integrity of slave families were trying to forestall abolitionist criticism of the slave trade in general and disapproval of their operations in particular. Abolitionists insisted that slavery's brutality was tied in large part to its ravages on the slave family. In an effort to squelch such protests, slave traders changed their marketing strategy. Doing so also served as an antidote to the testimony of former slaves who suffered family separation. Countless slave narratives of the nineteenth century recounted the agony of bondspeople who became the property of speculators. Should traders plausibly differentiate themselves from association with such stories, then they could discredit the slaves. Creating the perception that slaves exaggerated for effect could be a powerful way to mitigate the growing abolitionist movement.

As traders worked hard to dissociate themselves from their reputation for destroying slave families, they deemphasized the speculative aspects of the slave trade. In doing so, they took on the trappings of a planter. For instance, an anonymous advertiser in a Richmond paper promised to pay a higher price for slaves "that have been raised together on one farm, as they are not wanted for speculation." The intention here was to spend a little more money to buy slaves in families and keep them together rather than use them for speculative gain. Traders tried to tap into this sentiment.

21. Ingraham, *South-West by a Yankee*, 2:203 (first quotation); Winfield H. Collins, *The Domestic Slave Trade of the Southern States* (New York, 1904), 104; *Liberator*, March 5, 1836, 39 (second quotation).

Edwin Lee, a well-known trader in Norfolk, advertised that he wanted to buy ten to fifteen young bondservants for an estate in the Southwest. Abner Robinson tried the same tactic, advertising in Richmond for forty to sixty slaves. They were for a New Orleans resident who wanted them for his own use, with Robinson adding that "Satisfactory assurance can be given, that they will not be bought for re-sale." This strategy of arranging sales for a specific buyer, whether it be genuine or not, enabled speculators to pose as brokers. The very fact that traders mentioned the particular circumstances surrounding a purchase such as this indicates that they assumed it would give them an edge in the highly competitive world of slave buying. Instead of wantonly purchasing slaves, they could be viewed as arranging a transaction with the goal of satisfying a specific individual rather than speculating on the price of bondservants. Traders who used this tactic hoped that owners who might not normally deal with them would be persuaded to part with their slaves if they knew the bondservants were going to a specific owner rather than out on the speculative market. They also tried to modify any public perception that traders were becoming too prevalent and enticing owners to give in to the temptation to speculation. Once owners convinced themselves that selling to a speculator did not lead to personal corruption, they could sell slaves without regret.[22]

Traders appear to have been effective in putting the best face possible on a sickening business. One writer grew so weary of speculators' proclaiming their virtue that he mocked their false sensitivity to the slaves and masters' dissembling. When he read that a man sent $16,000 worth of slaves to Liberia he could hardly believe his eyes. Without firsthand knowledge as to the truth, he would have thought the "story was fabricated by some pious negro-seller" on the James River. It was there, he said sarcastically, that "humane breeders" send "eight thousand black cattle" annually out of the state. Lundy, too, commented on the pervasiveness of the slave traders' posturing. In examining Woolfolk's tactics he deduced that most Baltimore residents disliked the abominable business. Woolfolk, though, deliberately put on "the guise of humanity" and pretended to be "a great stickler for fair and

22. *Richmond Enquirer*, July 12, 1825 (first quotation); *Norfolk American Beacon*, March 30, 1820; *Richmond Enquirer*, December 10, 1831 (second quotation); *Baltimore American*, September 12, 1815, February 20, September 7, September 9, September 25, 1822, November 9, 1824; *Easton Republican Star*, May 18, 1824; *Princess Anne Village Herald*, September 14, 1830, as quoted in Bancroft, *Slave Trading*, 32.

legal dealing." Some of his tricks included turning in kidnappers, courting the favor of slavery opponents, and treating his slaves fairly well. By these means, he duped many an unsuspecting person. On another occasion, Lundy deplored Woolfolk's "despicable canting" and mocked the speculator's "sham '*humanity*.'" Woolfolk and other slave traders realized that since they were in an objectionable business, and one that relied on the good faith of the seller for high profits, they must work for the esteem of the community. By turning in kidnappers, pretending to keep families together, and bragging how good they were, traders separated themselves from illegal activity and, by extension, established their personal honesty. A few noteworthy and well-publicized incidents went a long way towards reducing hostility towards the trade. When they advertised their intention to serve as a type of broker rather than a speculator, they helped allay any remaining doubts. Franklin, Armfield, Woolfolk, and slave traders of their ilk transformed the interstate slave trade from its sporadic beginnings to its place as the lifeblood of the expanding South. They also helped effect a change in opinions toward speculation from initial skepticism to grudging acceptance.[23]

Even though traders softened southern attitudes towards speculation, being called a slave trader was still something most southern citizens wished to avoid. David Settle Reid learned this lesson when he ran for governor of North Carolina. The former United States congressman was accustomed to political attacks, but the accusation of speculation caught his supporters by surprise. The local paper in Craven County, the *Newbernian*, castigated Reid for voting for the Wilmot Proviso, opposing internal improvements, and being a slave trader. It wondered whether Democrats in the area were "snowed under" by "their Wilmot Proviso, anti-Newbern Railroad, negro-trading candidate." Reid's brother-in-law, Samuel F. Adams, moved quickly to minimize the damage. He confronted the newspaper's editor because Reid had never been a slave trader. Adams demanded a retraction. The editor apologized profusely and explained that some of his political friends supplied the erroneous information. He said it was "known to everyone" that Reid had a brother in eastern North Carolina who bought slaves "on specu-

23. *Western Luminary*, January 19, 1831, 322 (first three quotations); *Genius of Universal Emancipation*, August 26, 1826, 406 (fourth and fifth quotations, emphasis in original); Dillon, *Benjamin Lundy*, 34–54; *Genius of Universal Emancipation*, January 2, 1827, 109 (sixth and seventh quotations, emphasis in original).

lation." The natural assumption was that Reid was part of the business. The retraction soon followed. "So much for that thrashing machine," Adams told Reid proudly. The *Newbernian*'s editor printed an apology the next week. He explained it was a "common rumor" that Reid had bought and sold slaves for profit. The paper carefully distinguished between different types of slave sales and implied that "negro speculation" was worse than the mere selling of slaves.[24]

Traders had successfully created a caste system of speculation that the public eagerly adopted. Jackson's experience is helpful in analyzing the slave trader's place in southern society. Theodore Parker, in reading two antislavery publications, noticed the allegations against Jackson. One boldly proclaimed that it was well known that Old Hickory was a "soul driver" and that he escorted a coffle of slaves to Louisiana for sale. Parker accepted the accusations at face value and wrote a letter accusing Jackson of being a slave trader. The issue quickly became the topic of a public dispute. Parker, realizing that his reputation was at stake, fired off a letter to James Birney, a former slaveholder who moved north and became a dedicated abolitionist. He wanted to know specifically if Jackson ever sold a slave, if he had engaged in the slave trade, and if he brought a coffle of slaves to Louisiana. Birney, choosing his words carefully, did not defend Jackson's actions but could not describe Old Hickory as a slave trader. All people of influence in the South were slaveholders or came from slaveholding families, and as a consequence, all have sold, exchanged, or bought slaves, Birney explained. Jackson was no exception, and the fact that he had fewer slaves at his death than might be expected demonstrates that he sold some of them. Even though Jackson sold slaves, Birney thought that calling him a slave trader "according to slave-holding idiom" was an improper use of the term. However, "were I to say of him, that he dealt in slaves, without any conscientious restraint, *whenever he chose*—or that he was an *occasional* slave dealer, I should not regard myself as departing more from the truth."[25]

Birney used his musings about Jackson to instruct Parker on the place of

24. *New Bern Newbernian*, July 9, 1850, July 16, 1850; Samuel F. Adams to David Settle Reid, July 11, 1850, David Settle Reid Papers, NCDAH.

25. Weld, *American Slavery as It Is*, 174 (first quotation); Weld and Thome, *Slavery and the Internal Slave Trade*, 68; *Boston Post*, June 14, 1848; Theodore Parker to James Birney, June 17, 1848, and July 5, 1848 (remaining quotations, emphasis in original), Theodore Parker Papers.

the slave trade in southern society. In reflecting on his life there twenty years earlier, Birney admitted that it was "a difficult matter" for someone who had not lived in the South to "come precisely at what is meant *there* by Slave-dealer or Slave-trader." There was a "discernible difference" between the two, with the latter being "more obnoxious." It was the slave trader who had "no other business by which he makes his living than buying up slaves to sell again." He should not be confused with a "reputable" southerner who "occasionally" sold a slave for the highest price. Such a person had another occupation that defined him. Selling slaves was only of secondary importance to this person. He should not be identified as a slave trader, "a word of no small reproach at the South," according to Birney.[26]

To make his point as clearly as possible, Birney borrowed the example of gambling. A man with a reputable calling may gamble and not be called a gambler, unlike the man who made gambling the basis of his livelihood. Just like the distinction between a slave dealer and a slave trader, the line was often indistinct. Most southerners understood the difference between a professional gambler and a social gamester. Birney noted that southern states passed strict laws against the former but ignored the latter. The assumption was that the professionals subverted the process by manipulating the terms of the contest. Cheating could find no home in the South's stringent honor code. It violated the sense of order and propriety upon which the southern society depended.[27]

A similar point could be made about the men who bought and sold slaves in the South. Insisting on distinctions between different types of speculators was more than asserting a difference without a distinction. Here, the distinction of not being involved in the lowly activities of traders—manipulating the appearance of slaves or concealing the true nature of their past—was key. Those who were not traders could assert their genuine motives in a culture that often depended on a person's word. Even while the actions of a speculator and a private citizen may not have been appreciably different, the perceptions of them were worlds apart. Southerners wanted to believe that there was a small group of itinerant and underhanded traders who created most of the difficulties and who sold most of the bondspeople. It was this type of speculator, most thought, who destroyed slave families, escorted coffles, sold diseased slaves, concealed the flaws of bondservants,

26. Theodore Parker to James Birney, July 5, 1848, Theodore Parker Papers.

27. Wyatt-Brown, *Southern Honor*, 340–50.

and corrupted whites through speculation. All others who bought or sold slaves, even if they did so on a full-time basis, were innocent. That is how someone like Isaac Franklin avoided being classed as a slave trader. Speculators successfully parsed the negative perceptions of slave trading from their business because, in part, most southerners wanted them to do so.

There is evidence that slave traders knew they could not be fully accepted into society if they retained their association with speculation. When the Reverend John Jones refused to acknowledge the presence of a slave trader, the trader retaliated. As a stunned Jones recorded in 1825, "this dealer in human flesh rudely knocked off my hat, and began to abuse me for 'not speaking to a *gentleman.*'" Jones turned the other cheek, retrieved his hat, and rode off. Bacon Tait, who operated a slave jail in Richmond, also understood why a speculator could never attain full honor in the South. Tait wanted to quit the interstate slave trade and start a "negro auction & commission business." Buying and selling slaves on commission appealed to him because it could be conducted "with perfect fairness." Tait was trying to present himself as merely a go-between in the transfer of bondservants, as someone who was still worthy of respect. Once his slave auction was well established, he planned to phase in the sale of real estate and commercial goods. In this way, Tait could slowly disconnect himself from the speculative aspects of the slave trade. Traders relied on other subtle methods, as well. Pulliam and Company, well-known Richmond slave traders, even used its letterhead to educate customers about the finer points of speculators and traders. On a letter describing the Richmond slave market was the heading "Auctioneers for the Sale of Negroes, *Have no connection with the Negro Trade* THEY SELL ONLY ON COMMISSION." In disassociating themselves from speculation, traders hoped to prove their good intentions. They did not want to be known as men who profited from the pain of slaves, nor did they want the reputation of profit-takers. Slave traders were trying to have it both ways. On the one hand, they refused to admit that their profession was based on misery and money, but on the other they could hardly avoid the connection to profit taking. Slave traders tried to shed the skin of dishonorable activity and assume the guise of respectability.[28]

28. John G. Jones, "Autobiography," 75–76, manuscript in MDAH (first quotation, emphasis in original); Bacon Tait to Rice C. Ballard, January 14 (second and third quotations), January 31, 1838, Ballard Papers; Pulliam and Company letter, November 15, 1860, Negro Collection, DU (final quotation, emphasis in original).

Perceptions of the interstate slave trade changed during the first three decades of the nineteenth century. Speculators effectively countered bondservants' efforts to test the limits of slavery and undermine white authority. In the same way they asserted control over slave coffles, traders successfully uncoupled their activities from the more objectionable features of their business. They made their activities more palatable by concealing the offensive portions of the trade: coffles, kidnapping, and the separation of slave families. Traders also persistently lobbied to convince southern citizens that they merely facilitated slave sales rather than profited from them. As a result, the outrage over speculative activities declined, since the trade came to be seen as less about profit at slaves' expense and more about providing a service to slaveholders. Speculators reinforced this idea by cultivating the notion that there were different types of slave traders and that established speculators could be trusted while itinerant traders could not. The former, once they could effectively distance themselves from the stench of speculation, could attain a type of honorable position in the South. In short, speculators succeeded in shaping southern attitudes toward their profession. They did so during a rapid expansion of the interstate slave trade. Slave sales were more common, and more frequent exposure to slave auctions and coffles inured southerners to the suffering of bondservants. A mounting external threat, moreover, solidified this new attitude and gave rise to the ultimate justification for speculators' existence.

CHAPTER 7

Speculation Triumphant

On January 7, 1829, John C. Weems took the floor of the House of Representatives and offered up a systematic defense of the interstate slave trade. He vigorously rebutted the charges of Charles Miner, a representative from Pennsylvania, who graphically described the devastating effects of speculation. Some of Miner's more provocative allegations included slave pens infested with "vermin, disease, and misery," rampant kidnapping in Washington, and slaves left heartbroken and miserable. His ultimate conclusion was that the interstate slave trade justified legislating slavery. Weems knew he must speak up when Miner used the interstate slave trade as a justification for legislation that would restrict slavery's growth. In an effort to squelch what the *United States Gazette* called the "greatest excitement" of the session, Weems tactfully observed that his colleague's "mistaken zeal" had suppressed his "usual good judgment." The lengthy rebuttal was a turning point, because Weems responded with the first known public defense of the interstate slave trade by a citizen of the Upper South. His answer to Miner was a precursor of the arguments southerners would use throughout the 1830s and beyond in their defense of the interstate slave trade and of slavery. It is also indicative that Upper South attitudes about slavery and speculation were catching up to those in the Deep South.[1]

1. *Register of Debates,* 20th Cong., 2nd sess., 176 (first quotation); *Niles' Weekly Register,* January 10, 327–28, January 17, 340–41, February 7, 1829, 396; *Washington Daily National Intelligencer,* February 7, 1829, April 23, 1829; Clipping of *Washington United States Gazette,* January 8, 1829, John Agg Papers, DU (second quotation); *Register of Debates,* 20th Cong., 2nd sess., 181–86 (remaining quotations); Lightner, "Door to the Slave Bastille," 235–52;

Weems explained that slavery was so benign that masters rarely sold their slaves. On such occasions, slaveholders were not to blame. He used the circumstances surrounding the recent sale of a woman and her children to demonstrate his point. A free black man bought his family on credit but could not pay off the loan. The creditor did all he could, but had to sell the family to satisfy the obligation. Weems insinuated that market forces were to blame in such cases, especially since he personally intervened to prevent the sale. Nothing could be done, so the woman and children were sold to Georgia. This story had a happy ending, according to Weems. The woman wrote her spouse that she belonged to a "good and humane" master and was as happy as ever, "save the separation from her husband." The moral of the story was, of course, on the rare occasions when slaves happened to be sold south, their condition was improved. Weems was politely telling outsiders that they should not try to fix something that was not broken.[2]

Slavery's newest public apologist went further, however. He related the story of a colleague in Congress who wanted to buy several families of slaves for his sugar plantation, provided, of course, they were willing to move. Weems approached his brother, whose kind treatment of his slaves and low prices for crops had brought him to the point of unloading some of his land because he "could not bear the idea of selling his slaves." Weems persuaded his brother to sell twenty slaves in families. When asked if they would be willing to go, the bondservants "put up their thanks to God" even though they hated to leave their master. On the sale day, the slaves left "most cheerfully and happily." Weems's brother felt the opposite emotions. "He never recovered his feelings" and died a short time later, presumably of a broken heart. Weems explained that he took so much time clarifying this situation because he resented Miner's personal attacks. Slavery, if fully examined, was not objectionable. Moreover, Weems continued, the Bible supported slavery. He cited the curse of Ham, the fact that Old Testament patriarchs owned slaves, and Paul's admonition to Philemon to have mercy on a bondservant. Since slavery was part of the social fabric in both the Old Testament and the New Testament, Weems could not understand why someone would question it.

This maudlin description was standard fare for the defense of slavery, but

---

Lightner, "Interstate Slave Trade in Antislavery Politics," 119–36; Deyle, "Domestic Slave Trade," 144–210; Newman, *Transformation of American Abolitionism*, 50–51.

2. All of Weems's quotations in this and the following paragraphs are taken from *Register of Debates*, 20th Cong., 2nd sess., 181–86.

Weems also exonerated slave traders of wrongdoing. There might be "some truth" to Miner's description of the "dealers in human flesh," but not much. Speculators were "very useful citizens" because they purchased convict slaves and felonious free men and housed them in jail before starting south. Weems would rather see slaves in local jails than to have "worse than wild beasts of the forest, let loose amongst us." Lest representatives from Louisiana, Mississippi, and Alabama become alarmed, Weems was certain that the slave trade rehabilitated its participants. When bondservants realized they had no chance of escape, they became "more than usually valuable" and turned into "the most sprightly fellows." In Weems's hands, slave traders became a species of social workers who redeemed the dregs of society. He discounted any widespread destruction of slave families and denied that money motivated speculators. Instead of being detrimental to the South as Miner alleged, the slave trade was advantageous. As the capstone of his argument, Weems had used a creative interpretation of speculation but one that showed the transitional nature of southern thinking about the interstate slave trade. He did not decry speculation as his predecessors did, nor did he employ the stereotype of an evil, money-grubbing parasite as his successors would. As speculation came under increasing attack in the 1830s, southerners modified their defense of slavery by relying on a caricature of speculators. They exaggerated the supposed benefits of slave traders and softened their harsh features.

When Weems finished, Richard H. Wilde tried to end the discussion by moving the previous question. Moderate Ichabod Bartlett wanted to soothe matters and suggested Miner withdraw his preamble, which was the chief cause of trouble. When Miner declined, Mark Alexander moved to table the resolutions. His motion failed, 107 to 66. Even though the House agreed to move ahead, it did so cautiously. A subsequent vote to adopt the preamble lost by an even more lopsided margin. The House postponed any action on the matter by creating a committee to "inquire into the slave trade as it exists in, and is carried through, the District." It was reminiscent of the artful dodging that happened when John Randolph raised the issue thirteen years earlier. This resolution carried on the strength of northern representatives, although 18 southerners voted for it. All of these men, however, came from the slave-exporting states of Maryland (5), Delaware (1), Virginia (4), North Carolina (3), Tennessee (1), and Kentucky (4). A third resolution, to inquire into gradual abolition in the District of Columbia, failed 114 to 66. Only 11 representatives of slaveholding states, all of them slave-exporting states, sided with northern representatives in this vote. The willingness of Upper South congressmen to question the interstate slave trade or slavery was fading.[3]

The Committee for the District of Columbia reported its findings on the slave trade about a month later. Southerners controlled the committee, and the report reflected their influence. In a masterstroke of disingenuous language, the committee described the situation of slaves who were sold from Washington as being improved by moving to a "more genial and bountiful clime." Even though "violence may sometimes be done to their feelings," the laws of society could not be avoided. The representatives remained convinced that the slaves' condition was bettered and they became happier because of the interstate slave trade's rehabilitative effects. The report, rather than being a product of a thorough investigation, was a gloss of Weems's melodramatic performance.[4]

The debates surrounding Miner's proposal show that residents of the Upper South were rapidly changing their attitude about the interstate slave trade. Where they once ignored or questioned its harmful effects, they now explained and justified the trade's presence. Virginia decisively rejected a proposal to emancipate and deport its slaves in 1832, while colonization itself became a dead issue in the rest of the South. With no possibility of shedding slavery and no foreseeable solution to the problem of "excess" bondservants, the interstate slave trade became a more attractive option. Northerners, furthermore, were more strident in their demands to abolish slavery. They used the interstate slave trade as a powerful illustration of the institution's evil effects. With slavery penned in and under attack, southerners chose to defend it without reservation. Since many speculators consciously softened the sharp edges of the interstate slave trade, moreover, it was easier to explain away its presence. Southerners employed various methods, but the eventual result was a stereotype of itinerant slave traders, slaves, owners, and abolitionists. Moreover, southerners demonstrated a solid grasp of capitalism as they blamed market forces for circumstances beyond their control. They, in effect, had to deny the reality of the interstate slave trade before they could fully accept slavery.

Amid this climate of shifting beliefs, and in the wake of the Nat Turner

3. *Register of Debates*, 20th Cong., 2nd sess., 191–92; *Washington Daily National Intelligencer*, January 10, 1829. The vote was 141–36.

4. *Washington National Intelligencer*, February 7, 1829 (quotations); Jay, *Miscellaneous Writings*, 54; Weld and Thome, *Slavery and the Internal Slave Trade*, 211.

rebellion, Virginia embarked on a public debate over the future of slavery in that state. Since the Old Dominion easily had the most slaves amongst the states that were net exporters of bondservants, the debate had enormous significance for the future of the interstate slave trade. Should the legislature decide to end slavery in Virginia, the number of slaves available for sale would plummet. The majority of bondservants in the slave markets of the Lower South came from Virginia, and their absence would have drastically driven up prices. Farmers in and migrants to the Deep South would have found it more difficult to make cotton production profitable. Abolition in the Upper South would have imperiled expansion of the entire South. Most southerners readily understood this point. A paper in South Carolina opined that selling slaves for "removal" to the Southwest was "connected with the wealth and prosperity of the entire south." Anything that impeded this movement would hinder "the consequent increase of wealth [and] important elements of political power." The slave trade was vital to expansion, which was essential for the maintenance of slavery.[5]

These facts were not lost on the debate's participants, and the interstate slave trade was an important part of the discussion. Delegates who favored some type of gradual emancipation usually linked their schemes to a plan of colonization. They realized that colonization and the interstate slave trade worked at cross purposes, so the debates inextricably linked the two. Supporters of colonization joined with opponents of slavery to show why the peculiar institution itself needed to be slowly snuffed out. Their efforts came to naught, and what the discussion convincingly demonstrated was slavery's entrenched position and how ineffectual were those who desired to rid the state of the peculiar institution. Moreover, it underscored the need to do something with Virginia's slaves, and with the lack of change came a renewed support of the interstate slave trade.

The public debate began when Thomas Jefferson Randolph proposed that any slave born on or after July 4, 1840, become state property, males at age twenty-one, and females at age eighteen. He called for a statewide referendum on the matter, and his plan became the fulcrum of the debate. Until they reached maturity, the bondspeople would work for pay in order to defray the cost of shipping them to Africa. Like most of the proponents of emancipation, Randolph realized speculation's significance for Virginia. He knew that a robust slave market increased prices and decreased the op-

5. Undated *Charleston Patriot*, as quoted in *Niles' Weekly Register*, September 19, 1835, 39.

portunity for colonization. As a consequence, he attacked the slave trade in the hopes of shaming his colleagues into listening to his proposals. Randolph accused Virginia slaveholders of converting the state into a "grand menagerie" where slaves were "reared for the market, like oxen, for the shambles." He hated how the ties of father, mother, husband, and child were broken when masters sold their slaves to "cruel taskmasters." Randolph drew upon personal experience in preparing his remarks. He assumed the debts of his grandfather, Thomas Jefferson, and promised to pay off all creditors. Part of that process involved selling slaves, which he described as a "sad scene." Although he tried his best to keep families together, the episode confirmed Randolph's disgust with the bitter fruit of slavery.[6]

Those who sided with Randolph knew they would have difficulty convincing their fellow delegates. Both friends and foes of emancipation recognized that one function of the trade was to inflate the price of slaves, a fact that rendered abolition a long shot because most slaveowners would have trouble resisting the financial gain. Thomas Marshall, who favored gradual abolition, advocated the sale of the state's public land to raise money for colonization. His scheme would never work, he admitted, if masters continued to sell slaves for gain. While humanity might prevent some masters from selling to interstate traders, enough other slaveholders did not restrain themselves and, as a result, drove up the prices of slaves. The greed of these masters was sufficient to make colonization too expensive and unworkable. Even if owners arranged for slaves to stay in the state, the buyer might change his or her mind someday. Marshall was concerned that this tension between humanity and commerce wrecked the chances of colonization.[7]

In a similar fashion, slavery's defenders also recognized the interstate slave trade's importance. William O. Goode fought against any attempt to speed Virginia towards free soil, but recognized that slavery naturally flowed to where it was most useful. In this fashion, the northern states had already rid themselves of the peculiar institution and Virginia would probably follow their course. "Natural causes," he explained, would accomplish a

6. Randolph, as quoted in Joseph C. Robert, *The Road from Monticello: A Study of the Virginia Slavery Debate of 1832* (Durham, 1941), 97; Freehling, *Drift toward Dissolution*, 132; Stowe, *Key to Uncle Tom's Cabin*, 291; Weld and Thome, *Slavery and the Internal Slave Trade*, 66; Jay, *Miscellaneous Writings*, 264–65.

7. Thomas Marshall, *The Speech of Thomas Marshall in the House of Delegates of Virginia, on the Abolition of Slavery* (Richmond, 1832), 10.

peaceful "removal of slavery from Virginia." He concluded there was no reason to entertain such foolish notions as gradual emancipation or colonization. In other words, Goode counted on the domestic slave trade and migration to rid Virginia of slaves. James H. Gholson had a similar opinion. He reasoned that Virginia's slaves constituted the "largest portion of our wealth" and that their value was tied directly to the demand for slave labor in the Old Southwest. Gholson reminded his listeners that should anything be done to close the slave markets, it "would essentially impair our wealth and prosperity." The slave trade, in other words, was a vital part of Virginia's economy. Goode and Gholson made the case for expediency. Virginia slaveholders might as well take advantage of a lucrative situation while they could.[8]

The proponents and opponents of colonization had similar assumptions about the interstate slave trade. Most delegates realized that the operation of the interstate slave trade was in direct contravention to any plan of gradual emancipation or colonization. The high price of slaves deterred owners from freeing their bondservants; it was difficult to pass up the financial windfall that could be found in the sale of a slave's body. In a similar fashion, the state government could hardly expect to raise enough money to pay prices that were artificially raised by the slave market. The state, in theory, had the option of legally prohibiting the sale of slaves to southern states, but such an idea was unthinkable. That course of action would have given too much power to the government and eroded the rights of the slaveholder. Both sides clearly saw how a thriving slave market ruined colonization's chances to succeed.

Randolph's plan went nowhere and lost by a lopsided margin. Slavery's defenders then went on the offensive to win full acceptance for the slave trade. The most notable early advocate was Thomas R. Dew. He wrote a commentary on the Virginia Debates, and his work is often cited in the shift to a more aggressive defense of slavery throughout the South, particularly the Upper South. His arguments have become quite familiar, but in his defense of slavery he also analyzed the slave trade. He mocked the idea of colonization by pointing out the folly of the state government trying to "overbid the Southern seeker." Dew thought Virginia would, given enough time, become a free state. Slaves would go further south and white laborers

8. *Richmond Constitutional Whig*, March 28, 1832, as quoted in Freehling, *Drift toward Dissolution*, 155; Gholson, as quoted in Robert, *Road from Monticello*, 68.

would naturally fill the void. He went further, though, and turned the argument for colonization on its head. Instead of ridding Virginia of slaves, colonization would augment their numbers by cutting off the flow to southern markets. Dew did not have to add that an excess of slaves invited a race war. Although his reasoning in this regard was faulty, since slaves would have continued to go south rather than become a burden to their owners, Dew's implicit threat of a rebellion was calculated to undercut any vestige of support for emancipation. He even reiterated the biblical justification for the slave trade. Dew added that other cultures, including the Irish, Africans, and Indians, sold their kin into slavery, so the institution was common to man and was therefore normal. The reasons more people did not sell themselves into slavery, according to Dew, were that the law forbade it or they could locate no purchasers. He concluded that bargain and sale were legitimate parts of slavery and natural consequences of the master-slave relationship. Thus, according to Dew, the slave trade was not only beneficial for Virginia, it was pleasant for the slave and a natural feature of human existence.[9]

Hoping to repair the damage caused by Dew's argument, the American Colonization Society selected Jesse B. Harrison to draft a rebuttal. His response showed the futility of colonization and emancipation in the face of a surging slave market. Like Dew, Harrison thought Virginia would eventually become a free state. He argued, however, that the process should be accelerated before slavery inflicted any more damage on whites. Harrison was quick to correct what he saw as Dew's misguided view of the slave trade. He drew a direct parallel between the African trade and the internal trade and wisely pointed out that if Virginians needed to sell their slaves to stave off economic need, then the state was in dire straits. A reliance on the "contaminated" internal trade illustrated the "degradation to which slavery may reduce its supporters!" Harrison invoked the names of Washington and Jefferson in order to shame any who bought or sold slaves for profit, noting that speculation in slaves was a source of "impure wealth" which must be resisted. Although his argument was logical, it illustrated the weakness of those who disliked the internal trade: they could do little to change the situation. Moral suasion was one method of trying to counter the growth of the trade, but there was no effective organization to channel the energies of

9. Dew, "Review of the Debate," 317 (quotation), 318–22, 359; Drew Gilpin Faust, ed., *The Ideology of Slavery: Proslavery Thought in the Antebellum South, 1830–1860* (Baton Rouge, 1981), 31.

those who wanted to end speculation. The best they could do was to emphasize the deleterious effects the trade had on masters. Moralizing proved ineffective in blunting the force of economic and social considerations.[10]

The discussion about gradually ending slavery in Virginia had little or no chance of success. It was simply too difficult to find a satisfying political solution to remove something that was an integral part of the society. Talk of colonization continued, but the idea had no chance of succeeding once the legislature refused to formally endorse or fund a program. "ASHMUN," writing in the *Petersburg Times*, conceded that public opinion about colonization was fluctuating in the wake of the Nat Turner revolt. While moderately in favor of the state buying slaves and shipping them to Africa, Ashmun pointed out that the interstate trade, "Painful as it is," accomplished the same purpose at no price to the state. Echoing the ideas of Harrison and Dew, he realized that the state could not compete with the slave trade and bluntly concluded, "Virginia cannot stop it." Others even taunted the colonization movement by accusing it of raising the price of slaves. One writer, calling himself "ANTI-ABOLITIONIST," argued that the only way to rid the state of slavery was to make slave labor less valuable. Doing so would invite slaveholders to give up a useless investment. He did not see such a scenario happening anytime soon. It was painfully clear to colonization's supporters that the operation of the interstate slave trade inflated prices at a time when a drop in the cost of slaves was necessary for any colonization scheme to work. With slave prices rising in the late 1820s and beyond, the cost of purchasing and deporting slaves became prohibitive.[11]

Once Virginia rejected the program of state-sponsored colonization, it became apparent that no other state was willing or able to coordinate and fund any colonization efforts. The ACS looked to Washington as the only viable alternative and stepped up its campaign to secure federal funds. Colonization adherents wanted to use the proceeds from the sale of public land to pay for buying and shipping slaves, but they only steered the organization in an antislavery direction. Democrats and Southerners were loath to do any-

10. [Jesse Burton Harrison], *Review of the Slave Question, extracted from the American Quarterly Review, Dec. 1832* (Richmond, 1833), 17, 32–33.

11. Undated *Petersburg Times*, as quoted in *Western Luminary*, January 11, 1832 (quotation); *Richmond Enquirer*, September 17, 1833. Jehudi Ashmun was a fund-raiser and spokesman for the American Colonization Society who also served in Liberia as a colonial agent and died there in 1828.

thing that gave the federal government any more power than it needed, especially when it came to the sensitive issue of slavery. Andrew Jackson's veto of the Distribution Bill in 1833, a measure that would have funded colonization with money from public land sales, effectively neutered the organization. When colonization became linked to the removal of slaves with federal funds, critics in the Lower South castigated the ACS as a tool of abolitionists. They were concerned that removal of all the slaves would cause the southern economy to collapse. An unstated concern was that the ACS would serve as a competitor to the supply of slaves and raise prices. Furthermore, as slaves left the country, those who remained would become strident about asserting claims to freedom. Most citizens of the Deep South refused to have any contact with an organization they saw as a threat to slavery.[12]

Colonization, more of a sentiment than a solution, faltered in the face of reality. It offered comfort that somehow slavery could be removed without disturbing society or making sacrifices. Those who adhered to its precepts underestimated how deeply slavery had become enmeshed in the culture; they offered a simple solution to a complex problem. Colonization, moreover, could not compete with the slave markets of the Lower South. In the twenty-five years after its formation in 1816, the ACS sent just over 3,800 slaves to Africa, or about 150 per year. State organizations probably doubled this total, but their combined efforts did not make a dent in the slave population. The interstate trade far outstripped these numbers. More importantly, speculation did not rely on government funding and even brought economic benefits to the South's economy. The largest drawback of the trade was its methods, because most southerners envisioned a more benign way to remove slaves. As speculation became acceptable, Upper South residents could abandon their commitment to colonization and rest easy that the trade reduced the slave population.[13]

Besides the competition with the slave market, colonization was becoming an anachronism. It was a moderate solution at a time when moderation was evaporating. The ACS tried to find a middle way between the extremes of unimpeded slavery and abolition, but could not. Southerners were less

12. Staudenraus, *African Colonization Movement*, 184–87; Fredrickson, *The Black Image in the White Mind*, 25–26.

13. Staudenraus, *American Colonization Movement*, 251; T. Michael Miller, "'Out of Bondage': A History of the Alexandria Colonization Society," *Alexandria History* 7 (1987): 27.

likely to be introspective as they faced the harsh glare of abolitionist assaults in the 1830s and beyond. The Upper South, a bastion of support for colonization, was less inclined to consider the idea when speculation siphoned off many of its slaves. In this sense, the interstate slave trade fulfilled one of the major functions of the American Colonization Society—removing slaves. It had the added bonus of being more remunerative to masters than colonization.

If citizens of the Upper South were still divided over speculation when support for colonization evaporated, an outside threat dispelled most of their doubts. The interstate slave trade, in fact, was one of the easiest points of attack for slavery's opponents, and those assaults prompted doubters to rally to the trade's defense. Abolitionists portrayed slavery in the worst possible light, and a natural way to do that was to provide information about the slave trade. Lurid stories detailing the trade's abuses became a focal point of the radical abolitionist campaign to annihilate slavery. Speculation was a convenient target because it destroyed slave families and implied that masters let personal profit triumph over concern for slaves. Publications such as the *Genius of Universal Emancipation*, *Freedom's Journal*, and the *Liberator* regularly contained stories on the trade, reprinted advertisements of slave sales, and included harsh editorials about the buying and selling of human beings. The *Liberator*, for instance, printed the woodcut of a slave sale on its masthead and had a regular feature entitled the "Black List," which featured the slave trade's abuses. From its inception, the American Anti-Slavery Society called for congressional action to end to the trade. Prominent abolitionists such as William Jay, Henry B. Stanton, Alvan Stewart, Benjamin Lundy, and William Lloyd Garrison all were vocal about the need to put a stop to the trade. The torrent of abuse directed towards commerce in slaves was so great that even a casual visitor to the United States noticed that "the slave-trade is now become more than formerly a subject of discussion."[14]

14. C. D. Arfwedson, *The United States and Canada, in 1832, 1833, and 1834*, 2 vols. (London, 1834), 1:352 (quotation); Mayer, *All on Fire*, 75; Lightner, "Door to the Slave Bastille," 235–52; Lightner, "Interstate Slave Trade in Antislavery Politics," 119–36; Deyle, "Domestic Slave Trade," 144–210, Dillon, *Slavery Attacked*, 162–200; James Brewer Stewart, *Holy Warriors: The Abolitionists and American Slavery* (New York, 1976), 33–73; Bertram Wyatt-Brown, *Lewis Tappan and the Evangelical War against Slavery* (Cleveland, 1969), 98–125.

One of the abolitionists' first tactics was to flood Congress with petitions to terminate the interstate slave trade and abolish slavery. Although most of them focused on the District of Columbia, by 1837 the House of Representatives received petitions signed by 23,405 people that called for an end to the interstate trade. As we have seen, northerners realized that the slave trade was vital to slavery's existence because it kept bondservants valuable in the Upper South and supplied the labor demand for the Lower South. They attacked the slave trade as being brutal, transforming humans into property, operating contrary to God's law, corrupting white morals, and fostering greed by encouraging slaveholders to sell their slaves for high prices. In essence, they repeated all of the misgivings that Upper South residents had voiced in the 1820s. The abolitionists' tone, however, was different from that of Upper South residents. Opponents of slavery were more willing to attack slavery in specific detail rather than general terms. Instead of condemning slavery in the abstract, abolitionists seized upon vivid accounts of beatings, murders, mutilations, escapes, and auctions as the most effective way to illustrate the horrors of the peculiar institution. Their critique of slavery brought criticism of slaveowners to a personal level. Masters were no longer the victims of an unfortunate labor system, but were active participants in an evil and exploitative regime. Those southerners who did nothing to eradicate slavery were equally culpable.[15]

Southerners, however, did not allow the consistent and growing criticism of slavery pass without a response. The growth of an external threat to slavery that was vocal and personal triggered an aggressive defense of the peculiar institution. In public debates and official pronouncements slavery was less and less an evil, but was more and more a positive good. Instead of being a benighted institution that hindered southern development, it was superior to the North's grimy capitalism. Southern politicians outdid themselves to prove their loyalty to slavery. Not only did southerners rally around slavery, but they also defended speculation in slaves. The Deep South had long been aware of its dependence on the interstate slave trade, but it took several years for the Upper South to swing around to a defense of the trade. A recognition of the trade's necessity helped bring uniformity to southern opinions about slavery. This outside attack also effectively neutralized southern concerns about how speculation affected whites, an idea

15. *Liberator*, June 23, 1837, 102; Lightner, "Door to the Slave Bastille," 243–44; Deyle, "Domestic Slave Trade," 182–85.

that was probably the strongest objection to the trade. Slaveholders had once been deeply concerned that speculation corroded personal virtue and threatened free government. No longer. As attacks multiplied, southerners found ways to deny the reality of speculation.[16]

The simplest way to defend the interstate slave trade was to minimize its importance. If southerners could make the argument that speculation was of little consequence for the South, then they would effectively counter claims that masters exploited their slaves. They could also reassure themselves that it would not imperil white society. Slave traders had been making these arguments for years, but it took some time for other southerners to come around to that viewpoint. Thomas Cooper, for instance, framed his defense of slavery around six assertions about the peculiar institution. One of the charges described the trade as cruel, tyrannical, and unjust because it meted out punishment, separated husbands and wives, and prohibited education. Cooper carefully rebutted each of the accusations. He suggested that separation of families occurred in every country and in every time, so the trade could not be singled out for causing wanton cruelty. In the South, he claimed, such a thing "may occur occasionally . . . but, for the most part, husbands and wives are not parted." If, on the odd chance, slaves happened to be sold, "in nine cases out of ten" a neighbor purchased them. The evil was so unusual no legislation was necessary. Even if slaves were separated from their families, "the very slight bonds of concubinage" meant that they were hardly bothered. In other words, the slave trade was so rare that northerners need not waste their time trying to reform it. The *Charleston Patriot* echoed this idea. Any sound or fury about the trade signified nothing, since the debate about the interstate trade was based on "the false philanthropy or mawkish sensibility of the abolitionists" and not on a realistic appraisal of the situation. Northerners, in other words, were overwrought about something of minor importance and should drop the matter.[17]

Underestimating the volume of the interstate slave trade was essential to an aggressive defense of the peculiar institution. The debate over slavery in

16. William J. Cooper Jr., *The South and the Politics of Slavery, 1828–1856* (Baton Rouge, 1978), 58–69; Larry E. Tise, *Proslavery: A History of the Defense of Slavery in America, 1701–1840* (Athens, Ga., 1987); William Sumner Jenkins, *Pro-Slavery Thought in the Old South* (Chapel Hill, 1935); David Donald, "The Proslavery Argument Reconsidered," *JSH* 37 (1971): 3–18.

17. *Southern Literary Journal*, November 1835, 190 (Cooper quotations); undated *Charleston Patriot*, as quoted in *Niles' Weekly Register*, September 19, 1835.

the 1830s increasingly turned on moral issues. James Henry Hammond stressed the notion that southern society was perfectly ordered, thus the master-slave relationship was beneficial for all involved. There was an implied contract between master and slave, he explained, where the latter received "*peace, plenty, security*" in exchange for labor. Hammond and many other southerners wanted to believe their culture possessed high morals because slaveowners usually had the best interests of their people in mind. This explains the great consternation at the thought of the interstate slave trade; it demonstrated the opposite reality. Speculation had to be minimized or explained away to preserve faith in a well-structured and virtuous society. Once southerners could convince themselves the trade was rare, then they could have confidence in their attitudes and actions. In an amazing display of mental flexibility, most southerners denied the ubiquity of the interstate slave trade even when it was a fixture in their society.[18]

Closely connected to soft-pedaling the interstate slave trade's activity was emphasizing the kind and gentle nature of slavery. The general thrust of the argument was that if southerners treated their slaves like persons, they would have scant inclination to use the interstate slave trade. Southerners hated the idea that slaves had become chattels, or merely a species of property. Spokesmen for the peculiar institution vigorously rejected any suggestion that "slaves are merely chattels and not persons." Any thinking along that line was a "radical error, and one that has been too long circulated uncontradicted by the abolitionists." Robert J. Walker explained how the master-slave relationship was "reciprocal" in that masters provided lifetime care for slaves that included food, clothing, shelter, and medicine. His disgust with the description of slaves as "chattel" reflects southerners' dislike for the term, especially because of its frequent use by abolitionists. The argument about whether bondservants were treated like persons or like chattel went to the heart of the slavery controversy, since it would be hard to attack a benign type of servitude. Southerners did all they could to disprove northern assertions that slaves were no more than property. Instead they erected a paternalistic ideal that masters had their slaves' best interests at heart.[19]

18. Jenkins, *Pro-Slavery Thought*, 112 (emphasis in original); Tise, *Proslavery*, 110–11, 116–21.

19. *Groves et al. v. Slaughter*, 40 U.S. (15 Peters), lv–lvi (quotations); Wyatt-Brown, *Southern Honor*, 377–78.

Walker was not the only southerner to find the word *chattel* repellent. John Hartwell Cocke held moderate views on slavery but was perturbed by the agitation over the issue and took it as a personal affront that abolitionists described slaves as chattel. Such language demeaned and cheapened the master-slave relationship. In an essay entitled "Negroes not Chattels," he argued that using the word *chattel* to describe slavery was deceptive. Cocke thought it an "adroit slander" and an insult, since *chattel* implied that masters cared only for the property aspect of their slaves and slighted the Christian belief that slaves had souls. It was apparent that the "ultra-abolitionists of the North" were stirring up trouble with their insistence that slaves were chattel. Walker's argument echoed these thoughts and took them one step further by accusing the abolitionists themselves of treating slaves as chattel. Only those northerners who demanded congressional regulation of the interstate slave trade wanted slaves to be treated as property. He adroitly turned the situation on its head by implying that abolitionists' extreme tactics indicated their disingenuousness. The definition of slaves was a means to an end. For Walker, and perhaps for many southerners, the antislavery activists were playing a deadly political game where ruthlessness was rewarded. It was northerners who treated slaves as things and southerners who protected them from such abuse.[20]

On the few occasions when speculation happened, apologists claimed, its effects were exaggerated. If they could demonstrate that the trade had no harmful effects on slaves, then they would effectively rebut abolitionists' claims of cruelty. Southerners made an extra effort, moreover, to argue that bondservants were treated better than northern whites. Charles Cotesworth Pinckney, speaking in South Carolina, seized upon this essential point. He knew that outsiders described the slave trade as "an outrage on humanity." They were wrong. The sale of slaves was usually beneficial and improved the lives of bondservants. In Pinckney's view, the slaves usually consented to be separated from their relatives. In those unusual cases where slaves were forced apart, they were better off than the working class of the North, who faced "more real perils and hardships" than could be found in "the romantic catalogue of the horrors of slavery." Judge William Harper covered much the same ground in his four-part defense of slavery. The second in-

20. John Hartwell Cocke Sr., "Negroes not Chattels," undated essay, Cocke Family Papers (Cocke quotations); *Groves v. Slaughter*, lv (Walker quotations); Baptist, "'Cuffy,' 'Fancy Maids,' and 'One-Eyed Men,'" 1631–33.

stallment of the series concerned itself mostly with disproving the alleged evils of slavery. Harper trotted out a list of the usual suspects: no legal protection, excessive labor, cruel punishment, no opportunity for moral or intellectual advancement, marriage was essentially equivalent to concubinage, and families were torn apart. He then tried to disprove each assertion. Most of the charges were distorted, he thought, especially since worse things happened in a free society. The relation of the master to the slave was naturally one of kindness, so there was more tenderness than brutality. Harper did admit that slaves were "liable" to be sold, but charged that free laborers were separated from their families more frequently. Besides, Harper continued, the "native character and temperament" of bondservants made the separation "much less severely felt." Harper's awkward defense of the slave trade was really not much of a defense at all. Things in the North were worse, he argued, so northerners should focus their crusading energies on themselves rather than torturing the South.[21]

The interstate slave trade, the most blatant form of capitalistic exploitation in the South, became a means to assert the South's precapitalistic nature. It was a strange and perverse twist of logic. Southerners frequently blasted the North as a land of economic corruption that ran roughshod over its poor, defenseless workers. They extolled the virtues of slavery as it upheld morals and provided security for the slave. Free labor, the argument ran, undermined public virtue because it pitted management against labor in a competition for scarce resources. Not so with slavery. It harmoniously blended the needs of masters and slaves. Extending this line of thinking to speculation meant that the interstate slave trade had virtually no negative effects, since it was infrequent and in the slaves' best interest.[22]

The core of this transformation of the interstate slave trade into a bulwark of proslavery thought was the intense desire to repel any outside interference in the slaveholders' power. Any such meddling could corrupt the master-slave relationship. It was no small stretch for southerners to read abolitionist rhetoric about the necessity to end slavery and then assume that

21. *Genius of Universal Emancipation*, September 6, 1829, 66 (Pinckney quotations); Mathews, *Religion in the Old South*, 72; "Judge Harper's Memoir on Slavery," *Southern Literary Journal*, February 1838, 81–97 (Harper's quotations).

22. Eugene D. Genovese, *The Slaveholders' Dilemma: Freedom and Progress in Southern Conservative Thought, 1820–1860* (Columbia, 1992), 33–37; Jenkins, *Pro-Slavery Thought*, 296–300.

slaves imbibed such notions. How slaves could incorporate these ideas, since most could not read and did not have contact with northerners, usually went unexplained. After Nat Turner's rebellion, Governor A. B. Roman of Louisiana blamed abolitionists for inciting Virginia slaves to revolt. Cooper also blamed abolitionists for degrading the master-slave relationship because they "render it necessary to draw the cords of subjugation tighter instead of relaxing them." Not only were attacks on the interstate slave trade undermining the master-slave relationship, they were part of a broad conspiracy to destroy the South. Abolitionists were rash and dangerous, according to a Huntsville, Alabama, newspaper. It protested that the "fanatics" sent "seditious and incendiary doctrines" through the mail. Perhaps even worse was their interference in property rights. This obnoxious tendency took several forms, including emancipation in the District of Columbia or the territories, and inhibiting the transportation of slaves from one state to another. Defense of the slave trade, then, was integral to an overall explanation of slavery.[23]

This argument reached its apotheosis in a Supreme Court case that involved the legality of Mississippi's trade prohibition. Robert Walker, who argued on behalf of abrogating debts to slave traders, carefully explained why the slave trade existed. Significant numbers of slaves in the Upper South had been "indoctrinated for years on the principles of abolition." According to Walker, they were rampant in Virginia, Maryland, and Kentucky. They were ready to spread "their emancipating creed" among the gullible Lower South slaves. The result would be a dangerous, worthless, and sullen workforce. Such slaves spread their deadly poison to others, forcing owners to sell rebellious bondservants to traders. According to Walker, the primary reason that the South tolerated speculators was that they were necessary to defuse the instability caused by abolitionists. The South was "united," he said, in wanting to abolish the interstate slave trade. Should the abolitionists cease their agitation, then the interstate slave trade would hardly be necessary. According to another southerner, the "multiplication of slave-gangs" was "one of the sad effects of the doctrine and practice of

23. *New Orleans Louisiana Courier*, November 16, 1831; *Louisiana Senate Journal*, extra 10th sess. (New Orleans, 1832), 1; *Southern Literary Journal*, November 1835, 190 (Cooper quotation); *Huntsville Southern Advocate*, September 10, 1833 (remaining quotations); *Woodville Republican*, January 9, 1836; Henry I. Tragle, ed., *The Southampton Slave Revolt of 1831* (Amherst, 1971), 275.

abolitionists." These ideas repeated one of the key components of the slave trade defense: masters were not to blame for the interstate slave trade. Speculators, even though reduced to a stereotype, were not at fault either. It was the abolitionists who caused the South's problems. Southerners, moreover, had come to accept the most commercial dimension of their society only because that aspect was supposedly foreign to them. Speculation, in this scenario, was reluctant and infrequent. Only the evils of northern society could corrupt the South. In this way southerners could claim to be distinct and better than northerners because they hated speculation. The slave trade, in a perverse twist of logic, proved the South's superiority to the North.[24]

These arguments about the interstate slave trade, moreover, also were a type of longing for a yesteryear that did not exist. When slave trade apologists explained away the presence of speculation, they were, in a sense, trying to imagine an ideal South free from strife. Their imagined South was full of "cohesion, unity, and grace." They wanted to believe that there was a type of organic unity to the South, where slaves cheerfully respected and obeyed their owners because of the kind treatment they received. White southerners mused about a paternalist paradise that never existed. Doing so required a foil—and northern capitalism proved useful. When apologists continually referred to a North riven by strife, where workers were set against owners, they almost seemed to be saying that such an environment could not happen in the South. In short, an imagined North full of evil was a way to ignore or explain away similar problems closer to home.[25]

This aggressive position made itself felt in the halls of Congress. Northern congressmen became more assertive in their efforts to shame southerners into admitting the evil effects of the interstate trade. Southerners, in turn, were increasingly outspoken about resisting any and all attempts to use the trade as a way to attack slavery. Miner's speech was an early salvo, but northern assaults became more frequent in the 1830s. The trade in the District of Columbia was a favorite target because it made for good press back home, and it could plausibly be argued that the federal government had the authority to intervene in Washington's affairs. In 1835, for instance, northern representatives from Maine, Massachusetts, and New York intro-

24. *Groves v. Slaughter*, lv–lvi (Walker quotations); J. Blanchard and N. L. Rice, *A Debate on Slavery held in the City of Cincinnati* (Cincinnati, 1846), 28; Donald, "Proslavery Argument," 12.

25. Donald, "Proslavery Argument," 17.

duced petitions to abolish slavery in the District of Columbia. One of their tactics was reading local slave traders' advertisements in the hopes of disgracing southerners into admitting the wretchedness of slavery. The tactic failed. Two years later, in the Senate, Samuel L. Southard of New Jersey tried to find some of the shrinking middle ground during another debate on ending slavery in the District of Columbia. Northern petitions variously asked for the abolition of slavery in Washington or the end of the slave trade there. Southard made a distinction between the two when he called for an end to the slave trade in the District but denied that he wanted to touch slavery itself. He explicitly disavowed the right of the federal government to interfere with slavery. William C. Preston of South Carolina vigorously opposed Southard's proposal. Preston called the separation of the slave trade from slavery "a distinction without a difference" and objected to all interference in the matter. Southerners were "sore on the subject" and their "nerves were irritated" by the "violent and incessant attacks." Propositions to meddle with the slave trade in the District were an entering wedge in a campaign to destroy slavery, according to Preston. The South Carolinian was peeved that southerners were assumed to be transgressors of God's laws who lived in vice and wickedness. When Preston finished his outburst, Southard continued and clarified his position. He was not an abolitionist and was not condemning the South or southerners. He merely joined "distinguished Southern gentlemen" in opposing the character of the trade in the District. All Southard asked was for a distinction to be made between the abolition of slavery in Washington and the suppression of slave trafficking there. Preston could not keep quiet. He admitted that John Randolph had once made that argument, but times had changed. "The country," he explained, "had not then been filled with abolition principles." What might have been done safely then was dangerous now, because to touch slavery in the District was to affect the entire South. Preston had no doubt that if Randolph were present he would disavow his earlier statements and vehemently defend the interstate slave trade.[26]

Other southerners jumped into the fray and fended off the attacks. Alfred Cuthbert of Georgia thought that if Congress touched the "smallest mite" connected with slavery, the result would send "a thrill of dread and horror

26. *Register of Debates in Congress*, 23rd Cong., 2nd sess., pt. 2, February 16, 1835 (Washington, 1830), 1392–93; *Register of Debates*, 24th Cong., 2nd sess., pt. 1, February 6, 1837, 713 (all quotations).

through all the South." Even the smallest concession would be seized by the abolitionists as a triumph. William C. Rives said he witnessed the whole discussion with "pain and mortification." There was no justification for the view that Congress could regulate the internal slave trade. The Virginian contended that "the gratuitous exhibitions of these horrid pictures of misery" had no basis in fact. He thought the petitioners, and those senators who listened to them, were just trying to stir up trouble. John Calhoun then closed the matter when he asserted that slavery was a "great good." The Senate made no progress and voted to table the petition along a sectional vote. One speculator who closely followed the debates knew that southerners would not allow anything to happen that would jeopardize his livelihood. The abolitionists' petitions, he told a northerner, were an attempt to legislate morality. He thought it would "blow over" soon. The man, who refused to describe himself as a slave trader, noted that "the slave-traders tell us they don't care a d—— for it—they ain't afraid of it."[27]

As this speculator knew, the southern position had emerged with great clarity and increasing unity across the South. Twenty years earlier congressmen representing the Upper South were wary of supporting the domestic trade because of its troublesome aspects. By the mid-1830s, they were willing to accept it as fundamental to their society. In doing so, they denied the validity of earlier southern concerns about speculation. Southerners were convinced that times had changed and that northerners were now going to hammer away at the slave trade in order to undermine slavery's support. James Birney, who moved out of the South to oppose slavery, understood the situation. He pointed out that abolitionists had a "very injurious" effect in the South because they furnished "a kind of justification of slavery itself to the Southern slaveholders." Southerners assumed that any attempt to meddle with the buying and selling of bondservants, even in the District of Columbia, was the first step on the road to abolition. The slave trade, then, had to be protected, and southerners rallied to resist federal interference with slavery. One southern newspaper, for example, wondered how anyone could support Martin Van Buren after one of his papers attacked the Washington trade. It pointed out that the South could not afford to lose too many political battles and still hope to protect servitude. A European visitor sensed the vehemence of southern attitudes. He thought that all southern-

27. *Register of Debates*, 24th Cong., 715–23 (quotations on 715, 717, 719, 723); *Liberator*, April 20, 1838, 61 (final quotation).

ers had "an interest in protecting this infernal trade of slave-driving" because the physical expansion—and the future—of their society depended on it. Those who wanted to preserve slavery had to be willing to defend all of its aspects, even something as ugly as the interstate slave trade. They were willing to justify speculation's horrible features in order to erect a comprehensive defense of their peculiar institution. As southerners did so, especially in the Upper South, they modified their beliefs about slavery. It no longer had any flaws, because admitting weakness would open the door to even more northern denunciation. All negative aspects of slavery had to be blamed on those who were outside the mainstream of society.[28]

The slave trade was important to southerners in another way. Many assumed that slavery had to expand or there would be grave consequences. Sons of slaveowners and yeomen wanted new land on which to locate their farms. Those with established farms in the Deep South wanted to augment their workforce. Masters in the Upper South wanted an outlet for potentially idle bondspeople. Southerners also desired more territory in order to maintain influence in national politics. The interstate slave trade was the foundation for all of these aspirations, since it was vital to adjusting the cloak of slavery to fit the expanding South. To deny the significance of the interstate slave trade was to deny the need for slavery's expansion. Speculation was of psychological and tangible importance to southerners.

As more southerners acknowledged the vital nature of the interstate slave trade, it was increasingly difficult to defend slavery and maintain an opposition to speculation. The *Western Luminary*, in deploring masters who sold their slaves to speculators, did not want to level indiscriminate accusations. Some of the "best citizens" of the South held slaves, but did so in accordance with the "principle of humanity and justice." These owners showed that it was not necessary to deal with slave traders. The paper also made it clear that it was not in league with abolitionists. It distinguished itself from "a certain class in some section of our country" and forcefully asserted the right to hold slaves. The paper was in the minority, though, and did little to shape people's thoughts. This chorus of extremism drowned out voices of moderation.[29]

28. Dwight L. Dumond, ed., *Letters of James Gillespie Birney, 1831–1857* (New York, 1938), 1:90 (first and second quotations); *Woodville Republican*, March 9, 1839; Featherstonhaugh, *Excursion through the Slave States*, 37 (final quotation).

29. *Western Luminary*, November 23, 1831.

More typical was the position of William Haile, who ran for state representative in Mississippi on an openly antiabolitionist platform. He realized that it was useless to differentiate between slavery and the slave trade. Haile accused seminaries and antislavery societies of conspiring to "destroy the domestic institutions of the South." Campaigning in the aftermath of the Turner revolt, Haile pledged to keep Mississippi open to all slave importation. He ticked off a number of reasons why a law restricting the entry of slaves should be opposed: it would only help the large slaveholder, it would be evaded, a similar law in Louisiana had failed, it would reduce immigration, and too many legal restraints demoralized a community. Haile thought that as "long as slavery is recognized, it cannot be restrained without a violation of right." Interference with the slave trade was the first step to limiting the rights of slaveholders, according to this view. The absolute power of masters had to be defended absolutely.[30]

Once masters had realized the importance of speculation, all that remained was to fill in the gaps. It was at this point that the stereotype of the ruthless slave trafficker emerged with clarity and force. This caricature was everything that slaveowners did not want to be, but were afraid they would become due to speculation's corrosive effects. The trader broke up families, emphasized profit above piety, manipulated reality, and ruined paternalism. The stereotype had all the qualities that slaveowners were supposed to control. When they could not meet this ideal, the speculator was one way to explain their failure. The emergence of the slave trader stereotype reflected the southern mentality that masters did not want to admit they thought of their slaves in commercial terms. The interstate slave trade was the epitome of treating slaves in such a fashion, since, by its very nature, speculation was concerned with the value of the slave rather than his or her character. This notion was the most difficult one for southerners to defend or explain away, especially in light of the abolitionists' efforts to portray slavery in the worst possible way. For those who tried to justify the presence of the interstate slave trade, it was essential to defy the very nature of the transaction. They blamed all others—banks, debt, abolitionists, the slaves themselves—for the slave trade because to admit their own culpability would have undermined the whole basis of their society. If others were at fault for the trade, then southern qualms about speculation became a nonissue.[31]

30. *Woodville Republican*, October 10, 1833.

31. Tadman, *Speculators and Slaves*, 179–92, has a different interpretation of the existence of the slave trader stereotype.

This stereotype had a powerful resonance in the South because it reflected the "double character" of slaves and slaveowners. It has long been understood that southerners grappled with the dual nature of slaves as both people and property. What is becoming more clear is that a southern culture of honor and one of commerce could be reconciled through slavery. The interstate slave trade became a powerful way to bring together these two seemingly contradictory ideals. Southerners needed to reassure themselves that slavery had significant benefits for bondservants. After all, the master could argue, slaves received food, clothing, shelter, and medical care for the length of their lives in exchange for their labor. Owners prided themselves on the benevolent care of their slaves, but speculation contradicted this illusory vision. In explaining away the interstate slave trade, and defying its essential commercial nature, southerners relied on a defense of slavery where owners were concerned with the welfare of their slaves, not profit. Southerners needed to believe they were better than they actually were.[32]

Slaveowners needed the stereotype of the evil slave trader, moreover, to preserve their way of life. Southerners widely considered it more humane to keep bondservants' families together than to wantonly separate them. Some owners might even have had good intentions when selling an entire family of slaves to a trader. But, as a traveler through the South observed, "such kindnesses are of no avail after the victims come into the southern markets," since traders did not hesitate to separate families. It is clear that southerners were uneasy about the fact that they destroyed slave families. Slaveowners were quick to assure visitors that they had kind feelings towards their people. Adverse public opinion, they continued, operated as a "powerful check against the parting of kindred." Others claimed they made great sacrifices from a sense of duty because owners thought it wrong to abandon slaves to an unknown purchaser. Masters hardly had to worry about abandoning their slaves; most received ample compensation in their transactions. Southerners were able to convince some visitors, and themselves, that they had the best interests of their slaves at heart. A Philadelphia druggist was not fooled, however. He observed that the slave trade, although "frowned upon and called an 'exceptional case'" was really "an essential and integral part of the system." He thought that in private sales, families were less prone to be separated, but public auctions were another story. Callous slave traders

32. Gross, *Double Character*, 47–71.

found it in their interest to buy a whole family at a reduced price and then sell them separately to make a greater profit. Such practices were carried on to "an *enormous extent*," and there was no shortage of slave traders combing the countryside in search of bargains.[33]

It is also clear that the interstate slave trade was helping to unite the various regions of the South. Whereas traders in the Upper South had earlier been greeted with indifference or scorn, they now were vital to the maintenance of domestic tranquility. Such men ensured that "excess" slaves would not be problematic but would instead be converted into a ready source of cash. In a similar fashion, the Deep South became even more dependent upon the new arrivals for its expansion and prosperity. It no longer viewed imported slaves as some type of infectious disease. In both cases, the convenient stereotype of a speculator who existed only because of northern meddling, served to balance the competing visions. The slave trader, then, was a vital means by which southerners reconciled some of the contradictory aspects of slavery.

Even though southerners rebutted moral attacks on speculation through the stereotype of an evil slave trader, they knew they had to shore up its legality. Central to a forceful defense of the slave trade and, by extension, slavery, was the issue of whether the movement of bondservants was subject to the interstate commerce clause of the Constitution. Northerners who wanted to regulate the trade insisted that the federal government could legislate the matter. Southerners admitted no such thing because they wanted no interference in the master-slave relationship. It was a delicate subject. The justification of slave sales hinged upon the assumption that slaves were property. The Constitution, however, gave the federal government the authority to regulate interstate commerce. Southerners were trying to have it both ways in denying and affirming the property nature of slaves. This dual approach to property rights helps explain the peculiar southern stance on the interstate slave trade and on speculators. One newspaper admitted as such when it admitted that slaves were "in the nature of commodities" but argued that they should not be regulated because the rights of ownership supersede any commercial implications.[34]

33. *Liberator*, May 17, 1834, 77; Lyell, *Second Visit to the United States*, 1:209–10 (first and second quotations); Francis C. Yarnall Diary, 14–15, DU (remaining quotations, emphasis in original).

34. Undated *Charleston Patriot*, as quoted in *Niles' Weekly Register*, September 19, 1835, 39.

Southerners asserted, moreover, that most bondservants willingly took part in the interstate slave trade. This notion not only put masters' motives and actions in the best possible light, but also presented the elaborate system of interstate trading as a voluntary migration of slaves. Two ideas were at work here. First, the emphasis on migration countered the abolitionist attack on slavery's cruelty. If slaves were voluntary participants in the trade, then exposés revealing speculators' cruelty were shams. There was no reason to question slavery because if the most objectionable aspect was acceptable, then the whole system was good. Second, if slaves willingly moved to new territory, then they could not be articles of commerce. There was no need to abolish or regulate the interstate slave trade because the bondservants moved voluntarily, were well-treated, and experienced improved material conditions as a result of sale.

The thorny issue of regulating interstate commerce came to a head in an 1841 Supreme Court case. As we have seen, Mississippi was in the unenviable position of constitutionally prohibiting the interstate slave trade even while taxing it. Governor Charles Lynch presciently warned the legislature in 1837 that this contradictory position opened the door to litigation, so he proposed a change. Besides forestalling lawsuits, Lynch hoped to steady a shaky economy by keeping money in Mississippi. The legislature responded by passing a bill that imposed penalties on those who imported slaves. It also declared all notes subsequently arising from the trade to be null and void. Mississippi, in essence, tried to shut down the trade. The legislature did not anticipate the mischief it would create. When the panic of 1837 hit with full force, creditors scrambled to collect debts. Slave traders felt an extreme burden because they held promissory notes that might not be paid. They tried to force payment, but Mississippi's high court ruled that state citizens could not collect money from fellow residents.[35]

An 1840 decision in federal court took a similar position. In *Hickman v. Rose*, a federal court ruled that all contracts for the sale of slaves in Missis-

35. *Woodville Republican*, January 21, 1837; *Richmond Enquirer*, May 16 and 19, 1837; Sydnor, *Slavery in Mississippi*, 167; Drake, "Constitutional Development in Mississippi," 182–83; Gross, *Double Character*, 57–61; Maurice G. Baxter, *Henry Clay the Lawyer* (Lexington, Ky., 2000), 93–101; Bacon Tait to Rice C. Ballard, October 14, 1840, Ballard Papers; Meredith Lang, *Defender of the Faith: The High Court of Mississippi, 1817–1875* (Jackson, Miss., 1977), 54–55; Helen T. Catterall, ed., *Judicial Cases concerning American Slavery and the Negro*, 5 vols. (Washington, D.C., 1926), 3:289–90. Two cases, *Green v. Robinson* and *Glidewell v. Hite*, affirmed this decision.

sippi since May of 1833 were illegal, and thus null and void. Should this decision stand, it had the potential to ruin slave trading in Mississippi, cripple speculation in general, and negatively affect slavery. The amount of money at stake was enormous. A Natchez newspaper estimated that nearly ten thousand slaves were sold in Mississippi in the twelve months after November 1, 1835. Their value was at least ten million dollars. Louisiana, too, would have suffered immensely from a negative ruling. A New Orleans newspaper estimated that the potential loss by depreciation of slave property could bankrupt the state. Bacon Tait, a slave trader in Richmond, confided to a colleague just what was at stake. He knew that the inability to collect his notes would make it difficult to secure financing for the next slave-trading season. That was just the start of his worries, because he also wondered what would happen to the country. Tait thought the court's decision would certainly accelerate the sectional crisis and probably "produce a dissolution of the Union." The federal government, in his opinion, was "subservient to non-slaveholders since it could now rule *slaves are not property*."[36]

Speculators like Tait had a keen insight into the possible ramifications of a negative court decision. They feared that the abrogation of debts was the first step towards national regulation of the trade. Should that result, it took little imagination to believe that the North would someday legislate slavery in a general sense. Mississippi's contradictory legislation, then, had the potential to cause trouble for the entire South. What began as a dispute over money quickly escalated into a matter of principle that touched the whole region. Southerners who supported slavery found themselves in the uncomfortable position of having to defend speculation and come to terms with the market economy. Attitudes towards speculation had undergone a rapid turnaround since the formative days of the slave trade. Something that was an "ideological embarrassment" had become the "lynch-pin of slavery's defense."[37]

The end result was a Supreme Court case, *Groves v. Slaughter*, where speculators sued to recover their money. Robert Slaughter had imported

36. *Niles' Weekly Register*, February 1, 1840, 368; undated *Newark Sentinel*, as quoted in *Liberator*, January 3, 1840, 2; undated *Natchez Courier*, as quoted in *Liberator*, May 12, 1837, 78; Bacon Tait to Thomas Boudar, January 1, 1840, Bacon Tait to Rice C. Ballard, January 3, 1840 (quotations, emphasis in original), Ballard Papers.

37. Tadman, *Speculators and Slaves*, 184.

slaves into Mississippi in 1836 and sold them for notes totaling $7,000. He sued when he could not collect. This case became a collaborative effort on the part of several traders. They pooled their money and hired some of the best available legal talent. Besides Walter Jones, Henry Clay and Daniel Webster, the "Ajax and Achilles of the bar," argued on their behalf. United States attorney general Henry D. Gilpin and Mississippi senator Robert J. Walker opposed Clay, Webster, and Jones. On February 12, 1841, the week-long case commenced. Since it involved issues of great substance, vast sums of money, and prominent attorneys, it generated much interest. Crowds, which included a "large proportion of well-dressed ladies," packed the courtroom to hear the eloquent arguments. The case's surprising length pushed back the starting date for the celebrated *Amistad* case, next on the court's docket.[38]

The justices had a number of issues to decide. Most obviously, they had to rule whether the Mississippi constitution was a ban in and of itself or whether it needed prohibitory legislation to become effective. John Quincy Adams, who listened to the case while preparing to argue for the *Amistad* slaves, grasped this point. He thought the *Groves* case turned on whether a state could "constitutionally prohibit" the interstate slave trade. Southerners extended the issue even further and saw the case as a test of state sovereignty. One newspaper feared for the future should the court rule against state authority. If that should happen, states could no longer protect themselves against abolitionists whose "fanaticism would provoke every species of excess against our laws and institutions." The court also had to address the question of whether slaves were persons or were articles of commerce. This area could cause enormous difficulties. Should the court rule that slaves were not articles of commerce, then it could be argued that bondser-

38. *Groves v. Slaughter*, 449–517, i–lxxxviii (first quotation on 477); undated *Baltimore American*, as quoted in *Washington Niles' National Register*, February 20, 1841, 400; Allan Nevins, ed., *The Diary of Philip Hone, 1828–1851*, 2 vols. (New York, 1927), February 19, 1841, 2:523 (final quotation); *Charleston Southern Patriot*, March 4, 1841; *Boston Massachusetts Spy*, February 24, 1841, clipping in Carl Swisher Papers, Library of Congress, Washington, D.C.; Charles Warren, *The Supreme Court in United States History*, 3 vols. (Boston, 1922), 2:342–46; Charles Sydnor, *The Development of Southern Sectionalism, 1819–1848*, vol. 5 of *A History of the South*, ed. Wendell Holmes Stephenson and E. Merton Coulter (Baton Rouge, 1948), 246–47; Carl B. Swisher, *The Taney Period, 1836–64*, vol. 5 of *The Oliver Wendell Holmes Devise History of the Supreme Court of the United States*, ed. Paul A. Freund (New York, 1974), 365–69; Sydnor, *Slavery in Mississippi*, 165–68.

vants were persons and the interstate slave trade infringed on their constitutional rights. If the court ruled that slaves were property, then it could deem that they were subject to the interstate commerce clause. Southerners had reason to fear such a decision. Abolitionists had already signaled their intentions to oppose the interstate slave trade whenever possible, and a ruling favorable to them would probably unleash a renewed attempt to regulate the trade to the point of extinction. The *Richmond Enquirer* sensed the danger. It believed the case involved the "right claimed by Abolitionists, for Congress to prohibit the transportation of slaves from State to State." The decisive issue for southerners, then, was a fear that the Supreme Court would shackle the interstate slave trade and cause slavery to wither away.[39]

Once the case began, Clay, Webster, and Jones argued that Mississippi's constitutional clause was no prohibition in itself, being merely a suggestion rather than a directive. Since it did not interdict trade, purchasers could not contest sales on the grounds of illegality. Clay forcefully argued that "no one questioned the right to introduce slaves for sale" after the constitution took effect. It was only during difficult economic times that it became convenient to avoid debt because hard-pressed Mississippi residents would be less willing to honor such contracts. In other words, the fundamental issue did not change, but people hoped to use economic trouble to avoid their obligations. More importantly, Clay accused the plaintiffs of being on the "abolition side of the question" when it came to the regulation of interstate commerce. He was implying that southerners who denied the trade's legitimacy were no better than northern agitators. Clay also tried to establish that Mississippi's prohibitory clause superseded the United States Constitution. "Regulation," in Clay's words, "implies continued existence." The abolitionists were trying to prevent the exercise of this commerce. Although Mississippi might not currently want the slave trade, it reserved the sole right to regulate it, he said. Clay finished by asserting that the slave trade was, in essence, a constitutional right. He flatly stated that "to deny the introduction of slaves, as merchandise, into a state, from another state, is an interference with the Constitution of the United States." In this view, the Constitution affirmed the right of state authority. If one were to take Clay

39. Charles Francis Adams, ed., *Memoirs of John Quincy Adams, Comprising Portions of his Diary from 1795 to 1848*, 12 vols. (Philadelphia, 1876), February 19, 1841, 10:427 (first quotation); *Milledgeville Georgia Journal*, January 26, 1841 (second quotation); *Richmond Enquirer*, April 9, 1841 (third quotation).

at his word, the regulation of the interstate slave trade was a litmus test for the southern argument to prevent any and all regulation of the peculiar institution and to preserve state authority.[40]

Clay's argument was "splendid," according to one observer, because he used the abolitionists as a scapegoat. Southerners had good reason to be pleased with his argument because this new line of thought forcefully outlined the emerging southern view of slavery. Webster, however, dissented from his partner's opinion. He carefully separated slavery and the slave trade—something southerners were reluctant to do. Webster argued that the United States Constitution recognized slaves as property and gave Congress the "power and duty to regulate commerce between the states." He thus tried to undo Clay's efforts to fuse the slave trade with the regulation of slavery. Webster, though, carefully qualified his argument. He admitted that Congress could not interfere with state regulations as to slavery per se, but could address commerce. The statements of these eminent statesmen show just how far apart many in the North and the South were by 1841. Clay described slave trading as a constitutional right while Webster thought the federal government could regulate speculation.[41]

Walker had a challenging task when it came time for him to present the government's case. Being a southerner, he did not want regulation of the trade, but he also had to argue against collection of debts. He swept past the smaller issues in his rebuttal, a statement that ably elucidated the aggressive southern defense of the interstate slave trade. His argument, which was too lengthy to include in the case description, endeavored to prove that interstate commerce in slaves was purely a state issue even while establishing that bondservants were property. Walker combined legal reasoning, political argumentation, and emotional appeals into an effective statement of why the interstate trade must remain a state issue and not become a federal one. His position came directly from the Mississippi Supreme Court's ruling. That Walker made political appeals is inferred from the situation in Mississippi. The Democrats urged him to run for senator in 1839, and much of the campaign involved the national bank. His attack on banks and the credit system as being heartless in the *Groves* case fits neatly with his pronounce-

40. *Groves v. Slaughter*, 482 (first quotation), 488 (second quotation), 489 (third quotation).

41. *Charleston Southern Patriot*, March 4, 1841 (first quotation); *Groves v. Slaughter*, 495 (second quotation).

ments during the campaign. The fact that he was indebted for several hundred thousand dollars of slave purchases also influenced his statements.[42]

Walker quickly clarified why a southern state would prohibit something it desperately wanted to preserve. It was, he explained, a matter of self-defense. Walker claimed that the "unscrupulous negro-trader" brought in slaves "of depraved character." Such men flouted the law, endangered citizens, and challenged conventional morals. The state and not the federal government, he explained, was in the best position to decide how to deal with such evil. Walker clearly relied on the stereotype of itinerant traders that had become widespread in the South to explain away the interstate slave trade.[43]

Although Walker had fashioned a worthy defense of the slave trade, he spent several hours arguing that the federal government had no authority in the matter. He did so even though Clay and Webster explicitly made the same point. Walker argued that regulation of the slave trade would give Congress the power "*to regulate slavery*, both in and among the states." That step was "abolition in its most dangerous form, under the mask of a power to regulate commerce." Walker wanted to make sure the door was shut tightly against any federal meddling with slavery. He boldly proclaimed that the power to regulate interstate commerce was Congress's sole prerogative. If that body chose to legislate the interstate slave trade "in defiance of state authority," it would provoke a "most alarming and momentous" controversy. He warned the Supreme Court not to get involved in the question because no one could predict the consequences. The likely result would be federal authority trampling on state control. Free states might find themselves in the uncomfortable position of having the federal government make slavery uniform throughout the entire country. Although this line of reasoning might seem absurd, Walker anticipated northern reaction to the *Dred Scott* case. He wanted the court to deem slavery to be "the unquestionable power of a state, and over which congress [*sic*] has no control or supervision." This analysis fit neatly into the emerging doctrine of states' rights. He rested his assertions on the bedrock of state authority rather than on federal control. At its base, Walker's defense of slavery and the slave trade encapsulated the essential southern position. He attached protection of the

42. *Groves v. Slaughter*, ix; James P. Shenton, *Robert John Walker: A Politician from Jackson to Lincoln* (New York, 1961), 27–30; Sydnor, *Slavery in Mississippi*, 166.

43. *Groves v. Slaughter*, xxxv–xxxvi.

slave trade to a vigorous assertion of states' rights. The implication was that defending speculation was ultimately worth the risk of secession.[44]

The court rendered its verdict on the day before it ruled on the *Amistad* case, and both decisions had the potential to cause much friction between slaveholding and free states. By a margin of five to two, it upheld the circuit court's decision and ruled that statutory legislation was necessary before the constitutional ban took effect. More importantly, and in a major victory for the South, the court specifically directed that Congress possessed no power to regulate the interstate slave trade. Three of the justices had slightly different slants on the ruling. In oral comments, John McLean thought states could outlaw slavery and prohibit the entry of bondservants. He flatly stated that the "power over slavery belongs to the states respectively. It is local in its character, and in its effects." Chief Justice Roger Taney left no doubt as to his personal opinion. The power over the interstate slave trade lay "exclusively with the several states," and Congress could not affect state action. Henry Baldwin, who was ardently antislavery, could not keep quiet either. He differed from his colleagues in believing that slaves could become the subjects of federal commerce. Even so, Baldwin asserted the authority of the states to legislate the interstate slave trade. He agreed with Walker's contention that federal regulation of speculation could eventually have deleterious effects on the free states.[45]

Bacon Tait rejoiced at the decision. He wrote Rice C. Ballard that because of the decision, traders could soon collect their debts. Ballard certainly greeted the news with joy; speculators and southerners in general had good reason to be happy. The *Groves* decision effectively neutralized efforts in Congress to regulate the interstate slave trade. The *Richmond Enquirer* called for abolitionists to respect the Court and abandon their petitions regarding slave trafficking. This part of the "Abolition controversy," the paper intoned, had been "solemnly settled in favor of the South." The paper was too optimistic. Opponents of slavery did not abandon the fight, but concentrated their efforts on the District of Columbia. They ultimately succeeded, of course, in having the trade banned in the District during the Compromise of 1850. Their victory was a hollow one, since most of the slave sales took place

44. Ibid., li, xlix (emphasis in original).

45. Ibid., 496–517 (quotations on 508, 514); *Washington Globe*, March 27, 1841, clipping in Carl Swisher Papers; Swisher, *Taney Period*, 367–69. During the court's term, Justice John Catron became ill and Justice Philip P. Barbour died, so only seven justices decided the case.

in Alexandria anyway. Southerners probably realized they could compromise on the District in 1850, since they now had the weight of case law on their side in any debate about regulating the interstate trade between the states.[46]

The *Groves* case symbolized the southern embrace of the interstate slave trade. Although defenders of slave trafficking denied its ubiquity and their own culpability, they still needed to explain the presence of slave traders. After all, owners who had the best interests of their slaves at heart presumably would not sell to a speculator. Just as the qualms that many southerners had about dealing with traders were rapidly disappearing, there was an underlying need to preserve the fiction that most owners preferred not to sell their slaves to speculators. Southerners could not deny the presence of traders, so it became common to assert that they were rare and had contact with a relatively small number of bondservants. Those few speculators who did exist, the thinking went, were shunned from polite society and only survived because they duped a gullible public into buying their slaves. They only bought slaves, moreover, who had been induced by abolitionists to stir up trouble. The trader was a necessary evil who was not a product of slaveholders' greed but of northerners' interference.

James Stirling, who traveled through the United States in the mid-1850s, believed that the interstate trade of slaves was "a sore subject with the defenders of slavery." They made a scapegoat of the trader and loaded "all the iniquities of the system on his unlucky back." All questions about the inhumanity or barbarity of bondage had a simple answer: owners sold slaves not because they wanted to, but because they had to. Traders stepped in and took advantage of the situation. As a result, slavery was good, the South was purer than the North, slaveholders acted responsibly and with the best interests of their slaves at heart, and the only unacceptable feature of southern society was the slave trader. Since speculators themselves were outcasts and devoid of honor, the argument continued, they remained at the periphery of society and were not important.[47]

This stereotypical view of traders was linked, in southern minds, to northerners. Fanatical abolitionists induced slaves to run away, while ruinous economic policies caused hardship in the South, thereby necessitating the sale of bondservants in the first place. Southerners redirected abolition-

46. Bacon Tait to Rice C. Ballard, June 23, 1841, Ballard Papers; *Richmond Enquirer*, April 9, 1841.

47. James Stirling, *Letters from the Slave States* (London, 1857), 292.

ist attacks on the peculiar institution by essentially saying northerners caused the worst abuses of slavery. As a result, there was no need to reform southern society or interfere with the rights of the master to sell his bondservants. Constructing a stereotypical view was one way to hold together a society increasingly under siege. It was also a way to distinguish itself from the North and demonstrate its greater virtue.

The rhetoric of an evil slave trader enabled southerners to explain a problematic aspect of their society: the cruel treatment of slaves. Once speculators were to blame for the worst abuses of slavery, southerners could remain committed to the institution as a whole. Certainly masters were just as much to blame for the sale of slaves as traders. Most southerners, however, preferred not to consider the full consequences of the interstate slave trade because it did not conveniently fit the notions of their society. The reliance on a class of evil speculators that the South ritually condemned allowed slaveholders to evade blame for splitting up families, punishing slaves, or engaging in other objectionable acts that brought grief to their bondservants. The disagreeable portions of slavery that naturally flowed from the institution could be separated from the slaveholders and blamed on circumstances beyond the master's control: itinerant traders, northern meddlers, or unruly slaves. In this way, speculators, abolitionists, and slaves became responsible for the worst features of slavery, thus sparing slaveholders from having to shoulder any blame for the negative consequences of the peculiar institution. In the face of the personal nature of abolitionist criticism after 1830, southerners found a way to avoid personal responsibility.

The southern interpretation of the interstate slave trade shows just how far southerners were willing to go to deny reality. They reduced the relationship between master and slave to a crude caricature, where the slaves were rarely separated from their relatives and the masters were more concerned with pleasing their bondservants than with financial survival. On the rare occasions where the slave trade intruded on this happy existence, it sometimes operated as rehabilitative force on those slaves who deserved to be sold because of their antisocial behavior. Citizens of the Upper South abandoned their initial reservations about the slave trade in favor of a completely unrealistic picture. Those in the Deep South overlooked their uneasiness about importing additional bondspeople. Just as slavery was beneficial to slaves, all aspects of the institution had to be free from defects, as well. There was no room for the troublesome reality of the interstate slave trade, so southerners substituted an idealized and stylized dream for the bitter reality of whippings, auctions, coffles, family separations, and personal anguish.

EPILOGUE

A Troubled Legacy

Isaac Franklin retired at the top of his profession. He and his partner, John Armfield, sold their slave-trading business to Rice Ballard, a friend and business associate. Franklin, nicknamed "the old man" by his business associates, probably thought it time for younger men to seek their fortunes. Soon after retiring, he complained that his health was bad, his eye was out, and his shoulder was broken. The years of traveling across the United States had taken their toll on the aging slave trader. It is likely Franklin also wanted to care for something different—his legacy. Franklin carefully planned how he could make the transition from slave trader to plantation owner. Sometime around 1826 he enlisted Francis Routh to buy land and slaves along the Mississippi River in Louisiana. Routh put the title to all the 3,600 acres and 75 slaves in his own name, presumably to conceal Franklin's identity. It was by no means certain that the established planters of West Feliciana Parish would welcome a slave trader in their midst. By 1838 Routh had finished his assignment, and Franklin bought him out in two lump-sum payments, the second of which was $72,500. The slave trader eventually acquired a total of 8,500 acres and 550 slaves in Louisiana, dividing them into six plantations. He also bought clumps of land in Tennessee, one of which was Fairvue, a mansion about five miles west of Gallatin. The spot was advantageous for many reasons: it had easy access to a tributary of the Cumberland River, it possessed numerous salt licks, and it was fertile farmland. Franklin raised mainly grain and livestock on Fairvue, products he shipped to his Louisiana plantations. He concentrated on transforming Fairvue into a manor house worthy of an extremely wealthy man, spending nearly $10,000 furnishing the two-story brick mansion. Franklin also owned land in Texas, shares in the Commercial Bank of Manchester, the Nashville and Gallatin Turnpike Company, and the Nashville Racecourse. Clearly, he was one of the richest men in the United States.[1]

Franklin sealed his transition from slave trader to respectable planter by marrying into a prosperous and respectable Nashville family. In 1839 he took Adelicia Hayes as his wife, a woman twenty-eight years younger than the fifty-year-old Franklin. Her father once had a law partnership with Thomas Hart Benton, but then retired from the legal profession to become a Presbyterian minister. Whether it was a match of love or convenience is open to speculation, but it served both of them well. Franklin gained a measure of respectability that money could not buy, and Hayes set out to find out how much she could buy with Franklin's money.[2]

The marriage ended in seven years with Franklin's sudden death. His will spelled out specific plans for the disposition of his estate, and he made provision for Adelicia. She was to live off the proceeds of Fairvue and, if she remarried, receive $100,000 over a period of years. Franklin, moreover, laid out detailed plans for carving out more plantations from his Louisiana property on which to establish his children. The will also called for a surprise. Franklin wanted to establish the "Isaac Franklin Academy" on Fairvue's grounds to educate his children, nieces, and nephews. If money permitted (and it is difficult to understand how it would not), he also wanted the institute to serve the poor children of Sumner County and then become a permanent institution of learning. The Tennessee legislature soon followed suit and passed an act incorporating the school. Franklin's widow then sold

1. Jacob F. Purvis to George Kephart, December 4, 1837, Kephart Papers, New Jersey Historical Society, Trenton, N.J. (quotation); John Armfield to Rice C. Ballard, December 29, 1832, Isaac Franklin to Rice C. Ballard, March 5, 1838, Ballard Papers; titles to Franklin-Routh land, Acklen Family Papers, Tulane; Stephenson, *Isaac Franklin*, 94–96; *Succession of Isaac Franklin*, 273–304; Stephanie L. Perrault et al., *Cultural Resources Survey, Testing, and Exploratory Trenching for the Louisiana State Penitentiary Levee Enlargement Project, West Feliciana Parish, Louisiana* (Baton Rouge, 2001), 57–67.

2. *Succession of Isaac Franklin*, 486–500; Stephenson, *Isaac Franklin*, 18–21; Albert W. Wardin Jr., *Belmont Mansion: The Home of Joseph and Adelicia Acklen* (Nashville: Belmont Mansion Association, 1989), 4–5; *About Belmont: Belmont Mansion*, website, http://www.belmont.edu/about/mansion.cfm, accessed July 10, 2002.

her life interest in Fairvue to trustee William Franklin. It appeared that Franklin's dream was soon to become a reality.[3]

Adelicia changed her mind, however. In 1849 she married Joseph A. S. Acklen, a wealthy Alabama planter who is remembered for his pamphlet establishing rules for overseers. She then sued to forbid the use of Franklin's Louisiana property to establish the academy, presumably to ensure the payment of her money. The Louisiana supreme court ruled in her favor and, as a result, spoiled Franklin's plan for largesse. Fairvue remained a plantation, but the proceeds from it were not enough to build and staff an academy. Adelicia, however, hardly had time to pause at Fairvue. She and Acklen built the sumptuous Belmont Mansion in Nashville and apparently left Fairvue vacant until 1869. Franklin, rather than being remembered as the benefactor of a school, will forever be known as a slave trader.[4]

Franklin's partner John Armfield also appears to have been concerned with how posterity would consider him. He proved more successful than Franklin in establishing an identity other than that of a slave trader. Armfield purchased a resort in Beersheba Springs, Tennessee, and converted the establishment into a type of spa. Beersheba Springs was modeled after the hot baths in Virginia, where wealthy Americans could "take the waters." The baths were valued not only for their warmth, but also for their exclusivity. Armfield added an elaborate two-story hotel, created twenty private cabins, and imported chefs and musicians from New Orleans. Beersheba Springs attracted wealthy visitors from across the South and enjoyed lively social seasons until the Civil War. Like his slave-trading partner, Armfield wanted to be remembered as a patron of education. He was instrumental in establishing the University of the South at Sewanee. It is instructive that Franklin and Armfield, linked forever through the slave trade, also sought similar means to distance themselves from the foul odor of speculation.[5]

3. *Succession of Isaac Franklin*, 447 (quotation), 397–403; Stephenson, *Isaac Franklin*, 116–19; *New Orleans Daily Picayune*, October 7, 1846; *New Orleans Daily Delta*, December 19, 1849; Wardin, *Belmont Mansion*, 5.

4. *Succession of Isaac Franklin*, 397–403; Stephenson, *Isaac Franklin*, 116–19; Joseph A. S. Acklen, *Rules, Regulations and Instructions, for the Management, Government and Guidance of Overseers and Employees* (New Orleans, 1861); Wardin, *Belmont Mansion*, 7–8.

5. Margaret Brown Coppinger, *Beersheba Springs: 150 Years, 1833–1983: A History and a Celebration* (Beersheba Springs, Tenn., 1983), 10–12; Isabel Howell, "John Armfield, Slave-Trader," *Tennessee Historical Quarterly* 2 (1943): 3–29; Isabel Howell, "John Armfield of Beersheba Springs," *Tennessee Historical Quarterly* 3 (1944): 46–64, 156–67; *The Tennessee Encyclopedia of History and Culture* (Nashville, 1998), s.v. "Beersheba Springs."

What is striking about these slave traders—two men who succeeded in a difficult and controversial business—is their later efforts to use their wealth as an entrée into polite society and establish their reputations within the southern culture of honor. What Franklin and Armfield knew better than most is that the interstate slave trade was at the center of a battle over the contested meaning of the antebellum South. Was slavery, as most white southerners wanted to believe, a beneficial and useful institution? Or was it, as most African Americans understood, a brutal and degrading business? White southerners had to find a way to reconcile these two incredibly variant interpretations. As a result, they willingly endorsed the creation of "classes" of slave traders in order to reduce their culpability with the brutal aspects of the peculiar institution. A class of evil slave traders could be publicly and ritually condemned for wreaking havoc in the lives of slaves so that ordinary slaveholders would feel no remorse for engaging in essentially the same activities. Franklin and Armfield understood this idea and tried to jettison their difficult past in order to achieve a more acceptable future for themselves and their children.

Just as the interstate slave trade lay at the crossroads of meaning for the Old South, it is also fundamental to modern-day perceptions of that society. The contested image of the interstate slave trade has made itself known in two diametrically opposite interpretations of the Old South. A real estate developer has bought the Fairvue estate. He planned to convert the land into a gated suburban community, transform the mansion into a clubhouse, and turn the old slave quarters into bed-and-breakfast suites. The developer renamed the estate "The Last Plantation," conjuring up images of belles in hoop skirts surrounded by dashing young men. It is the moonlight-and-magnolias myth writ large. The marketing of the "The Last Plantation" is canny. In an amazing display of historical amnesia, Fairvue has been cleansed of anything that might indicate slavery's essential brutality. Just like the those who wanted to believe the best of the interstate slave trade, "The Last Plantation" is a measure of the unwillingness of many to submit to a complex reality. Its message is one of a white master class asserting its dominance over a docile and well-treated African American workforce. "The Last Plantation" portrays an image of the Old South that would make U. B. Phillips proud.[6]

6. *The Last Plantation*, website of the Last Plantation, http://www.thelastplantation.com, accessed July 10, 2002. Ulrich Bonnell Phillips was a southern historian in the early twentieth century. His works have been identified as minimizing slavery's negative aspects.

There is another way to measure Franklin's legacy. It is grimly ironic that his favorite Louisiana plantation, Angola, is now the Louisiana State Penitentiary. Where slaves once labored, about 5,100 inmates bide their time. Approximately 3,800 of those prisoners are African Americans. In the prison's first days, it housed inmates in the slave quarters. The location of a state penitentiary on a slave trader's plantation might be coincidental, but the jail itself is eerily reminiscent of slavery. Although slavery has been compared to a concentration camp, perhaps a more fitting comparison would be a jail. Although less brutal and dehumanizing than a concentration camp, jails employ some of the same methods of slavery: confinement, the constant threat of physical punishment, certain opportunities to carve out a niche based on human initiative, and hard work for minimal rewards.[7]

There is a third way between these two extremes. Another interpretation of the slave trade lay in Franklin and Armfield's slave jail in Alexandria. It had served as a slave jail until 1861, when the United States Army occupied the building. The army immediately recognized the utility of the fortress and converted it into a prison for Union soldiers who had been drunk and disorderly or who had tried to desert. Not surprisingly, the "Slave Pen Prison" had one of the best records for preventing escape, a reality that could have been attested to by the tens of thousands of slaves who had been locked in its cages. The building began to shed its symbolism as the enslaver of African Americans and became an instrument in the fight for freedom. Black soldiers stationed just across the street at the L'Ouverture military hospital lived in a portion of the slave pen. The hospital, for black soldiers only, doubled as a schoolhouse and temporary home for slaves who had seized their freedom and run to the Union army.[8]

The building continues its process of redemption today. The Urban League of Northern Virginia has acquired the building and is converting

7. *Louisiana State Penitentiary*, website of the Louisiana Department of Public Safety and Corrections, http://www.corrections.state.la.us/LSP, accessed July 10, 2002; *Demographic Profiles of the Adult Correctional Population*, website of the Louisiana Department of Public Safety and Corrections, http://www.corrections.state.la.us/stats2.htm, accessed July 10, 2002; Stanley Elkins, *Slavery: A Problem in American Institutional and Intellectual Life* (1959; 3rd ed. Chicago, 1976); Wyatt-Brown, *Shaping of Southern Culture*, 3–30.

8. Artemel, Crowell, and Parker, *Alexandria Slave Pen*, 41–47; James W. Loewen, *Lies across America: What Our Historic Sites Get Wrong* (New York: 1999), 290–94; *To Witness the Past: African-American Archaeology in Alexandria, Virginia*, website, http://oha.ci.alexandria.va.us/archaeology/ar-exhibits-witness-4.html, accessed January 6, 2003.

the basement into a museum to interpret slavery and the slave trade in Virginia and the District of Columbia. It was in the basement that many of the slaves were confined prior to shipment to the Deep South, and it is here that prison bars and slave chains are still attached to the walls. This building's name carries its own moral freight. "Freedom House" is designed to capture the struggle of enslaved people to assert their individuality and work out a place for human agency within the confined space of slavery. While a long way from the ideological implications of "The Last Plantation," or the Louisiana State Penitentiary, "Freedom House" has its own message. Rather than seeing antebellum southern society in romantic terms, or as a society that fostered only brutality, "Freedom House" believes that the basement, with its slave cages, "represents our past, but the first floor and above represents our future." Regardless of which interpretation one believes, the legacy bequeathed to America from slavery and the interstate trade is troublesome.[9]

9. *Freedom House*, website of the Northern Virginia Urban League, http://www.novaul.org/freedomhouse.html, accessed July 11, 2002.

APPENDIX

TABLE I

Estimated Interregional Migration of the White Population, 1810–1840

Age	0–10	10–20	20–30	30–40	40+	Total
1810–1820						
Old South	–82,368	–55,349	–36,035	–20,957	–28,069	–222,777
Percentage	37.0	24.8	16.2	9.4	12.6	
New South	30,442	28,175	15,066	9,384	12,242	95,309
Percentage	31.2	29.6	15.8	9.8	12.8	
1820–1830						
Old South	–78,768	–52,803	–35,730	–19,834	–25,516	–212,651
Percentage	37.0	24.8	16.8	9.3	12.0	
New South	22,571	31,646	19,660	8,606	7,788	90,271
Percentage	25.0	35.1	21.8	9.5	8.6	
1830–1840						
Old South	–118,297	–97,871	–61,900	–30,545	–35,119	–343,732
Percentage	34.4	28.4	18.0	8.9	10.2	
New South	–6,663	24,495	15,782	4,316	1,775	39,705
Percentage	N/A	N/A	N/A	N/A	N/A	

Age groupings indicate age at the beginning of the decade.

Old South: Delaware, Maryland, Virginia, North Carolina, South Carolina.

New South: Georgia, Florida, Tennessee, Alabama, Mississippi, Arkansas, Louisiana.

Source: Peter D. McClelland and Richard J. Zeckhauser, *Demographic Dimensions of the New Republic: American Interregional Migration, Vital Statistics, and Manumissions, 1800–1860* (New York, 1982), 138–43.

TABLE 2

Estimated Interregional Migration of the African American Population, 1810–1840

Age	0–10	10–20	20–30	30–40	40+	Total
1810–1820						
Old South	–36,545	–11,874	–5,623	–6,722	–2,433	–63,197
Percentage	57.8	18.8	8.9	10.6	3.8	
New South	29,868	7,811	4,311	5,059	2,500	49,549
Percentage	54.2	15.8	9.3	10.9	5.0	
1820–1830						
Old South	–49,061	–24,181	–10,002	–3,312	–5,474	–92,030
Percentage	53.3	26.3	10.9	3.6	5.9	
New South	44,208	21,143	8,962	2,531	4,578	81,422
Percentage	54.3	26.0	11.0	3.1	5.6	
1830–1840						
Old South	–84,722	–51,562	–28,962	–12,020	–13,426	–190,962
Percentage	44.4	27.0	15.2	6.3	7.0	
New South	71,179	47,167	5,307	8,812	10,715	163,180
Percentage	43.6	28.9	15.5	5.4	6.6	

Age groupings indicate age at the beginning of the decade.
Old South: Delaware, Maryland, Virginia, North Carolina, South Carolina.
New South: Georgia, Florida, Tennessee, Alabama, Mississippi, Arkansas, Louisiana.

Source: Peter D. McClelland and Richard J. Zeckhauser, *Demographic Dimensions of the New Republic: American Interregional Migration, Vital Statistics, and Manumissions, 1800–1860* (New York, 1982), 159–64.

BIBLIOGRAPHY

PRIMARY SOURCES

MANUSCRIPT COLLECTIONS

Alabama Department of Archives and History, Montgomery

Alabama Governors' Papers
James Dellet Papers
Bolling Hall Papers
Pickens Family Papers
Pitts Family Papers
Tait Family Papers
Walker Family Papers

American Antiquarian Society, Worcester, Mass.

Lucy Chase Family Papers
R. H. Dickinson and Brother Day Book
Dickinson and Hill, Company Account Book

Auburn University Archives, Auburn, Ala.

Tait Collection

Boston Public Library, Boston, Mass.

Anti-Slavery May Papers
Ziba B. Oakes Papers
Slave Trade Collection

Chicago Historical Society, Chicago

Hector Davis and Company, Slave sales record books
R. H. Dickinson Papers
William Gaston Collection

Columbia University, New York

Butler Library

Frederic Bancroft Papers

Duke University, Durham, N.C.

Perkins Library

John Agg Papers
Angus Blakely Papers
Reuben Dean Bowen Papers
Archibald H. Boyd Papers
Campbell Papers
William Crow Letters
John E. Dennis Papers
Joseph and Washington Dickinson Papers
Obadiah Fields Papers
William A. J. Finney Papers
Tyre Glen Papers
Robert S. Gracey Papers
James Graham Papers
William Haynie Hatchett Papers
Edward B. and D. S. Hicks Papers
Edward Hooker Papers
John H. Howard Papers
Jarratt-Puryear Papers
Daniel W. Jordan Papers
William W. Jordan Diary
John Knight Papers
John Robert Middleton Papers
James A. Mitchell Papers
Sterling Neblett Papers
Negro Collection
John O'Neale Papers
William C. F. Powell Papers
D. M. Pulliam Papers
Francis Everod Rives Papers
Langhorne Scruggs Papers
James Sheppard Papers
James A. Tutt Papers
David G. Waller Papers
Floyd L. Whitehead Papers
Matthew J. Williams Diary

Samuel O. Wood Papers
Francis Yarnall Papers

Georgia Department of Archives and History, Atlanta
William G. Ponder Papers
Slave Importation Registers for Elbert County, Drawer 2, Box 76

Harvard University, Cambridge, Mass.
Houghton Library
Paul Pascal Papers
Slavery Papers

Library of Congress, Washington, D.C.
Manuscript Division
Black History Collection
Cornelius Chase Family Papers
Franklin H. Elmore Papers
William A. Galbraith Papers
Turner Reavis Papers
Carl Swisher Papers

Louisiana State University, Baton Rouge
Hill Memorial Library
Anonymous Letter number 3416
John Bisland Papers
Samuel R. Browning Letter
Owen B. Cox Papers
John W. Gurley Papers
William S. Hamilton Papers
William Kenner Papers
John McDonogh Letters
Joseph Meek Letter
U.S. Customs Service Records. Port of New Orleans, La., Inward Slave Manifests, 1807, 1819–1860 (microfilm)
Douglas Walworth and Family Papers
David Weeks and Family Papers

Kentucky, University of, Lexington
King Library
Allen-Butler Papers
J. Winston Coleman Papers
Gordon Family Papers
Fountain and Roderick Perry Papers

Maryland Department of Archives and History, Annapolis
Talbot County Land Records

Massachusetts Historical Society, Boston
Theodore Parker Papers

Mississippi Department of Archives and History, Jackson
Adams County Papers, Auction Sales of Slaves, 1827–1830, Record Group: Natchez Reel, 157.
Adams County Papers, Certificates of Negro Traders, 1833, Record Group: Natchez, Reel 36.
Adams County Papers, City of Natchez Health Officer Reports, Record Group: Natchez, Reel 57.
Adams County Papers, City of Natchez Minute Books, Minute Book Number 6, 1820–1875, Record Group: Natchez, Reel 2.
Adams County Papers, City of Natchez Municipal Records, Record Group: Natchez, Reel 45.
Adams County Papers, City of Natchez Ordinances, 1829–1854, Record Group: Natchez, Reel 45.
Adams County Papers, City of Natchez Petitions, 1824–1833, Record Group: Natchez, Reel 47.
Adams County Papers, Lists of Sales of Slaves, 1833, Record Group: Natchez, Reel 157.
J. F. H. Claiborne Papers
John G. Jones Autobiography
John G. Jones Journal
James T. Magruder Papers

National Archives, Washington, D.C.
Papers of the Select Committee to Inquire into the Existence of an Inhuman and Illegal Traffic in Slaves . . . in the District of Columbia, HR 14A-C.17.4.

New Jersey Historical Society, Newark
Raritan Bay Union and Eagleswood Military Academy Collection
Papers of George Kephart

New Orleans Public Library, New Orleans
New Orleans, Office of the Mayor. Lists of Slaves Imported for Sale in the City of New Orleans, 1831.
New Orleans Conseil de Ville (City Council). Records of Proceedings.
New Orleans Parish Court. Declarations of Individuals Importing Slaves into New Orleans, 1831–1833.

New York Public Library, New York
Hector Davis and Company Day Book
H. N. Templeman Account Book

North Carolina Division of Archives and History, Raleigh
Badgett Family Papers
John W. Bond Papers
Jesse H. Cobb Letter
Elias W. Ferguson Papers
Southgate Jones Papers
William Long Papers
David S. Reid Papers
Mary Jeffrey Rogers Collection
Joseph S. Totten Papers
Randolph Webb Papers
Elizabeth Winston Collection
Witherspoon and McDowell Papers

North Carolina, University of, Chapel Hill
Southern Historical Collection
Rice C. Ballard Papers
James Thomas Harrison Papers
Ernest Haywood Collection
E. V. Howell Papers
Jackson and Prince Family Papers
Lenoir Family Papers
David Outlaw Papers
Pettigrew Family Papers
Abram David Pollock Papers
Springs Family Papers
Templeman and Goodwin Account Book
Waddy Thompson Papers
John Walker Papers
Floyd L. Whitehead Papers
Witherspoon and McDowall Papers

Tennessee State Library and Archives, Nashville
James Bradley Letter
Felix Grundy Papers, in the Whitefoord R. Cole Collection
Emil Edward Hurja Collection, Peter Force Materials
Wallace Alexander Jones Papers, Memoir of Norman Smith
Thomas Hardin Perkins Papers

Winchester and Erwin Family Papers
Wynne Family Papers

Tennessee, University of, Knoxville
James D. Hoskins Library
David Burford Papers

Texas, University of, Austin
Center for American History
Barnes-Willis Family Papers, Natchez Trace Slavery Collection
"Entry of Slaves in Concordia Parish, Louisiana, 1826–1831," Natchez Trace Slavery Collection
Steamboat receipts, Natchez Trace Steamboat Collection

Tulane University, New Orleans
Howard-Tilton Memorial Library
Acklen Family Papers
John McDonogh Papers
James E. Winston, "New Orleans as a Slave Mart before 1860." Typescript in the Slavery Manuscript Series

Virginia Historical Society, Richmond
[C. Abner] Letter
Beverley Family Papers
Blow Family Papers
Branch and Company Records
Benjamin Brand Papers
James T. Harrison Papers
Joseph Meek Papers
Tayloe Family Papers
William M. Waller Papers

Virginia, Library of, Richmond
Goshen Association Minutes
Silas Omohundro Papers

Virginia, University of, Charlottesville
Alderman Library
Argosy Collection
Austin Brockenbrough Papers
Cocke Family Papers
Philip St. George Cocke Papers
Dearing Family Papers
Harris-Brady Collection

Carter H. Harrison Diary
Hooe-Harrison Letters
Kennon Family Papers
Morton-Halsey Papers
Silas and R. R. Omohundro Slave Sales Book
Palmore Family Papers
Pocket Plantation Papers
Southside Papers
Richard H. Stuart Papers
Floyd L. Whitehead Papers
Robert N. Windsor Papers

GOVERNMENT DOCUMENTS

Acts passed at the first Session of the second General Assembly of the State of Mississippi. Natchez: Marschalk and Evans, 1819.

Debates and Proceedings in the Congress of the United States. Washington: Gales and Seaton, 1854.

A Digest of the Ordinances and Resolutions of the General Council of the City of New-Orleans. New Orleans: J. Bayon, 1845.

A Digest of the Ordinances, Resolutions, By-laws and Regulations of the Corporation of New-Orleans, and a Collection of the Laws of the Legislature relative to the said City. New Orleans: Gaston Brusle, 1836.

Groves et al. v. Slaughter, 40 U.S. (15 Peters).

Journal of the Senate of the State of Alabama, 13th sess. Montgomery: The Senate, 1832.

Laws of the State of Mississippi, 8th sess. Jackson: 1825.

Louisiana Senate Journal, Extra 10th sess., 1831. Baton Rouge: 1832.

Register of Debates in Congress. Washington: Gales and Seaton, 1830.

Succession of Isaac Franklin. n.p., n.d.

NEWSPAPERS

Alabama
Huntsville Southern Advocate, 1825–1834
Huntsville Weekly Democrat, 1827–1829
Mobile Commercial Register, 1821–1831
District of Columbia
Daily National Intelligencer, 1812–1833
Georgetown National Messenger, 1817–1819
Niles' Weekly Register, 1816–1842

Georgia
Augusta Chronicle and Georgia Gazette, 1820–1827
Milledgeville Georgia Journal, 1810–1831
Milledgeville Southern Recorder, 1820–1832
Savannah Republican, 1817–1820
Kentucky
Lexington Kentucky Gazette, 1815–1830
Lexington Public Advertiser, 1820–1821
Paris Western Citizen, 1812, 1821, 1831–1838
Louisiana
Baton Rouge Gazette, 1831
New Orleans Bee, 1830–1834
New Orleans Louisiana Advertiser, 1820, 1826–1835
New Orleans Louisiana Courier, 1810–1837
New Orleans Louisiana Gazette, 1818–1826
New Orleans Picayune, 1840–1841
Maryland
Annapolis Maryland Gazette, 1810–1824
Baltimore American and Commerical Advertiser, 1815–1825
Easton Republican Star and General Advertiser, 1821–1828
Mississippi
Natchez Ariel, 1825–1828
Natchez Courier and Journal, 1835–1836
Natchez Gazette, 1806–1808
Natchez Mississippi Journal and Natchez Advertiser, 1833
Natchez Mississippi Republican, 1813–1824
Natchez Mississippi State Gazette, 1820–1824
Natchez Mississippi Statesman and Natchez Gazette, 1827
Woodville Republican and Wilkinson Weekly Advertiser, 1824–1836
North Carolina
New Bern Newbernian, 1850
Raleigh Register and North Carolina Gazette, 1815–1823
Raleigh Star and North Carolina State Gazette, 1828
South Carolina
Charleston Courier, 1815–1820
Charleston Mercury, 1822–1841
Charleston Southern Patriot and Commercial Advertiser, 1816–1817
Tennessee
Nashville Republican and State Gazette, 1824–1831
Nashville Whig, 1812–1829
National Banner and Nashville Whig, 1819–1827

Virginia
Alexandria Phenix Gazette, 1825–1827
Fredericksburg Virginia Herald, 1815–1826
Lexington Intelligencer, 1823–1831
Norfolk American Beacon and Commercial Diary, 1815–1820
Richmond Enquirer, 1820–1837
Warrenton Palladium of Liberty, 1817–1820

OTHER PERIODICALS

Abolition Intelligencer and Missionary Magazine
African Observer
Genius of Universal Emancipation
Liberator
Port Folio
Religious Remembrancer
Southern Literary Journal
Western Luminary

BOOKS AND ARTICLES

Abdy, E. S. *Journal of a Residence and Tour in the United States of North America*, 3 vol. London: John Murray, 1835.

Acklen, Joseph A. S. *Rules, Regulations and Instructions, for the Management, Government and Guidance of Overseers and Employees.* New Orleans: P. O'Donnell, 1861.

Adams, Charles Francis, ed. *Memoirs of John Quincy Adams, Comprising Portions of his Diary from 1795 to 1848.* 12 vols. Philadelphia: J. B. Lippincott, 1876.

Adams, Nehemiah. *South-side View of Slavery: or Three Months at the South in 1854.* 3rd ed. Boston: T. R. Marvin, 1855.

"American Convention [of] Abolition Societies, Minutes, 1828." *Journal of Negro History* 6 (July 1921): 326–28.

Andrews, Ethan A. *Slavery and the Domestic Slave-Trade in the United States.* Boston: Light and Stearns, 1836.

Arfwedson, C. D. *The United States and Canada, in 1832, 1833, and 1834*, 2 vols. London: Richard Bentley, 1834.

Ball, Charles. *Slavery in the United States: A Narrative of the Life and Adventures of Charles Ball, a Black Man.* 1837; reprint, New York: Negro Universities Press, 1969.

Bernhard, Duke of Saxe-Weimar Eisenach. *Travels through America, during the Years 1825 and 1826.* 2 vols. Philadelphia: Carey, Lea, and Carey, 1828.

Bibb, Henry. *Narrative of the Life and Adventures of Henry Bibb, an American Slave.* 1850; reprint, New York: Negro Universities Press, 1969.

Birkbeck, Morris. *Notes on a Journey in America.* 1818; reprint, Ann Arbor, Mich.: University Microfilms, 1966.

Blackford, L. Minor. *Mine Eyes have seen the Glory: The Story of a Virginia Lady Mary Berkeley Minor Blackford 1802–1896 who taught her sons to hate Slavery and to love the Union.* Edited by F. Nash Boney. Cambridge, Mass.: Harvard University Press, 1954.

Blanchard, J., and N. L. Rice. *A Debate on Slavery held in the City of Cincinnati.* Cincinnati: William H. Moore, 1846.

[Blane, William H.] *An Excursion through the United States and Canada during the years 1822–23.* 1824; reprint, New York: Negro Universities Press, 1969.

Blassingame, John W., ed. *Slave Testimony: Two Centuries of Letters, Speeches, Interviews, and Autobiographies.* Baton Rouge: Louisiana State University Press, 1977.

Boney, F. Nash, ed. *Slave Life in Georgia: A Narrative of the Life, Sufferings, and Escape of John Brown, a Fugitive Slave.* Savannah: Beehive Press, 1972.

Bontemps, Arna, ed. *Great Slave Narratives.* Boston: Beacon Press, 1969.

———. *Five Black Lives: The Autobiographies of Venture Smith, James Mars, William Grimes, the Rev. G. W. Offley, James L. Smith.* Middletown, Conn.: Wesleyan University Press, 1971.

Brandon, Nellie Wailes, and W. M. Drake, eds. *Memoir of Leonard Covington by B. L. C. Wailes.* 1861; reprint, n.p., 1928.

Breeden, James O., ed. *Advice among Masters: The Ideal in Slave Management in the Old South.* Westport, Conn.: Greenwood Press, 1980.

Bremer, Fredrika. *Homes of the New World: Impressions of America.* 2 vols. Translated by Mary Howitt. New York: Harper and Brother, 1854.

[Brown, Henry Box]. *Narrative of Henry Box Brown.* Boston: Brown and Stearns, 1849.

Brown, William Wells. *Narrative of William Wells Brown: A Fugitive Slave.* Boston: Anti-Slavery Office, 1847.

Buckingham, James S. *The Slave States of America.* 2 vols. London: Fisher and Son, 1842.

Butler, Lindsey S., ed. *The Papers of David Settle Reid.* Vol. 1, 1829–1852. Raleigh: Department of Archives and History, 1993.

Chambers, William. *Things as they are in America.* London: William and Robert Chambers, 1854.

Chevalier, Michael. *Society, Manners and Politics in the United States: Being a Series of Letters on North America.* Boston: Weeks, Jordan, and Company, 1839.

Child, Lydia M. *The Patriarchical Institution, as described by Members of its own Family.* New York: American Anti-Slavery Society, 1860.

Clay, Thomas S. *Detail of a Plan for the Moral Improvement of Negroes on Plantations.* N.p., 1833.

Cobb, Thomas R. R. *An Inquiry into the Law of Negro Slavery in the United States of America.* Vol. 1. Philadelphia: T. and J. W. Johnson, 1858.

Committee of the Synod of Kentucky. *An Address to the Presbytery of Kentucky, Proposing a Plan for the Instruction and Emancipation of their Slaves.* Cincinnati: Taylor and Tracy, 1835.

Conway, Moncure D. *Testimonies Concerning Slavery.* London: Chapman and Hall, 1864.

Cossitt, F[ranceway] R. *The Life and Times of Rev. Finis Ewing.* 3rd ed. Louisville: Morton and Griswold, 1853.

Criswell, Robert. *"Uncle Tom's Cabin" contrasted with Buckingham Hall, the Planter's Home, or a fair View of both Sides of the Slavery Question.* New York: D. Fanshaw, 1852.

Crowe, Eyre. *With Thackeray in America.* London: Caswell, 1893.

Davis, Edwin Adams. *Plantation Life in the Florida Parishes of Louisiana, 1836–1846 as reflected in the Diary of Bennet H. Barrow.* New York: Columbia University Press, 1943.

Davis, Stephen. *Notes of a Tour in America, in 1832 and 1833.* Edinburgh, Scotland: Waugh and Innes, 1833.

Dew, Thomas R. "Review of the Debate in the Virginia Legislature of 1831 and 1832." As reprinted in *The Pro-Slavery Argument as Maintained by the Most Distinguished Writers of the Southern States.* Philadelphia: Lippincott, Grambo, 1853.

Dodge, N. S. "A Charleston Vendue in 1842." *Galaxy Magazine,* January 1869, 119–23.

Douglass, Frederick. *My Bondage and My Freedom.* 1855; reprint, New York: Arno Press, 1968.

———. *Life and Times of Frederick Douglass.* 1881; reprint, Secaucus, N.J.: Citadel Press, 1983.

Drago, Edmund L., ed. *Broke by the War: Letters of a Slave Trader.* Columbia: University of South Carolina Press, 1991.

Drew, Benjamin, ed. *The Refugee: or the Narratives of Fugitive Slaves in Canada.* Boston: John P. Jewett, 1856.

Dumond, Dwight L., ed. *Letters of James Gillespie Birney, 1831–1857.* 2 vols. New York: D. Appleton, 1938.

Eastman, Mary H. *Aunt Phillis's Cabin: of Southern Life as It is.* Philadelphia: Lippincott and Grambo, 1852.

Elliott, Charles. *History of the Great Secession from the Methodist Episcopal Church in the Year 1845.* Cincinnati: R. P. Thompson, 1855.

[Erwin, Andrew]. *A Brief Account of General Jackson's Dealings in Negroes, in a Series of Letters and Documents by his own Neighbors.* N.p., [1828].

———. *Gen. Jackson's Negro Speculations, and his Traffic in Human Flesh, examined and established by Positive Proof.* N.p., [1828].

———. *Supplement to Andrew Jackson's Negro Speculations.* N.p., [1828].

"Estimates of the Value of Slaves, 1815." *American Historical Review* 19 (July 1914): 813–38.

Evans, Estwick. *A Pedestrious Tour of Four Thousand Miles, through the Western States and Territories during the Winter and Spring of 1818.* Concord, Mass.: Joseph C. Spear, 1819.

Faust, Drew Gilpin, ed. *The Ideology of Slavery: Proslavery Thought in the Antebellum South, 1830–1860.* Baton Rouge: Louisiana State University Press, 1981.

Fearon, Henry B. *Sketches of America: A Narrative of a Journey of Five Thousand Miles through the Eastern and Western States of America.* London: Longman, Hurst, Rees, Orme, and Brown, 1818.

Featherstonhaugh, George W. *Excursion through the Slave States, from Washington on the Potomac to the Frontier of Mexico.* 1844; reprint, New York: Negro Universities Press, 1968.

Finch, I. [John]. *Travels in the United States of America and Canada.* London: Longman, Rees, Orme, Brown, Green, and Longman, 1833.

Garland, Hugh A. "The Domestic Slave Trade." *Western Journal and Civilian* 14 (November 1855): 406–11.

"Governor Charles Goldsborough's Views on Slavery." *Maryland Historical Magazine* 39 (December 1944): 332–34.

Grandy, Moses. *Narrative of the Life of Moses Grandy, Late a Slave in the United States of America.* Boston: Oliver Johnson, 1844.

Hall, Basil. *Travels in North America in the Years 1827 and 1828.* 2 vols. Philadelphia: Carey, Lea, and Carey, 1829.

Hall, Francis. *Travels in Canada, and the United States, in 1816 and 1817.* London: Longman, Hurst, Rees, Orme, and Brown, 1818.

Hamilton, Thomas. *Men and Manners in America.* 2 vols. London: T. Cadell, 1833.

[Harrison, Jesse Burton]. *Review of the Slave Question, extracted from the American Quarterly Review, Dec. 1832.* Richmond: T. W. White, 1833.

Hodgson, Adam. *Remarks during a Journey through North America in the Years 1819, 1820, and 1821.* New York: Samuel Whiting, 1823.

———. *Letters from North America, written during a Tour in the United States and Canada.* 2 vols. London: Hurst and Robinson, 1824.

Hogan, William R. and Edwin A. Davis, eds. *William Johnson's Natchez: The Ante-Bellum Diary of a Free Negro.* Baton Rouge: Louisiana State University Press, 1993.

Hundley, Daniel R. *Social Relations in Our Southern States.* 1860; reprint, Baton Rouge: Louisiana State University Press, 1979.

———, ed. *The Sunny South; or, The Southerner at Home.* Philadelphia: G. G. Evans, 1860.

Ingraham, Joseph H. *The South-West by a Yankee.* 2 vols. 1835; reprint, Ann Arbor, Mich.: University Microfilms, 1966.

Jay, William. *A View of the Action of the Federal Government in behalf of Slavery.* New York: J. S. Taylor, 1839.

———. *Miscellaneous Writings on Slavery.* Boston: John P. Jewett, 1853.

Jefferson, Paul, ed. *The Travels of William Wells Brown.* New York: Markus Wiener, 1991.

Jeter, Jeremiah. *Recollections of a Long Life.* Richmond: Religious Herald, 1891.

"John Owen's Journal of His Removal from Virginia to Alabama in 1818." *Publications of the Southern History Association* 1 (April 1897): 89–97.

Jones, Charles Colcock. *A Catechism of Scripture, Doctrine, and Practice, for Families and Sabbath Schools, Designed also for the Oral Instruction of Colored Persons.* Savannah: T. Purse, 1837.

Junkin, George. *The Integrity of Our National Union vs. Abolitionism.* Cincinnati: R. P. Donogh, 1843.

Kemble, Frances Anne. *Journal of a Residence on a Georgia Plantation, 1838–1839.* New York: Harper and Brothers, 1863.

Kennedy, John P. *Swallow Barn, or a Sojourn in the Old Dominion.* 1832; reprint, New York: G. P. Putnam, 1856.

Knight, Henry C. [Arthur Singleton]. *Letters from the South and West.* Boston: Richardson and Lord, 1824.

Lambert, John. *Travels through Lower Canada and the United States of North America.* 3 vols. London: Richard Philips, 1810.

Lyell, Charles. *A Second Visit to the United States of North America.* 2 vols. New York: Harper and Brothers, 1849.

Marryat, Frederick. *A Diary in America with Remarks on Its Institutions.* 1839; reprint, Westport, Conn.: Greenwood Press, 1962.

Marshall, Thomas. *The Speech of Thomas Marshall in the House of Delegates of Virginia, on the Abolition of Slavery.* Richmond: Thomas W. White, 1832.

Matlack, Lucius C. *The History of American Slavery and Methodism, from 1780 to 1849, and History of the Wesleyan Methodist Convention of America.* 2 parts. 1849; reprint, Freeport, N.Y.: Books for Libraries Press, 1971.

May, Samuel Joseph. *Some Recollections of our Anti-Slavery Conflict.* Boston: Fields, Osgood, 1869.

McTyeire, H. N., C. F. Sturgis, and A. T. Holmes. *Duties of Masters to Servants: Three Premium Essays.* Charleston: Southern Baptist Publication Society, 1851.

Melish, John. *Travels through the United States of America, in the Years 1806 and 1807, and 1809, 1810, and 1811.* London: Longman, Hurst, Rees, Orme, and Brown, 1818.

A Mississippian. "Slavery and the Slave Trade in the District of Columbia." *American Review* 28 (April 1850): 332–40.

Nevins, Allan, ed. *The Diary of Philip Hone, 1828–1851.* 2 vols. New York: Dodd, Mead, 1927.

Northrup, Solomon. *Twelve Years a Slave.* Edited by Sue Eakin and Joseph Logsdon. Baton Rouge: Louisiana State University Press, 1968.

Olmsted, Frederick Law. *A Journey in the Back Country.* 2 vols. 1860; reprint, New York: G. P. Putnam's Sons, 1907.

———. *A Journey in the Seaboard Slave States.* New York: Mason Brothers, 1861.

———. *The Cotton Kingdom: A Traveller's Observations on Cotton and Slavery in the American Slave States.* Edited by Arthur M. Schlesinger. New York: Alfred A. Knopf, 1953.

Page, J. W. *Uncle Robin in His Cabin in Virginia, and Tom without One in Boston.* Richmond: J. W. Randolph, 1853.

Palfrey, John G. *The Inter-State Slave Trade: Anti-Slavery Tract No. 5, 1855.* Reprint in *Anti-Slavery Tracts, Series I, Numbers 1–20, 1855–1856.* New York: Universities Press, 1970.

Palmer, John. *Journal of Travels in the United States of North America, and in Lower Canada, Performed in the Year 1817.* London: Sherwood, Neely, and Jones, 1818.

Paulding, James Kirke. *Letters from the South, Written during an Excursion in the Summer of 1816.* 2 vols. New York: James Eastburn, 1817.

———. *Works.* Vol. 5. New York: Harper, 1835.

Paxton, J. D. *Letters on Slavery; Addressed to the Cumberland Congregation, Virginia.* Lexington, Ky.: Abraham T. Skillman, 1833.

Phillips, Ulrich B., and John Commons, et al., eds. *A Documentary History of American Industrial Society.* Vol. 2, *Plantation and Frontier Documents.* Edited by Ulrich B. Phillips. Cleveland: Arthur H. Clark, 1910.

Power, Tyrone. *Impressions of America during the Years 1833, 1834, and 1835.* 2 vols. Philadelphia: Carey, Lea, and Blanchard, 1836.

Purefoy, George W. *A History of the Sandy Creek Baptist Association from its Organization in A.D. 1758, to A.D. 1858.* New York: Sheldon, 1859.

Randolph, J. Thornton. *The Cabin and Parlor; or, Slaves and Masters.* Philadelphia: T. T. Peterson, 1852.

Raymond, Daniel. *The Missouri Question.* Baltimore: Schaeffer and Maund, 1819.

Reed, Andrew, and James Matheson. *A Narrative of the visit to the American Churches.* 2 vols. New York: Harper and Brothers, 1835.

A Resident. *New Orleans as it is: Its Manners and Customs—Morals—Fashionable Life—Profanation of the Sabbath—Prostitution—Licentiousness—Slave Market—and Slavery, &c. &c. &c.* Utica, N.Y.: De Witt C. Grove, 1849.

Roper, Moses. *A Narrative of the Adventures and Escape of Moses Roper, from American Slavery.* 1838; reprint, New York: Negro Universities Press, 1970.

Sawyer, George S. *Southern Institutes; or, An Inquiry into the Origin and early prevalence of Slavery and the Slave-Trade.* Philadelphia: J. B. Lippincott, 1859.

Schoolcraft, Mrs. Henry R. *The Black Gauntlet: A Tale of Plantation Life in South Carolina.* Philadelphia: J. B. Lippincott, 1861.

"Slavery in the District of Columbia." *American Quarterly Review* 14 (September and December 1833): 54–65.

Smylie, James. *Review of a Letter, from the Presbytery of Chillicothe, to the Presbytery of Mississippi, on the subject of Slavery.* Woodville, Miss.: William A. Norris, 1836.

A South Carolinian [Edwin C. Holland]. *A Refutation of the Calumnies Circulated against the Southern and Western States.* Charleston: A. E. Miller, 1822.

Stirling, James. *Letters from the Slave States.* London: John W. Parker and Son, 1857.

Stowe, Harriet Beecher. *The Key to Uncle Tom's Cabin.* 1854; reprint, Salem, N.H.: Ayer, 1987.

Sturge, Joseph. *A Visit to the United States in 1841.* London: Hamilton and Adams, 1842.

Sullivan, Edward. *Rambles and Scrambles in the United States of North America.* 3 vols. London: John Murray, 1835.

Thornwell, J. H. *Report on the Subject of Slavery presented to the Synod of South Carolina, at their Sessions in Winnsborough, November 6, 1851.* Columbia: A. S. Johnston, 1852.

Torrey, Jesse. *A Portraiture of Domestic Slavery in the United States.* 1817; reprint, St. Clair Shores, Mich.: Scholarly Press, 1970.

Tragle, Henry I., ed. *The Southampton Slave Revolt of 1831.* Amherst: University of Massachusetts Press, 1971.

[Tucker, George]. *Letters from Virginia, translated from the French.* Baltimore: Fielding Lucas, Jr., 1816.

———. *The Valley of the Shenandoah; or, Memories of the Graysons.* 2 vols. New York: Charles Wiley, 1824.

Weld, Theodore D. *American Slavery as It Is: Testimony of a Thousand Witnesses.* New York: American Anti-Slavery Society, 1839.

Weld, Theodore D., and James Thome. *Slavery and the Internal Slave Trade in the United States of North America.* London: Thomas Ward, 1841.

Williams, James. *Narrative of James Williams, an American Slave.* New York: American Anti-Slavery Society, 1838.

SECONDARY SOURCES

BOOKS

Abernethy, Thomas Perkins. *The Formative Period in Alabama, 1815–1828.* 1922; reprint, Tuscaloosa: University of Alabama Press, 1990.

Adams, Alice D. *The Neglected Period of Anti-Slavery in America.* Boston: Ginn, 1908.

Alley, Reuben E. *A History of Baptists in Virginia.* Richmond: Virginia Baptist General Board, n.d.

Aptheker, Herbert. *"One Continual Cry": David Walker's Appeal to the Colored Citizens of the World, 1829–1830.* New York: Humanities Press, 1965.

———. *Nat Turner's Slave Rebellion.* New York: Humanities Press, 1966.

Artemel, Janice G., Elizabeth A. Crowell, and Jeff Parker. *The Alexandria Slave Pen: The Archaeology of Urban Captivity.* Engineering Science: Washington, 1987.

Bailey, David T. *Shadow on the Church: Southwestern Evangelical Religion and the Issue of Slavery, 1783–1860.* Ithaca, N.Y.: Cornell University Press, 1985.

Ballagh, James C. *A History of Slavery in Virginia.* Baltimore: Johns Hopkins University Press, 1902.

Bancroft, Frederic. *Slave Trading in the Old South.* 1931; reprint, Columbia, S.C.: University of South Carolina Press, 1996.

Baptist, Edward E. *Creating an Old South: Middle Florida's Plantation Frontier before the Civil War.* Chapel Hill: University of North Carolina Press, 2002.

Bassett, John S. *Slavery in the State of North Carolina.* 1899; reprint, New York: AMS Press, 1972.

Baxter, Maurice G. *Henry Clay the Lawyer.* Lexington: University Press of Kentucky, 2000.

Bennett, William W. *Memorials of Methodism in Virginia, from its Introduction into the State, in the Year 1772, to the Year 1829.* 2nd ed. Richmond: published by the author, 1871.

Berlin, Ira. *Slaves without Masters: The Free Negro in the Antebellum South.* New York: Pantheon Books, 1975.

———. *Many Thousands Gone: The First Two Centuries of Slavery in North America.* Cambridge, Mass.: Harvard University Press, 1998.

Berlin, Ira, and Ronald Hoffman, eds. *Slavery and Freedom in the Age of the American Revolution.* Charlottesville: University of Virginia Press, 1983.

Berlin, Ira, and Philip D. Morgan, eds. *Cultivation and Culture: Labor and the Shaping of Slave Life in the Americas.* Charlottesville: University of Virginia Press, 1993.

Birney, William. *James G. Birney and His Times.* New York: D. Appleton, 1890.

Bogger, Tommy L. *Free Blacks in Norfolk, Virginia, 1790–1860: The Darker Side of Freedom.* Charlottesville: University Press of Virginia, 1997.

Bohner, Charles H. *John Pendleton Kennedy: Gentleman from Baltimore.* Baltimore: Johns Hopkins University Press, 1961.

Boles, John B. *The Great Revival, 1787–1805: The Origins of the Southern Evangelical Mind.* Lexington: University Press of Kentucky, 1972.

———, ed. *Masters and Slaves in the House of the Lord: Race and Religion in the American South, 1740–1870.* Lexington: University Press of Kentucky, 1988.

Boyd, Jesse L. *A Popular History of Baptists in Mississippi.* Jackson, Miss.: Baptist Press, 1930.

Brackett, Jeffrey R. *The Negro in Maryland: A Study in the Institution of Slavery.* Baltimore: John Murphy, 1889.

Brown, Herbert Ross. *The Sentimental Novel in America, 1789–1860.* Durham: Duke University Press, 1940.

Bucke, Emory S., ed. *The History of American Methodism.* 2 vols. New York: Abingdon Press, 1964.

Buckley, James M. *Constitutional and Parliamentary History of the Methodist Episcopal Church.* New York: Methodist Book Concern, 1912.

Calhoon, Robert M. *Evangelicals and Conservatives in the Early South, 1740–1861.* Columbia: University of South Carolina Press, 1988.

Campbell, Randolph B. *An Empire for Slavery: The Peculiar Institution in Texas.* Baton Rouge: Louisiana State University Press, 1989.

Cashin, Joan E. *A Family Venture: Men and Women on the Southern Frontier.* New York: Oxford University Press, 1991.

Catterall, Helen T., ed. *Judicial Cases concerning American Slavery and the Negro.* 5 vols. Washington, D.C.: Carnegie Institution of Washington, 1926.

Coleman, J. Winston, Jr. *Slavery Times in Kentucky.* Chapel Hill: University of North Carolina Press, 1940.

Collins, Winfield H. *The Domestic Slave Trade of the Southern States.* New York: Broadway Publishing, 1904.

Cooper, William J., Jr. *The South and the Politics of Slavery, 1828–1856.* Baton Rouge: Louisiana State University Press, 1978.

———. *Liberty and Slavery: Southern Politics to 1860.* Baton Rouge: Louisiana State University Press, 1983.

Coppinger, Margaret Brown. *Beersheba Springs: 150 Years, 1833–1983: A History and a Celebration.* Beersheba Springs, Tenn.: Beersheba Springs Historical Society, 1983.

Craven, Avery. *The Coming of the Civil War.* Chicago: University of Chicago Press, 1942.

Crum, Mason. *Gullah: Negro Life in the Carolina Sea Islands.* Durham: Duke University Press, 1940.

Daly, John P. *When Slavery Was Called Freedom: Evangelicalism, Proslavery, and the Causes of the Civil War.* Lexington: University Press of Kentucky, 2002.

David, Paul A., Herbert G. Gutman, Richard Sutch, Peter Temin, and Gavin Wright. *Reckoning with Slavery: A Critical Study in the Quantitative History of American Negro Slavery.* New York: Oxford University Press, 1976.

Davis, David B. *The Problem of Slavery in the Age of Revolution, 1770–1823.* Ithaca, N.Y.: Cornell University Press, 1975.

———. "American Slavery and the American Revolution." In *Slavery and Freedom in the Age of the American Revolution,* edited by Ira Berlin and Ronald Hoffman. Charlottesville: University of Virginia Press, 1983.

Davis, William C. *A Way through the Wilderness: The Natchez Trace and the Civilization of the Southern Frontier.* New York: HarperCollins, 1995.

Degler, Carl. *The Other South: Southern Dissenters in the Nineteenth Century.* New York: Harper and Row, 1974.

Delke, James A. *History of the North Carolina Chowan Baptist Association, 1806–1881.* Raleigh, N.C.: Edwards, Broughton, 1882.

Denson, John V. *Slavery Laws in Alabama.* Auburn, Ala.: Alabama Polytechnic Institute Historical Studies, 1908.

Dillon, Merton L. *Benjamin Lundy and the Struggle for Negro Freedom.* Urbana: University of Illinois Press, 1966.

———. *Slavery Attacked: Southern Slaves and Their Allies, 1619–1865.* Baton Rouge: Louisiana State University Press, 1990.

Du Bois, W. E. Burghardt. *The Suppression of the African Slave-Trade to the United States of America, 1638–1870.* 1896; reprint, Baton Rouge: Louisiana State University Press, 1965.

Dupre, Daniel S. *Transforming the Frontier: Madison County, Alabama, 1800–1840.* Baton Rouge: Louisiana State University Press, 1997.

Dusinberre, William. *Them Dark Days: Slavery in the American Rice Swamps.* New York: Oxford University Press, 1996.

Eaton, Clement. *The Freedom-of-Thought Struggle in the Old South.* Durham: Duke University Press, 1940.

Elkins, Stanley M. *Slavery: A Problem in American Institutional and Intellectual Life.* 3rd ed. Chicago: University of Chicago Press, 1976.

Escott, Paul D. *Slavery Remembered: A Record of Twentieth-Century Slave Narratives.* Chapel Hill: University of North Carolina Press, 1979.

Essig, James D. *The Bonds of Wickedness: American Evangelicals against Slavery, 1770–1808.* Philadelphia: Temple University Press, 1982.

Faust, Drew Gilpin. *James Henry Hammond and the Old South: A Design for Mastery.* Baton Rouge: Louisiana State University Press, 1982.

Fehrenbacher, Don E. *The South and the Three Sectional Crises.* Baton Rouge: Louisiana State University Press, 1980.

Fields, Barbara Jeanne. *Slavery and Freedom on the Middle Ground: Maryland during the Nineteenth Century.* New Haven: Yale University Press, 1985.

Flanders, Ralph B. *Plantation Slavery in Georgia.* Chapel Hill: University of North Carolina Press, 1933.

Fogel, Robert W. *Without Consent or Contract: The Rise and Fall of American Slavery.* New York: W. W. Norton, 1989.

Fogel, Robert W., and Stanley L. Engerman. *Time on the Cross: The Economics of American Negro Slavery.* Boston: Little, Brown, 1974.

Fox, Early Lee. *The American Colonization Society, 1817–1840.* Baltimore: Johns Hopkins Press, 1919.

Fredrickson, George M. *The Black Image in the White Mind: The Debate on Afro-American Character and Destiny, 1817–1914.* New York: Harper and Row, 1971.

Freehling, Alison Goodyear. *Drift toward Dissolution: The Virginia Slavery Debate of 1831–1832.* Baton Rouge: Louisiana State University Press, 1982.

Freehling, William W., ed. *Slavery and Freedom.* New York: Oxford University Press, 1982.

———. *The Road to Disunion.* Vol. 1, *Secessionists at Bay, 1776–1854.* New York: Oxford University Press, 1990.

Genovese, Eugene D. *Roll, Jordan, Roll: The World the Slaves Made.* New York: Random House, 1972.

———. *The Slaveholders' Dilemma: Freedom and Progress in Southern Conservative Thought, 1820–1860.* Columbia: University of South Carolina Press, 1992.

Goen, C. C. *Broken Churches, Broken Nation: Denominational Schisms and the Coming of the American Civil War.* Macon, Ga.: Mercer University Press, 1985.

Gracy, David B., Jr. *Moses Austin: His Life.* San Antonio: Trinity University Press, 1987.

Gray, Lewis Cecil. *History of Agriculture in the Southern United States to 1860.* 2 vols. Washington, D.C.: Carnegie Institution of Washington, 1933.

Green, Constance McLaughlin. *Washington: Village and Capital, 1800–1878.* 2 vols. Princeton: Princeton University Press, 1962.

Greenberg, Kenneth S. *Honor and Slavery: Lies, Duels, Noses, Masks, Dressing as a Woman, Gifts, Strangers, Humanitarianism, Death, Slave Rebellions, the Proslavery Argument, Baseball, Hunting, and Gambling in the Old South.* Princeton: Princeton University Press, 1996.

Gross, Ariela J. *Double Character: Slavery and Mastery in the Antebellum Southern Courtroom.* Princeton: Princeton University Press, 2000.

Gutman, Herbert G. *Slavery and the Numbers Game: A Critique of "Time on the Cross."* Urbana: University of Illinois Press, 1975.

Gutman, Herbert G., and Richard Sutch. "The Slave Family: Protected Agent of Capitalist Masters or Victim of the Slave Trade?" in Paul A. David, et al., *Reckoning with Slavery: A Critical Study in the Quantitative History of American Negro Slavery.* New York: Oxford University Press, 1976.

Hamer, Philip M., ed. *Tennessee: A History, 1673–1932.* 2 vols. New York: American Historical Society, 1933.

Harrison, Lowell H. *The Antislavery Movement in Kentucky.* Lexington: University of Kentucky Press, 1978.

Henry, H. M. *The Police Control of the Slave in South Carolina.* Emory, Va.: Emory and Henry College, 1914.

Heyrman, Christin Leigh. *Southern Cross: The Beginnings of the Bible Belt.* New York: Alfred A. Knopf, 1997.

Hinks, Peter P. *To Awaken My Afflicted Brethren: David Walker and the Problem of Antebellum Slave Resistance.* University Park: Pennsylvania State University Press, 1997.

James, D. Clayton. *Antebellum Natchez.* Baton Rouge: Louisiana State University Press, 1993.

Jenkins, William Sumner. *Pro-Slavery Thought in the Old South.* Chapel Hill: University of North Carolina Press, 1935.

Jervey, Theodore D. *The Slave Trade: Slavery and Color.* Columbia, S.C.: State Company, 1925.

Johnson, Walter. *Soul by Soul: Life inside the Antebellum Slave Market.* Cambridge: Harvard University Press, 2000.

Jones, Norrece T., Jr. *Born a Child of Freedom yet a Slave: Mechanisms of Control and Strategies of Resistance in Antebellum South Carolina.* Hanover, N.H.: Wesleyan University Press, University Press of New England, 1990.

Jordan, Winthrop. *White over Black: American Attitudes toward the Negro, 1550–1812.* Chapel Hill: University of North Carolina Press, 1968.

Kilbourne, Richard H., Jr. *Debt, Investment, Slaves: Credit Relations in East Feliciana Parish, Louisiana, 1825–1885.* Tuscaloosa: University of Alabama Press, 1995.

Kirk, Russell. *John Randolph of Roanoke: A Study in American Politics.* Chicago: Henry Regnery, 1964.

Kulikoff, Allan. "Uprooted Peoples: Black Migrants in the Age of the American Revolution, 1790–1820." In *Slavery and Freedom in the Age of the American Revolution,* edited by Ira Berlin and Ronald Hoffman. Charlottesville: University of Virginia Press, 1983.

———. *The Agrarian Origins of American Capitalism.* Charlottesville: University of Virginia Press, 1992.

Lang, Meredith. *Defender of the Faith: The High Court of Mississippi, 1817–1875.* Jackson: University Press of Mississippi, 1977.

Levine, Lawrence. *Black Culture and Black Consciousness: Afro-American Folk Thought from Slavery to Freedom.* New York: Oxford University Press, 1977.

Loewen, James W. *Lies across America: What Our Historic Sites Get Wrong.* New York: New Press, 1999.

Loveland, Anne C. *Southern Evangelicals and the Social Order, 1800–1860.* Baton Rouge: Louisiana State University Press, 1980.

MacLeod, Duncan J. *Slavery, Race, and the American Revolution.* New York: Cambridge University Press, 1977.

Malone, Ann Patton. *Sweet Chariot: Slave Family and Household Structure in Nineteenth-Century Louisiana.* Chapel Hill: University of North Carolina Press, 1992.

Mathews, Donald G. *Slavery and Methodism: A Chapter in American Morality, 1780–1845.* Princeton: Princeton University Press, 1965.

———. *Religion in the Old South.* Chicago: University of Chicago Press, 1977.

Mayer, Henry. *All on Fire: William Lloyd Garrison and the Abolition of Slavery.* New York: St. Martin's Press, 1998.

McCardell, John. *The Idea of a Southern Nation: Southern Nationalists and Southern Nationalism, 1830–1860.* New York: W. W. Norton, 1979.

McClelland, Peter D., and Richard J. Zeckhauser. *Demographic Dimensions of the New Republic: American Interregional Migration, Vital Statistics, and Manumissions, 1800–1860.* New York: Cambridge University Press, 1982.

McColley, Robert. *Slavery and Jeffersonian Virginia.* Champaign: University of Illinois Press, 1964.

McCoy, Drew R. *Last of the Fathers: James Madison and the Republican Legacy.* New York: Cambridge University Press, 1989.

McDougle, Ivan E. *Slavery in Kentucky, 1792–1865.* 1918; reprint, New York: Negro Universities Press, 1964.

McLaurin, Melton A. *Celia: A Slave.* New York: Avon Books, 1991.

McLean, Robert Colin. *George Tucker: Moral Philosopher and Man of Letters.* Chapel Hill: University of North Carolina Press, 1961.

Miles, Edwin Arthur. *Jacksonian Democracy in Mississippi.* Chapel Hill: University of North Carolina Press, 1960.

Miller, John Chester. *The Wolf by the Ears: Thomas Jefferson and Slavery.* New York: Free Press, 1977.

Miller, Stephen F. "Plantation Labor and Slave Life on the Cotton Frontier: The Alabama-Mississippi Black Belt, 1815–1840." In *Cultivation and Culture: Labor and the Shaping of Slave Life in the Americas,* edited by Ira Berlin and Philip D. Morgan. Charlottesville: University Press of Virginia, 1993.

Miller, William Lee. *Arguing about Slavery: The Great Battle in the United States Congress.* New York: Alfred A. Knopf, 1996.

Mooney, Chase C. *Slavery in Tennessee.* Bloomington: Indiana University Press, 1957.

Moore, Glover. *The Missouri Controversy, 1819–1821.* Lexington: Kentucky University Press, 1953.

Moore, John Hebron. *The Emergence of the Cotton Kingdom in the Old Southwest: Mississippi, 1770–1860.* Baton Rouge: Louisiana State University Press, 1988.

Morris, Thomas D. *Southern Slavery and the Law, 1619–1860.* Chapel Hill: University of North Carolina Press, 1996.

Murray, Andrew E. *Presbyterians and the Negro—A History.* Philadelphia: Presbyterian Historical Society, 1966.

Newman, Richard S. *The Transformation of American Abolitionism: Fighting Slavery in the Early Republic.* Chapel Hill: University of North Carolina Press, 2002.

Nye, Russell B. *Fettered Freedom: Civil Liberties and the Slavery Controvery, 1830–1860.* East Lansing: Michigan State College Press, 1949.

Oakes, James. *The Ruling Race: A History of American Slaveholders.* New York: Knopf, 1982.

———. *Slavery and Freedom: An Interpretation of the Old South.* New York: Random House, 1990.

Owens, Leslie H. *This Species of Property: Slave Life and Culture in the Old South.* New York: Oxford University Press, 1976.

Parton, James. *Life of Andrew Jackson.* 3 vols. Boston: Houghton, Mifflin, 1860.

Patterson, Caleb Perry. *The Negro in Tennessee, 1790–1865.* 1922; reprint, New York: Negro Universities Press, 1968.

Perrault, Stephanie L., et al. *Cultural Resources Survey, Testing, and Exploratory Trenching for the Louisiana State Penitentiary Levee Enlargement Project, West Feliciana Parish, Louisiana.* Baton Rouge: Coastal Environments, 2001.

Phillips, Christopher. *Freedom's Port: The African American Community of Baltimore, 1790–1860.* Urbana: University of Illinois Press, 1997.

Phillips, Ulrich Bonnell. *American Negro Slavery: A Survey of the Supply, Employment, and Control of Negro Labor as determined by the Plantation Régime.* New York: D. Appleton, 1918.

Posey, Walter B. *The Baptist Church in the Lower Mississippi Valley, 1776–1845.* Lexington: University of Kentucky Press, 1957.

Preston, Dickson J. *Young Frederick Douglass: The Maryland Years.* Baltimore: Johns Hopkins Press, 1980.

Raboteau, Albert J. *Slave Religion: The "Invisible Institution" in the Antebellum South.* New York: Oxford University Press, 1978.

Remini, Robert V. *Andrew Jackson and the Course of American Empire, 1787–1821.* New York: Harper and Row, 1977.

———. *Andrew Jackson and the Course of American Freedom, 1822–1832.* New York: Harper and Row, 1981.

Richards, Leonard L. *The Slave Power: The Free North and Southern Domination, 1780–1860.* Baton Rouge: Louisiana State University Press, 2000.

Risjord, Norman K. *The Old Republicans: Southern Conservatism in the Age of Jefferson.* New York: Columbia University Press, 1965.

Robert, Joseph Clarke. *The Road from Monticello: A Study of the Virginia Slavery Debate of 1832.* Durham: Duke University Press, 1941.

Robinson, Donald L. *Slavery in the Structure of American Politics, 1765–1820.* New York: Harcourt Bruce Jovanovich, 1971.

Roth, Hal. *The Monster's Handsome Face: Patty Cannon in Fiction and Fact.* Vienna, Md.: Nanticoke Books, 1998.

Savage, Beth L., ed. *African American Historic Places.* Washington, D.C.: Preservation Press, 1994.

Scarborough, Ruth. *The Opposition to Slavery in Georgia prior to 1860.* Nashville: George Peabody College for Teachers, 1933.

Schafer, Judith Kelleher. *Slavery, the Civil Law, and the Supreme Court of Louisiana.* Baton Rouge: Louisiana State University Press, 1994.

Sellers, Charles Grier. "The Travail of Slavery." In *The Southerner as American*, edited by Charles Grier Sellers. Chapel Hill: University of North Carolina Press, 1960.

———. *The Market Revolution: Jacksonian America, 1815–1846.* New York: Oxford University Press, 1991.

Sellers, James Benson. *Slavery in Alabama.* University, Ala.: University of Alabama Press, 1950.

Shade, William G. *Democratizing the Old Dominion: Virginia and the Second Party System, 1824–1861.* Charlottesville: University Press of Virginia, 1996.

Shenton, James P. *Robert John Walker: A Politician from Jackson to Lincoln.* New York: Columbia University Press, 1961.

Sistler, Byron, and Samuel Sistler. *Tennesseans in the War of 1812.* Nashville: Byron Sistler and Associates, 1992.

Smith, H. Shelton. *In His Image, But . . . : Racism in Southern Religion, 1780–1910.* Durham: Duke University Press, 1972.

Smith, Julia F. *Slavery and Plantation Growth in Antebellum Florida, 1821–1860.* Gainesville: University of Florida Press, 1973.

Snay, Mitchell. *Gospel of Disunion: Religion and Separatism in the Antebellum South.* New York: Cambridge University Press, 1993.

Sparks, Randy J. *On Jordan's Stormy Banks: Evangelicalism in Mississippi, 1773–1876.* Athens: University of Georgia Press, 1994.

Stampp, Kenneth. *The Peculiar Institution: Slavery in the Ante-Bellum South.* New York: Random House, 1956.

Startup, Kenneth Moore. *The Root of All Evil: The Protestant Clergy and the Economic Mind of the Old South.* Athens: University of Georgia Press, 1997.

Staudenraus, P. J. *The African Colonization Movement, 1816–1865.* New York: Columbia University Press, 1961.

Stephenson, Wendell Holmes. *Isaac Franklin: Slave Trader and Planter of the Old South.* Baton Rouge: Louisiana State University Press, 1938.

Stewart, James Brewer. *Holy Warriors: The Abolitionists and American Slavery.* New York: Hill and Wang, 1976.

Stokes, Melvyn, and Stephen Conway, eds. *The Market Revolution in America: Social, Political, and Religious Expressions, 1800–1880.* Charlottesville: University Press of Virginia, 1996.

Swaney, Charles B. *Episcopal Methodism and Slavery: With Sidelights on Ecclesiastical Politics.* 1926; reprint, New York: Negro Universities Press, 1969.

Sweet, William W. *Virginia Methodism: A History.* Richmond: Whitlet and Shepperson, 1955.

Swisher, Carl B. *The Taney Period, 1836–1864.* Vol. 5 of *The Oliver Wendell Holmes Devise History of the Supreme Court of the United States,* edited by Paul A. Freund. New York: Macmillan, 1974.

Sydnor, Charles Sackett. *Slavery in Mississippi.* New York: D. Appleton, 1933.

———. *The Development of Southern Sectionalism, 1819–1848.* Vol. 5 of *A History of the South,* edited by Wendell H. Stephenson and E. Merton Coulter. Louisiana State University Press and Littlefield Fund for Southern History of the University of Texas, 1948.

Tadman, Michael. *Speculators and Slaves: Masters, Traders, and Slaves in the Old South.* Madison: University of Wisconsin Press, 1989.

Takaki, Ronald T. *A Pro-Slavery Crusade: The Agitation to Reopen the African Slave Trade.* New York: Free Press, 1971.

Taylor, Joe Gray. *Negro Slavery in Louisiana.* Baton Rouge: Louisiana Historical Association, 1963.

Taylor, Orville W. *Negro Slavery in Arkansas.* Durham: Duke University Press, 1958.

Taylor, Rosser H. *Slaveholding in North Carolina: An Economic View.* Chapel Hill: University of North Carolina Press, 1926.

Thompson, Ernest T. *Presbyterians in the South.* Vol. 1, *1607–1861.* Richmond: John Knox Press, 1963.

Tise, Larry E. *Proslavery: A History of the Defense of Slavery in America, 1701–1840.* Athens: University of Georgia Press, 1987.

Tracy, Susan J. *In the Master's Eye: Representations of Women, Blacks, and Poor Whites in Antebellum Southern Literature.* Amherst: University of Massachusetts Press, 1995.

Tremain, Mary. *Slavery in the District of Columbia.* 1892; reprint, New York: Negro Universities Press, 1969.

Trese, Joel D., ed., *Biographical Directory of the American Congress, 1774–1996.* Alexandria, Va.: CQ Staff Directories, 1997.

Trexler, Harrison A. *Slavery in Missouri, 1804–1865.* Johns Hopkins University Studies in Historical and Political Science, series 32, no. 2. Baltimore: Johns Hopkins Press, 1914.

Tushnet, Mark V. *The American Law of Slavery, 1810–1860: Considerations of Humanity and Interest.* Princeton: Princeton University Press, 1981.

Wade, Richard C. *Slavery in the Cities: The South, 1820–1860.* New York: Oxford University Press, 1964.

Wallis, Frederick A., and Hambleton Tapp, eds. *A Sesquicentennial History of Kentucky.* 4 vols. Hopkinsville, Ky.: Historical Record Association, 1945.

Walsh, Lorena S. "Slave Life, Slave Society, and Tobacco Production in the Tidewater Chesapeake, 1620–1820." In *Cultivation and Culture: Labor and the Shaping of Slave Life in the Americas,* edited by Ira Berlin and Philip D. Morgan. Charlottesville: University of Virginia Press, 1993.

Wardin, Albert W., Jr. *Belmont Mansion: The Home of Joseph and Adelicia Acklen.* Nashville: Belmont Mansion Association, 1989.

Warren, Charles. *The Supreme Court in United States History.* 3 vols. Boston: Little, Brown, 1922.

Warren, Margaret Lindsley. *The Saga of Fairvue, 1832–1977.* Nashville: published for the author, 1977.

Watson, Harry L. *Liberty and Power: The Politics of Jacksonian America.* New York: Hill and Wang, 1990.

———. "Slavery and Development in a Dual Economy: The South and the Market Revolution." In *The Market Revolution in America: Social, Political, and Religious*

Expressions, 1800–1880, edited by Melvyn Stokes and Stephen Conway. Charlottesville: University Press of Virginia, 1996.

West, Carroll Van, ed. *The Tennessee Encyclopedia of History and Culture*. Nashville: Tennessee Historical Society, 1998.

West, John G., Jr. *The Politics of Revelation and Reason: Religion and Civic Life in the New Nation*. Lawrence: University Press of Kansas, 1996.

Whitman, T. Stephen. *The Price of Freedom: Slavery and Manumission in Baltimore and Early National Maryland*. Lexington: University Press of Kentucky, 1997.

Whitten, David O. *Andrew Durnford: A Black Sugar Planter in the Antebellum South*. New Brunswick, N.J.: Transaction Publishers, 1995.

Wilson, Carol. *Freedom at Risk: The Kidnapping of Free Blacks in America, 1780–1865*. Lexington: University Press of Kentucky, 1994.

Wyatt-Brown, Bertram. *Lewis Tappan and the Evangelical War against Slavery*. Cleveland: Press of Case Western Reserve University, 1969.

———. "Modernizing Southern Slavery: The Proslavery Argument Reinterpreted." In *Region, Race, and Reconstruction: Essays in Honor of C. Vann Woodward*, edited by J. Morgan Kousser and James M. McPherson. New York: Oxford University Press, 1982.

———. *Southern Honor: Ethics and Behavior in the Old South*. New York: Oxford University Press, 1982.

———. *Yankee Saints and Southern Sinners*. Baton Rouge: Louisiana State University Press, 1985.

———. *The Shaping of Southern Culture: Honor, Grace, and War, 1760s–1890s*. Chapel Hill: University of North Carolina Press, 2001.

Young, Jeffrey Robert. *Domesticating Slavery: The Master Class in Georgia and South Carolina, 1670–1837*. Chapel Hill: University of North Carolina Press, 1999.

ARTICLES

Allen, Jeffrey Brooke. "Were Southern White Critics of Slavery Racist? Kentucky and the Upper South, 1791–1824." *Journal of Southern History* 44 (May 1978): 169–90.

Baptist, Edward E. "'Cuffy,' 'Fancy Maids,' and 'One-Eyed Men': Rape, Commodification, and the Domestic Slave Trade in the United States." *American Historical Review* 106 (December 2001): 1619–50.

Barnett, Jim, and H. Clark Burkett. "The Forks of the Road Slave Market at Natchez." *Journal of Mississippi History* 63 (fall 2001): 168–87.

Basch, Norma. "Marriage, Morals, and Politics in the Election of 1828." *Journal of American History* 80 (December 1993): 890–918.

Bellamy, Donnie D. "Slavery in Microcosm: Onslow County, North Carolina." *Journal of Negro History* 62 (November 1977): 339–50.

Bellamy, Donnie D., and Diane E. Walker. "Slaveholding in Antebellum Augusta and Richmond County, Georgia." *Phylon* 48 (summer 1987): 165–77.

Berger, Max. "American Slavery as Seen by British Visitors." *Journal of Negro History* 30 (April 1945): 181–202.

Blight, David W. "Perceptions of Southern Intransigence and the Rise of Radical Antislavery Thought." *Journal of the Early Republic* 3 (summer 1983): 139–63.

Boyd, William M. "Southerners in the Anti-Slavery Movement, 1800–1830." *Phylon* 9 (second quarter 1948): 153–63.

Brady, Patrick S. "The Slave Trade and Sectionalism in South Carolina, 1787–1808." *Journal of Southern History* 38 (November 1972): 601–20.

Calderhead, William. "How Extensive Was the Border State Slave Trade? A New Look." *Civil War History* 18 (January 1972): 42–55.

———. "The Role of Professional Slave Trader in a Slave Economy: Austin Woolfolk, a Case Study." *Civil War History* 23 (September 1977): 195–211.

Cassell, Frank A. "Slaves of the Chesapeake Bay Area and the War of 1812." *Journal of Negro History* 47 (April 1972): 144–55.

Censer, Jane Turner. "Southwestern Migration among North Carolina Planter Families: 'The Disposition to Emigrate.'" *Journal of Southern History* 57 (August 1991): 407–26.

Chaplin, Joyce E. "Slavery and the Principle of Humanity: A Modern Idea in the Early Lower South." *Journal of Social History* 24 (winter 1990): 299–315.

———. "Creating a Cotton South in Georgia and South Carolina, 1760–1815." *Journal of Southern History* 57 (May 1991): 171–200.

Clark, Thomas D. "The Slave Trade between Kentucky and the Cotton Kingdom." *Mississippi Valley Historical Review* 21 (December 1934): 331–42.

Clephane, Walter C. "The Local Aspect of Slavery in the District of Columbia." *Records of the Columbia Historical Association* 3 (1900): 224–56.

Cohen, William. "Thomas Jefferson and the Problem of Slavery." *Journal of American History* 56 (December 1969): 503–26.

Coleman, J. Winston, Jr. "Lexington's Slave Dealers and Their Southern Trade." *Filson Club Historical Quarterly* 12 (January 1938): 1–23.

Crowther, Edward R. "Mississippi Baptists, Slavery, and Secession, 1806–1861." *Journal of Mississippi History* 56 (May 1994): 129–48.

Daniel, W. Harrison. "Virginia Baptists and the Negro in the Antebellum Era." *Journal of Negro History* 56 (January 1971): 1–16.

———. "Virginia Baptists and the Negro in the Early Republic." *Virginia Magazine of History and Biography* 80 (January 1972): 60–69.

Deyle, Steven. "'By Farr the Most Profitable Trade': Slave Trading in British Colonial North America." *Slavery and Abolition* 10 (September 1989): 107–25.

———. "The Irony of Liberty: Origins of the Domestic Slave Trade." *Journal of the Early Republic* 12 (spring 1992): 37–62.

Donald, David. "The Proslavery Argument Reconsidered." *Journal of Southern History* 37 (February 1971): 3–18.

Drago, Edmund, and Ralph Melnick. "The Old Slave Mart Museum, Charleston, South Carolina: Rediscovering the Past." *Civil War History* 27 (June 1981): 138–50.

Drake, Winbourne Magruder. "The Mississippi Constitutional Convention of 1832." *Journal of Southern History* 23 (August 1957): 354–70.

———. "The Framing of Mississippi's First Constitution." *Journal of Mississippi History* 29 (November 1967): 301–27.

Dumont, William H. "Through Richmond County, Georgia: Importers of Slaves, 1818–1824." *National Genealogical Society Quarterly* 58 (January 1970): 31–51.

Dunne, Gerald T. "Bushrod Washington and the Mount Vernon Slaves." *Supreme Court Historical Society 1980 Yearbook* (Washington, D.C.: Supreme Court Historical Society, 1980), 25–29.

Eggert, Gerald G. "A Pennsylvanian Visits the Richmond Slave Market." *Pennsylvania Magazine of History and Biography* 109 (October 1985): 571–76.

Elliot, Robert N. "The Nat Turner Insurrection as reported in the North Carolina Press." *North Carolina Historical Review* 38 (January 1961): 1–18.

Evans, Robert, Jr. "Some Economic Aspects of the Domestic Slave Trade, 1830–1860." *Southern Economic Journal* 27 (April 1961): 329–37.

Fede, Andrew. "Legal Protection for Slave Buyers in the U.S. South: A Caveat Concerning Caveat Emptor." *American Journal of Legal History* 31 (October 1987): 322–58.

Fike, Claude E. "The Gubernatorial Administrations of Governor Gerard Chittocque Brandon, 1825–1832." *Journal of Mississippi History* 35 (August 1973): 247–65.

Finnie, Gordon E. "The Antislavery Movement in the Upper South before 1840." *Journal of Southern History* 35 (August 1969): 319–42.

Foster, Gaines M. "Guilt over Slavery: A Historiographical Analysis." *Journal of Southern History* 56 (November 1990): 665–94.

Fredrickson, George M. "Masters and Mudsills: The Role of Race in the Planter Ideology of South Carolina." *South Atlantic Urban Studies* 2 (spring 1978): 34–48.

Freehling, William W. "James Henry Thornwell's Mysterious Antislavery Movement." *Journal of Southern History* 57 (August 1991): 383–406.

Freudenberger, Herman F., and Jonathan B. Pritchett. "The Domestic United States Slave Trade: New Evidence." *Journal of Interdisciplinary History* 21 (winter 1991): 447–77.

Gimelli, Louis B. "Louisa Maxwell Cocke: An Evangelical Plantation Mistress in the Antebellum South." *Journal of the Early Republic* 9 (spring 1989): 53–71.

Goldfarb, Stephen J. "An Inquiry into the Politics of the Prohibition of the International Slave Trade." *Agricultural History* 68 (spring 1994): 20–34.

Goodstein, Anita S. "Black History on the Nashville Frontier, 1780–1810." *Tennessee Historical Quarterly* 38 (winter 1979): 401–20.

Hardy, James D., Jr. "A Slave Sale in Antebellum New Orleans." *Southern Studies* 23 (fall 1984): 306–14.

Herring, Todd A. "Kidnapped and Sold in Natchez: The Ordeal of Aaron Cooper, a Free Black Man." *Journal of Mississippi History* 60 (winter 1998): 341–54.

Howell, Isabel. "John Armfield, Slave-Trader." *Tennessee Historical Quarterly* 2 (March 1943): 3–29.

———. "John Armfield of Beersheba Springs." *Tennessee Historical Quarterly* 3 (March 1944): 46–64, and 3 (June 1944): 156–67.

Huston, James L. "The Experiential Basis of the Northern Antislavery Impulse." *Journal of Southern History* 56 (November 1990): 609–40.

Jervey, Edward D., and C. Harold Huber. "The *Creole* Affair." *Journal of Negro History* 65 (summer 1980): 196–211.

Jones, Howard. "The Peculiar Institution and National Honor: The Case of the *Creole* Slave Revolt." *Civil War History* 21 (January 1975): 28–50.

Keir-Nash, A. E. "Negro Rights, Unionism, and Greatness on the South Carolina Court of Appeals: The Extraordinary Chief Justice John Belton O'Neall." *South Carolina Law Review* 21 (no. 1, 1968): 141–90.

Ketcham, Ralph L. "The Dictates of Conscience: Edward Coles and Slavery." *Virginia Quarterly Review* 36 (January 1960): 46–62.

Kotlikoff, Laurence J. "The Structure of Slave Prices in New Orleans, 1807–1862." *Economic Inquiry* 17 (October 1979): 496–518.

Laprade, William T. "The Domestic Slave Trade in the District of Columbia." *Journal of Negro History* 11 (January 1926): 17–34.

Lightner, David L. "The Door to the Slave Bastille: The Abolitionist Assault upon the Interstate Slave Trade, 1833–1839." *Civil War History* 34 (September 1988): 235–52.

———. "The Interstate Slave Trade in Antislavery Politics." *Civil War History* 36 (June 1990): 119–36.

———. "The Founders and the Interstate Slave Trade." *Journal of the Early Republic* 22 (spring 2002): 25–51.

Littlefield, Daniel C. "Charleston and Internal Slave Redistribution." *South Carolina Historical Magazine* 87 (April 1986): 93–105.

Lowe, Richard B., and Randolph B. Campbell. "The Slave-Breeding Hypothesis: A Demographic Comment on the 'Buying' and 'Selling' States." *Journal of Southern History* 42 (August 1976): 401–12.

Malone, Ann Patton. "Searching for the Family and Household Structure of Rural Louisiana Slaves, 1810–1864." *Louisiana History* 28 (fall 1987): 357–79.

Martin, Asa, E. "The Anti-Slavery Societies in Tennessee." *Tennessee Historical Magazine* 1 (December 1915): 261–81.

Mason, Matthew E. "Slavery Overshadowed: Congress Debates Prohibiting the Atlantic Slave Trade to the United States, 1806–1807." *Journal of the Early Republic* 20 (spring 2000): 59–81.

McDougle, Ivan E. "Slavery in Kentucky." *Journal of Negro History* 2 (July 1918): 211–328.

McGettigan, James W., Jr. "Boone County Slaves: Sales, Estate Divisions, and Families, 1820–1865." *Missouri Historical Review* 72 (January 1978): 176–97, and 72 (April 1978): 271–95.

McMillan, Richard. "A Journey of Lost Souls: New Orleans to Natchez Slave Trade of 1840." *Gulf Coast Historical Review* 13 (summer 1998): 49–59.

Miles, Edwin A. "The Mississippi Slave Insurrection Scare of 1835." *Journal of Negro History* 42 (January 1957): 48–60.

Miller, M. Sammy. "Patty Cannon: Murderer and Kidnapper of Free Blacks: A Review of the Evidence." *Maryland Historical Magazine* 72 (fall 1977): 419–23.

Miller, T. Michael. "'Out of Bondage': A History of the Alexandria Colonization Society." *Alexandria History* 7 (1987): 15–29.

Miller, William L. "A Note on the Importance of the Interstate Slave Trade of the Ante Bellum South." *Journal of Political Economy* 63 (April 1965): 181–87.

Phifer, Edward W. "Slavery in Microcosm: Burke County, North Carolina." *Journal of Southern History* 28 (May 1962): 137–65.

Phillips, Christopher. "The Roots of Quasi-Freedom: Manumission and Term Slavery in Early National Baltimore." *Southern Studies* 4 (spring 1993): 39–66.

Posey, Walter B. "Influence of Slavery upon the Methodist Church in the Early South and Southwest." *Mississippi Valley Historical Review* 17 (March 1931): 530–42.

———. "The Slavery Question in the Presbyterian Church in the Old Southwest." *Journal of Southern History* 15 (August 1949): 311–24.

Pritchett, Jonathan B., and Herman F. Freudenberger. "A Peculiar Sample: The Selection of Slaves for the New Orleans Market." *Journal of Economic History* 52 (March 1992): 109–27.

Purifoy, Lewis M. "The Methodist Anti-Slavery Tradition, 1784–1844." *Methodist History* 4 (1966): 3–16.

———. "The Southern Methodist Church and the Proslavery Argument." *Journal of Southern History* 32 (August 1966): 325–41.

Ransom, Roger, and Richard Sutch. "Capitalists without Capital: The Burden of Slavery and the Impact of Emancipation." *Agricultural History* 62 (summer 1988): 133–60.

Richter, William L. "Slavery in Baton Rouge." *Louisiana History* 10 (spring 1969): 125–45.

Russell, Thomas D. "A New Image of the Slave Auction: An Empirical Look at the Role of Law in Slave Sales and a Conceptual Reevaluation of Slave Property." *Cardozo Law Review* 18 (November 1992): 473–523.

———. "South Carolina's Largest Slave Auctioneering Firm." *Chicago-Kent Law Review* 68 (no. 2, 1993): 1241–82.

Schafer, Judith K. "The Immediate Impact of Nat Turner's Insurrection on New Orleans." *Louisiana History* 21 (winter 1980): 361–76.

———. "New Orleans Slavery in 1850 as seen in Advertisements." *Journal of Southern History* 47 (February 1981): 33–56.

———. "'Guaranteed against the Vices and Maladies prescribed by Law': Consumer Protection, the Law of Slave Sales, and the Supreme Court in Antebellum Louisiana." *American Journal of Legal History* 31 (October 1987): 306–21.

Smith, Julia F. "Slavetrading in Antebellum Florida." *Florida Historical Quarterly* 50 (January 1972): 252–61.

Southall, Eugene P. "The Attitude of the Methodist Episcopal Church, South, toward the Negro, from 1844 to 1870." *Journal of Negro History* 16 (October 1931): 359–70.

Sparks, Randy J. "Mississippi's Apostle of Slavery: James Smylie and the Biblical Defense of Slavery." *Journal of Mississippi History* 51 (May 1989): 89–106.

Stewart, James B. "Evangelicalism and the Radical Strain in Southern Antislavery Thought during the 1820s." *Journal of Southern History* 39 (August 1973): 379–96.

Stone, Alfred H. "The Early Slave Laws of Mississippi." *Publication of the Mississippi Historical Society for 1899* (1899): 133–45.

Sutch, Richard. "The Treatment Received by American Slaves: A Critical Review of the Evidence presented in *Time on the Cross.*" *Explorations in Economic History* 12 (October 1975): 335–438.

Sweig, Donald M. "Reassessing the Human Dimension of the Interstate Slave Trade." *Prologue.* 12 (spring 1980): 5–21.

Tadman, Michael. "The Hidden History of Slave Trading in Antebellum South Carolina: John Springs III and Other 'Gentlemen Dealing in Slaves.'" *South Carolina Historical Magazine* 97 (January 1996): 6–29.

Tansey, Richard. "Bernard Kendig and the New Orleans Slave Trade." *Louisiana History* 23 (spring 1982): 159–78.

Taylor, A. A. "The Movement of Negroes from the East to the Gulf States from 1830 to 1850." *Journal of Negro History* 8 (October 1923): 367–83.

Taylor, Joe G. "The Foreign Slave Trade in Louisiana after 1808." *Louisiana History* 1 (winter 1960): 36–43.

Terry, Gail S. "Sustaining the Bonds of Kinship in a Trans-Appalachian Migration, 1790–1811: The Cabell-Breckinridge Slaves Move West." *Virginia Magazine of History and Biography* 4 (October 1994): 455–76.

Trexler, Harrison A. "The Value and Sale of the Missouri Slave." *Missouri Historical Review* 8 (January 1914): 69–87.

Wahl, Jenny B. "The Jurisprudence of American Slave Sales." *Journal of Economic History* 56 (March 1996): 143–69.

Waldrep, Christopher. "Kentucky's Slave Importation Law in Lyon County: A Document." *Filson Club Historical Quarterly* 65 (October 1991): 505–12.

Wesley, Charles H. "Manifests of Slave Shipments along the Waterways, 1808–1864." *Journal of Negro History* 27 (April 1942): 155–74.

West, Emily. "Surviving Separation: Cross-Plantation Marriages and the Slave Trade in Antebellum South Carolina." *Journal of Family History* 24 (summer 1999): 212–31.

Whitten, David O. "Slave Buying in 1835 Virginia as revealed by the Letters of a Louisiana Negro Sugar Planter." *Louisiana History* 11 (summer 1970): 231–44.

Woods, James. "In the Eye of the Beholder: Slavery in the Travel Accounts of the Old South." *Southern Studies* 1 (spring 1990): 33–59.

Woolfolk, George. "Taxes and Slavery in the Antebellum South." *Journal of Southern History* 26 (January 1960): 180–200.

THESES AND DISSERTATIONS

Cobb, Jimmy Gene. "A Study of White Protestants' Attitudes toward Negroes in Charleston, South Carolina, 1790–1845." Ph.D. diss., Baylor University, 1976.

Coyner, Martin Boyd. "John Hartwell Cocke of Bremo: Agriculture and Slavery in the Ante-Bellum South." Ph.D. diss., University of Virginia, 1961.

Deyle, Steven H. "The Domestic Slave Trade in America." Ph.D. diss., Columbia University, 1995.

Drake, Winbourne Magruder, III. "Constitutional Development in Mississippi, 1817–1865." Ph.D. diss., University of North Carolina, 1954.

Green, Barbara Layenette. "The Slavery Debate in Missouri, 1831–1855." Ph.D. diss., University of Missouri, Columbia, 1980.

Johnson, Walter Livezey. "Masters and Slaves in the Market of Slavery and the New Orleans Trade, 1804–1864." Ph.D. diss., Princeton University, 1995.

Kramer, Ethel Elizabeth. "Slavery Legislation in Antebellum Louisiana, 1803–1860." Master's thesis, Louisiana State University, 1944.

Marr, Don H., Jr. "Slave Trading and Slave Traders in North Carolina." Master's thesis, East Carolina University, 1995.

Miller, James David. "South by Southwest: Planter Emigration and Elite Ideology in the Deep South, 1815–1861." Ph.D. diss., Emory University, 1996.

Ridgeway, Michael. "A Peculiar Business: Slave Trading in Alexandria, Virginia, 1825–1861." Master's thesis, Georgetown University, 1976.

Russell, Thomas David. "Sale Day in Antebellum South Carolina: Slavery, Law, Economy, and Court Supervised Sales." Ph.D. diss., Stanford University, 1993.

Stafford, Hanford Dozier. "Slavery in a Border City: Louisville, 1790–1860." Ph.D. diss., University of Kentucky, 1982.

Sweig, Donald M. "Northern Virginia Slavery: A Statistical and Demographic Investigation." Ph.D. diss., William and Mary College, 1982.

Thomas, Arthur Dicken, Jr. "The Second Great Awakening in Virginia and Slavery Reform, 1785–1837." Th.D. diss., Union Theological Seminary, Richmond, Va., 1981.

Troutman, Philip Davis. "Slave Trade and Sentiment in Antebellum Virginia." Ph.D. diss., University of Virginia, 2000.

Turner, Ian Bruce. "Antislavery Thought in the Border South, 1830–1860." Ph.D. diss., University of Illinois, 1977.

Woessner, Herman Charles, III. "New Orleans, 1840–1860: A Study in Urban Slavery." Master's thesis, Louisiana State University, 1967.

ELECTRONIC SOURCES

About Belmont: Belmont Mansion. Website of Belmont Mansion; http://www.belmont.edu/about/mansion.cfm.

Demographic Profiles of the Adult Correctional Population. Website of the Louisiana Department of Public Safety and Corrections; http://www.corrections.state.la.us/stats2.htm.

Freedom House. Website of the Northern Virginia Urban League; http://www.novaul.org/freedomhouse.html.

The Last Plantation. Website of the Last Plantation; http:www.thelastplantation.com.

Louisiana State Penitentiary. Website of the Louisiana Department of Public Safety and Corrections; http://www.corrections.state.la.us/LSP/.

To Witness the Past: African-American Archaeology in Alexandria, Virginia. Website of the Alexandria Archaeology Museum; http://oha.ci.alexandria.va.us/archaeology/ar-exhibits-witness-4.html.

INDEX